To Daniella
and
to Katie and Evie (who is exactly as old as this book)

Contents

Authors' Note

ON A RECENT morning, amid the daily hullabaloo at London's busiest transport hub, the commuters at Waterloo Station went about their Underground rituals, demonstrating some of the vital skills of living in their city – how to carry a smartphone and a cup of hot tea in the same hand; how to open an umbrella without causing a public-safety emergency; and how to absolutely, positively, never, ever make eye contact with anyone else.

And down by the news-stand near the escalators, the dozens who stopped to pick up their daily newspaper showcased one very particular everyday skill essential to British life: how to read a tabloid.

Like almost everything else in this country, it turns out there's a right and a wrong way to do that. The page numbers are merely a suggestion.

The right way starts with a glance at the headline pun on the front and an obligatory sigh for the state of humanity. Situation normal – all is not good.

But these Londoners didn't stop to read on. They knew what they were doing. Without batting an eye, they took a quick sip of tea and flipped the entire paper over to find the news that really mattered.

Starting from the back, over dozens of pages – almost one-third of the entire newspaper in some cases – they found stories dripping with urgency, intrigue, outrage, and absurd amounts of cash; a breathless global pursuit of billions of pounds driven by an ensemble of outsize talent and ego, the stakes of which, readers are assured, are nothing less than the fates of cities, regions, and nations.

This was the stuff they really needed to start their days: the latest from the Premier League. From west London, where a Russian oligarch keeps his club in a state of permanent revolution, to north London where warring factions are locked in a spiral of endless one-upmanship, to Manchester, the country's old industrial hub, where a sudden and dramatic power shift is rewiring the dynamic between two ancient institutions. Caught in the gears between these empires are the smaller teams in market towns and mining counties where football is the only thing that keeps them from falling off the map. And this whole world is constantly animated by oligarchs, sheikhs, American tycoons, Asian Tiger titans, and a bunch of secondary school dropouts who have been millionaires since their teens because of their skill with a ball at their feet.

All of which combines for a pretty full day of reading, more than enough Premier League excitement to compete with the stuff in the front of the papers about the latest parliamentary crisis and all that.

Far beyond the morning scramble at Waterloo Station, the speculation and vague nuggets of truth contained in the red-tops also powers an international rumour mill that, on a daily basis, captivates a dizzying number of fans around the world, reaching over to the other side of the Atlantic, clear through Asia, and all across Africa, with a few researchers in Antarctica probably keeping tabs on it all, too.

The rise of the English Premier League is a story about the sports world's wildest gold rush. In the span of twenty-five years, the league's twenty clubs have increased their combined value by more than 10,000 per cent, from around £50 million in 1992 to £10 billion today. During that time, the league has also exported its product to every corner of the planet.

How this happened is a tale of how the country that invented the world's favourite game reinvented it and how a handful of secret meetings in 1992 spawned a crazy quarter-century in which money, ambition, and uncommon drama turned an ancient league into the most obsessively followed sports product on planet earth.

The story of how English football took over the world is a business and entertainment saga for the global age. It's a familiar one, at that. It begins with a bright idea. What follows is a period of supercharged growth and frothy ambition, which leads to thrilling highs and unimagined riches. If you know anything about the dot-com boom or subprime mortgages, you know where this is heading.

The cracks start to appear. Lured by outlandish valuations, investors from far-off places pitch up to grab a slice of the action. Competitors emerge. Short-termism replaces sound judgment. And pretty soon the whole enterprise has degenerated into a tawdry mixture of peacock egos, pathological greed, and shocking profligacy.

The Premier League is a timeless tale of boom and bust, no different from all those other bubbles they warn you about in business-school textbooks. Except, that is, in one crucial respect.

In football, the bubble never burst.

As any train station news-stand will prove, here and now in the twilight of the newspaper era, one rule seems to be enough to keep no fewer than nine national dailies in business: there is no such thing as too many football pages. On any given morning, those nine newspapers will generate roughly one hundred pages of copy on the Premier League between them. And that's only in print media. Britain's fanatical coverage of its most popular product this side of the sandwich also buttresses twenty-four-hour sports news channels and fills the airwaves 24/7, 365 days a year. Even in the offseason.

And that's only in Britain.

Considering the fact that the Premier League is chronicled in such minute, neurotic detail every day of its existence, the idea of a complete history would be both impossible and laughable. It would be like trying to chronicle the ins and outs of stock market fluctuations over a period of twenty-five years – a lot of numbers, a lot of lunatics in pinstriped suits, and not at all fun to read.

But there is one aspect of English football's modern history that hasn't quite been unpacked: the inside story of how the Premier League became the Premier League Inc., not just a football product but the global sports, business, and entertainment behemoth it is today. This is the story we want to tell.

English football didn't begin in 1992. But that year, which marked the foundation of the Premier League, became the sport's BC/AD milestone, the defining moment when nothing would be recorded the same way again.

So how to tell the crazy story of everything that's happened since?

We started, unwittingly, by living through it. We were both raised in the UK in the 1980s, 1990s, and 2000s – the same period when English football transformed from a hyperlocal community activity into a worldwide entertainment monster. Our football afflictions independently led us to the same career as sportswriters and our coverage enabled us to chart an impressionistic, episodic history of the major inflection points in the league's development. Right in front of us was an impossible-not-to-tell version of the Premier League's first twenty-five years.

You couldn't talk about the founding of the league in 1992, for instance, without telling the story of Rupert Murdoch, Sky TV, and a dramatic breakaway by a handful of English club owners who had the radical idea of making money from football. And you couldn't track the league's explosive commercial growth without digging into those owners' secret obsession with the NFL while English football's weaponized merchandising and money-spinning brilliance had to be traced back to Manchester United's marketing revolution. There was also the confluence of stadium tragedies, fan behaviour, and economic factors that turned the match-going experience upside down and led to the construction of Arsenal's Emirates Stadium, the first of the Premier League's modern monuments to its own success. And all of that simply laid the table for foreign money to pour in, with two owners in particular irreparably altering the landscape: Russia's Roman Abramovich, who bought Chelsea in 2003, and a member of the royal family of Abu Dhabi, who acquired Manchester City five years later. In between them, of course, also came the invasion of American owners who learned the hard way that doing business in the cut-throat Premier League is nothing like running a hedge fund back home.

Any of those turning points could fill volumes by themselves. But take them collectively and the arc of the whole league emerges, from deeply parochial cultural concern to global phenomenon.

★

This book is not an exhaustive history of English football. This book is not about who won the league when or a catalogue of the greatest moments on grass. This is a tale of empire building.

In our telling, there are a collection of inflection points that have, in turn, set off subsequent successive waves in the Premier League's global conquest. And the book is organized around those moments, using each one to bring to life the characters who made them happen and probe the history, culture, and commerce that has accelerated the league's growth or, at times, has stood in desperate resistance to it.

For more than one hundred years in towns across England and Wales, football supporters have turned out to champion their local teams. These aren't 'franchises' in a 'league' in any American sense. These are deeply ingrained territorial and regional markers of English culture. No English club ever moves – they are too rooted in their communities; and if they ever die, it's basically of old age (or financial ruin).

But when the top division of English football became the Premier League, and as the deals blossomed and the money started to flow in, more foreign players started to follow that money to England; more foreign managers came across the Channel with less rugged, more refined styles; bigger stadiums shot up, and with them, so did the ticket prices, putting a financial and emotional hurt on even the most committed of supporters.

So this is the story of how the Premier League built one of the great global entertainment empires of our era, how it sustained its astonishing growth, and what it's willing to give up to keep plowing ahead.

Beyond our own attachment to the league, this book grew out of a combined decade of covering the English Premier League for the *Wall Street Journal*. Clegg became the *Journal*'s first European sports correspondent in 2009 and was succeeded by Robinson, who returned to Britain in 2012 after nine years in the United States. Clegg went on to edit the paper's football coverage from New York, and Robinson is still in London and press boxes around the UK.

In order to wrap our arms around a story of this size – and tell it through original reporting rather than combing through newspaper archives – we did the only reasonable thing and started at the beginning: the clandestine meetings that created the Premier League and the people who were in the room. The key players in those days were Arsenal vice chairman David Dein, Manchester United chairman Martin Edwards, and Tottenham Hotspur owner Irving Scholar. After speaking to that trio, we sat down with nearly one hundred other key figures from across the league's history, gaining unprecedented access. And for the first time in any retelling, we were able to secure rare interviews with decision makers and executives from each of the so-called Big Six clubs – Manchester City, Manchester United, Chelsea, Liverpool, Arsenal, and Tottenham. Those include sit-downs with a veteran of twenty-two years of management in the league, Arsène Wenger, and conversations with the billionaire owners of Liverpool (John W. Henry), Arsenal (Stan Kroenke) and the famously reclusive chairman of Tottenham (Daniel Levy).

We also tracked down dozens of less visible figures who were nonetheless crucial – and present – during major turning points in the Premier League's arc, from the signing of Cristiano Ronaldo by Manchester United, to Abramovich's acquisition of Chelsea, to the arrival of Emirati royals in Manchester.

Every scene in the book is reconstructed from direct accounts and our conversations with the people who lived them. And in several cases, we were able to retell those moments because we attended them in person as English football underwent its most radical upheaval in a century.

Joshua Robinson and Jonathan Clegg
London, May 2018

Prologue

London, November 2017

ONE BY ONE, they pulled up to the Churchill Hotel in Mayfair in black taxicabs, chauffeur-driven cars, and one silver Rolls-Royce.

They strode into the marble-floored lobby, sidestepped the tourists wheeling too much luggage, and briskly turned left towards the private meeting room where they were due at 10 a.m., hoping to look casual as they clocked which of their colleagues and nemeses had already arrived. These get-togethers were never simple. The last one had devolved into an argument about who contributed more to their little club and who deserved – no, who had the God-given right – to make the most money. They hoped this time that they could talk to one another with a bit more civility. This was a fancy place after all.

A cosmopolitan collection of millionaires, billionaires, and CEOs, they came from worlds as far apart as Wall Street, professional poker, and the greeting-card business. Most of this crowd would never have had any reason to cross paths. Nor did they particularly want to. They never chose one another – they barely even trusted one another – and yet here they were, on a Thursday morning in November, committed partners in the most popular live-entertainment business on the planet.

They were the owners, executives, and resident plutocrats of the twenty football clubs in the Premier League. And they were meeting to make sure that their collective cash cow, which generates more than $5.6 billion a season, kept fattening at the same astronomical rate as it had over the past quarter of a century. Since 1992, the Premier League's combined revenues have increased by an obscene 2,500 per cent. Not bad for a group of guys who mostly loathe one another.

But before this summit could begin, before the suits could get down to the business of England's most successful export this side of the English language, there was another age-old national ritual they needed to endure: milling around awkwardly at a social gathering.

By the hotel entrance, Liverpool Football Club's principal owner, the bespectacled hedge-fund billionaire John W. Henry, was making small talk with the grey-haired former sales rep in charge of the whole show, Premier League chief executive Richard Scudamore. Henry was fresh in from Boston to take stock of Liverpool's revival under a German coach whose horn-rimmed glasses, scruffy beard, and grey sweatpants meant he could easily pass for a Hackney dad. The team's only problem is that its owner knows plenty about winning, but in the wrong sport – Henry's other major hobby is running the Boston Red Sox.

Strutting past them without so much as a *buenos dias* came Ferran Soriano, a Catalan former rugby player, carrying himself with the swagger of a man whose club is in the process of running away with the Premier League title. That's because Manchester City were, in fact, crushing the competition – though technically it wasn't Soriano's club. He was there representing the interests of his boss, an Abu Dhabi sheikh who spent around £200 million to buy the team, another £1 billion on talent, attended one game in Manchester in 2010, and then never came back. But with Pep Guardiola, the sport's eccentric philosopher king and self-styled genius from Barcelona running the team back in Manchester, the club was in good hands.

Soriano wasn't alone on this morning. Trotting alongside him was Ivan Gazidis, a bald, Oxford-educated lawyer, standing in for his own absentee boss, the Arsenal owner 'Silent Stan' Kroenke, a rarely seen, never-heard real estate mogul who married a Walmart heiress and now seems less interested in owning sports teams – his portfolio also includes the NFL's Los Angeles Rams and the NBA's Denver Nuggets – than he is in owning the buildings they play in.

Those two made for a slightly awkward pairing since Manchester City had spent most of the previous decade on a personal mission to usurp Arsenal, signing away their best players and appropriating their gimmick of playing beautiful football above all else – with only one minor tweak. City actually won.

This had been a point of some consternation at the staid old Arsenal FC. The Gunners' manager, a sixty-eight-year-old Frenchman with a professorial air and a PhD in late-season chokes, was desperately trying to pull off one last coup before retirement. But Arsenal's fans didn't want to give him that chance. They'd staged protests and flown banners over the stadium urging Arsène Wenger to beat it – and take Silent Stan with him. The joke had been running for so long now that Wenger Out signs had become practically de rigueur at any gathering of more than twelve people. That same week, one was spotted at an anti-Robert Mugabe protest in Zimbabwe.

Soriano and Gazidis wasted no time in heading to the meeting room. Tony Bloom, the poker savant and professional gambler, took a little longer. Bloom, the owner of Brighton & Hove Albion, a seaside club whose name sounds like a Shakespearean battle cry, was briefly waylaid by a detour into the hotel restaurant to peruse their selection of cakes.

By the time Bloom was ready to enter the meeting, he was joined by Steve Parish, the fast-talking, exuberantly coiffed, bespoke-suited advertising millionaire who likes to race Porsches when he isn't putting out fires at his club, Crystal Palace. They entered through the thick white double doors and moved inside, at which point Parish took a seat directly next to Bruce Buck, the chairman of Chelsea. It wasn't because the two men were particularly close, but because the league still gets its owners, these billionaires, titans of business, and type-A personalities, to sit in alphabetical order, presumably to prevent any nasty cliques from forming.

Parish's Palace needed to pay close attention to the day's discussion of projected revenues because he was a little short of cash right then despite annual payouts of up to £150 million to each club. He was about to ask his business partners in New York, a pair of private-equity giants, to stump up millions of pounds to spend on new players as his team steeled itself for a battle in the second half of the season. (If results kept breaking against Palace, they faced relegation, allowing somebody else to sit next to Chelsea the following year.)

For defending champions Chelsea, sometimes known as Chelski on account of their owner, the free-spending Russian oligarch Roman Abramovich, who is worth more than £4 billion, the money would make less of a difference. That sort of wealth comes in handy when one of your more expensive habits is impulsively firing managers and then paying out handsome severance packages. Even as the meeting unfolded without him, Abramovich was weighing the fate of his operatically mannered Italian coach, Antonio Conte, who was set to become the oligarch's twelfth managerial victim in fourteen years. Still, Abramovich took a keen interest in the proceedings from a distance. For a forcefully discreet man, few things happen inside his team or around the league without his knowledge.

During the next two hours, the clubs in the room thrashed out the newest terms of their most valuable source of income: the Premier League's television broadcast rights, which were heading to auction in three months' time.

For twenty-five years, that sale had formed the backbone of the league's business. Its games now air in 185 countries – the United Nations recognize only 193 – and every weekend they are broadcast to a potential TV audience of 4.7 billion people. This wasn't a gathering of twenty football clubs. This was somewhere between a shareholders' conference and a production meeting for a reality-TV show that shoots each episode with a rotating cast of twenty-two men before a live studio audience.

So no one in the meeting batted an eyelash when Ed Woodward excused himself halfway through to take a pressing phone call. New York was on the line. As chief executive of the New York Stock Exchange-listed Manchester United, he needed to lead the first-quarter earnings call with investors and financial analysts. As a former JPMorgan investment banker, this was right in Woodward's wheelhouse. The business of actually running a successful football club, however, is a task he's less comfortable with. Woodward was terrified of upsetting Manchester United's own impulsive overlord, though he wasn't one of Woodward's direct bosses, the Florida-based billionaires who own the club. It was one of his own employees, the man he personally hired as the manager, the irascible Portuguese, José Mourinho, whose reputation for lifting trophies is matched only by his knack for driving opponents – and club chairmen – up the wall.

Mourinho, of course, never attended these meetings. He was still in Manchester, where he had lived in a luxury hotel for the previous year and a half instead of moving his family up from London. As far as that day's conference was concerned, the foremost needler of club chairmen in the room was the short, quiet man in glasses with a stake in Tottenham Hotspur. That man, chairman Daniel Levy, drives the hardest bargain in the league. He has proven so gifted at wringing out every penny from selling players to his opponents that Tottenham could afford to tear down the stadium where it had played since 1899 and move into a new £850 million complex situated exactly twenty yards away – with nearly twice the capacity and a removable turf pitch. The goal was to accommodate NFL games on any given Sunday and provide a fitting stage for Harry Kane, his twenty-four-year-old wonder boy with a silky touch and vacant expression who was being touted as the latest saviour of the England team.

No one in the room knew more about how difficult Levy could be than David Gold, the co-owner of West Ham. He sat a few seats down from Levy though he was easy to spot in the row of dark business attire. Gold was the white-haired eighty-two-year-old who rocked up in the silver Rolls-Royce Phantom sporting a green tartan suit, looking as if he'd just stepped out of a P. G. Wodehouse novel. And that wasn't the only thing that distinguished Gold from his fellow owners. He was also the only owner in the room to make his fortune in the one form of entertainment more popular among young men than football: porno mags.

By Gold's side was the lone female executive in the room, Baroness Brady of Knightsbridge, better known as Karren Brady or by her nickname, the 'First Lady of Football'. The West Ham vice chairperson was among the most feared executives at the table, not just for her ruthless professionalism – she famously married one of her own players and then sold him to a rival club, twice – but because she authored a weekly column in the *Sun*, where she routinely bad-mouthed rival Premier League executives.

But on this morning, everyone seemed to be on their best behaviour. They tolerated one another's presence because there was one fact they could all agree on: the Premier League wasn't merely the most watched sports league in the world. It was No. 1 and nothing else came remotely close.

None of the people in the Churchill Hotel on that November morning were particularly responsible for any of this. But without any real genius or acumen, the motley cast of characters that created the modern Premier League in 1992 had stumbled onto the sports equivalent of the iPhone. Pretty soon everyone everywhere wanted a piece. And in a remarkably short period, a small group of owners discovered the alchemy that turned ageing industrial cities and obscurely named clubs into the focus of compulsive global attention.

It would be generous to call too many of the outcomes in this story planned or credit genius to many of the individuals who pulled them off. But with packed stadiums, millions of viewers around the world, and TV money pouring in, life in the Premier League today was sweeter than anyone ever imagined.

Or it was in the executive boxes, at least. The business realities that weigh down other industries hadn't caught up to the Premier League just yet, but the owners were starting to realize that the league's octopus reach across the globe was beginning to strain ties at home, among the grass roots. As the windfalls of worldwide television and licensing contracts, shirt sales, merchandise, and international tours stacked up − and as the league sold itself off to the highest bidders − ticket prices soared, global football tourists flooded in (upsetting the parochial roots of football fandom), and the irresistible logic of commercial interests trumped the irrationality that bonded people and cities to teams that were, in many pockets of England, the only constants since before the First World War.

The result was an increasing tension between the aspirations of one of the world's biggest entertainment businesses and the native fans of English football − its original customers − whose identity is deeply intertwined with the product. This business, ultimately, embodied the challenges of globalization, of the push and pull between expansion and identity, about the universalization of a product that is steeped in decidedly non-universal customs.

When the meeting in the Churchill wrapped up, everyone in the room agreed to keep what they'd just discussed secret. But they headed back to the four corners of England and the wider world beyond with a complimentary cold sandwich in their hands and a smile on their faces. Because they were all convinced that by the time they got together next Scudamore, their favourite employee, would have sold the next raft of television rights at a healthy profit.

And the millionaire and billionaire members of this elite circle would all come back a little richer.

PART I

Breaking Away

'You could see the future.'
Irving Scholar, Tottenham Hotspur

I

IT WAS A little after 4 a.m. on 18 May 1992 when the phone rang in a twenty-fourth-floor apartment at Hampshire House, the New York co-op overlooking Central Park, and woke up the world's most powerful media magnate.

Rupert Murdoch groggily reached for the receiver and placed it to his ear.

The voice barked at him from 3,500 miles away, far too loud for this hour of the morning. 'We're going to need to put another £30 million on the table.'

Murdoch let the information sink in.

The thick twang on the line belonged to Sam Chisholm, a cantankerous New Zealand-born executive Murdoch had installed to turn around BSkyB, his fledgling British subscription-TV network. And the table in question belonged to the owners of England's top football teams, who were negotiating the sale of live TV rights to their matches. Thirty million was a sum that Murdoch could ill afford.

He closed his eyes and took a breath in the dark. The past few months had been some of the most draining of his life. Turnover at Fox in Los Angeles meant that he'd personally been running the network since February. Only weeks before, he had also emerged from a frantic two-year refinancing to dig the firm out of a debt crisis that threatened to force his News Corporation newspaper operation into liquidation. And all the while, he was locked in a fruitless struggle to get BSkyB off the ground in Britain. He felt like the whole ordeal had aged him twenty years.

'Is that okay?' Chisholm asked.

Murdoch exhaled. He was determined to make BSkyB a success – and not just because he had already plowed £2 billion into it.

More than anything, he wanted BSkyB to shut up the ghastly London dinner-party set, who reliably informed him at every social event that British television was simply the best in the world. This in a country with a meagre four channels, at least two of which seemed to be forever showing snooker. Murdoch had given up trying to argue. He knew exactly what the best television in the world looked like – he watched it every night at his home in the United States.

It had more channels. It had mass appeal. And it definitely did not involve bloody billiards.

But despite his expensive efforts, the British public had been slow to come around to his satellite offering. It had been five years since he had launched the subscription-TV network, and BSkyB were still losing £1 million per week and were 500,000 subscribers short of breaking even. Now Chisholm was asking him for an extra £30 million to trump a rival offer for the rights to broadcast a sport that he distinctly didn't care about.

English football.

Murdoch ran through the numbers in his mind. He winced.

In the years to come, signing off on an extra few million dollars for a prime piece of sports programming would become a no-brainer to Rupert Murdoch. By 1997, he would have spent some $5 billion on acquiring sports rights, brazenly signing megadeals for NFL, NHL, Major League Baseball, and NCAA college football games. But at 4 a.m. on that May morning in 1992, parting with a fortune to screen live English football didn't feel like a no-brainer. It felt absurd. The truth was, he didn't even like sport.

On the other hand, Murdoch sensed in his gut that if anything was going to put BSkyB on a path to growth it was live football. He of all people knew what the sport could do for a struggling business.

In 1969, Murdoch had acquired the *Sun*, then a failing leftist paper, and quickly transformed it into a populist tabloid filled with lowbrow gossip, topless models, and . . . at least a dozen pages of football every day. Within three years, it had become Britain's biggest-selling daily newspaper. Now, nearly a quarter of a century later, could football bail him out again? He and Chisholm had spoken many times about using the game's broad appeal to stick satellite dishes onto more middle-class homes. But how much were they willing to bet on it?

In the last few days, Chisholm had begun to express doubts about whether they could really afford the rights at all, that perhaps it was time to jump off this treadmill. The company's advisers, Arthur Andersen, had expressly cautioned against this kind of suicidal bid, arguing it was impossible to make money on such ludicrous terms.

'Well?' Chisholm prodded.

Murdoch paused to consider his options one final time. There would be no call to the BSkyB directors or other members of the board in London. Their opinions would have to wait. With Chisholm hanging on the line, Murdoch weighed a decision that would upend English football and redefine the world's media landscape. In the Manhattan predawn, it all came down to one simple question.

How high would he go?

Standing in the lobby of an upscale West London hotel with a sheaf of documents under his arm, a sealed envelope in his hand, and a look of weary bewilderment on his face, Rick Parry was asking himself the exact same thing.

Parry had arrived at the Lancaster Gate Hotel that morning ready for the most important moment of his professional life – and arguably the most important moment in English football since a group of Oxbridge graduates met in a Covent Garden pub in 1863 to approve the laws of the game. He was here to finalize plans for a new breakaway league composed of the country's top professional clubs, which would soon become the most popular enterprise in world sport. There was just one last piece of business to hash out before they could usher in this glorious new future. In an upstairs conference room at 10 a.m., Parry was due to address the twenty-two team owners – a crowd of self-made millionaires, small-time tycoons, and freewheeling entrepreneurs – and deliver his recommendation on which broadcaster should be awarded the television rights to their new enterprise.

This was no minor detail. For more than a decade, the men who ran English football had been squabbling over how, when, and where their games should be shown on television – and, more than anything, how much they should be paid for the privilege. Figuring out a solution to this problem once and for all had persuaded twenty-two men who couldn't agree on much of anything to put their differences aside and band together. This joint effort would upend the way football had been structured for more than a century, result in legal action from the sport's apoplectic governing body, and spark accusations of greed from the disapproving press, not to mention widespread hostility from football fans up and down the country.

Now, after two years of clandestine meetings, courtroom drama, and more late nights than Parry had worked during his two decades as an accountant, they were ready to put the finishing touches on something they called the Premier League.

All they had to do was pick a broadcaster for the Premier League's inaugural season. One proposal came from ITV. The other came from Murdoch's BSkyB, better known as Sky. No matter which way they went, their football teams were set to make more money than at any point in their history.

It was Parry's job as chief executive of the new league to advise this group of owners on which bid to accept. At that moment, no one in England had a firmer grasp of the details of the Premier League's fate than he did. For months, Parry had been in discussions with the key players from the rival camps. For weeks, he'd been running the numbers. For hours the night before, he had stayed up late in his hotel room drafting the presentation he was due to deliver that morning. But with hundreds of millions of dollars at stake and mere minutes to go until he was due to begin speaking, it dawned on Parry that he now had no earthly idea what he was going to say.

From across the hotel lobby, John Quinton, the bespectacled former head of Barclays bank and newly installed chairman of the Premier League, caught his eye and came over. He looked puzzled. 'What's going on?' he asked. Parry shrugged and glanced at his watch. He had twenty minutes to figure it out.

What was going on was that someone had moved the goalposts. With the final bids from both parties locked in, Parry had gone to bed the night before with his presentation finished and his mind made up: Sky would be the Premier League's first television partner.

Their bid worth £44.5 million a year outstripped ITV's by £12.5 million a year; plus, they had promised to show more matches and devote greater time to the broadcasts, transforming live football into a genuine television product. Sky's partnership with the BBC meant highlights would be available to anyone in Britain who owned a television set. The decision, in Parry's mind, was clear.

Or rather it had been until a little after 9 that morning, at which point Trevor East, an erstwhile football journalist and the head of football at ITV, arrived at the Lancaster Gate armed with two dozen sealed envelopes containing copies of a post-deadline counterbid from ITV, which he proceeded to distribute to each of the twenty-two team owners as they arrived.

Parry looked at the envelope in his hand now and shook his head. It was completely outside the rules, of course. He had personally instructed the rival bidders to put together their final offers and make presentations to the club chairmen on 14 May, four days earlier. But Quinton had warned him about just this sort of thing. 'There are no rules,' Quinton had said. 'There is a knock 'em down, drag 'em out negotiation, and the last man standing is the one who wins.' What was Parry supposed to do now? He couldn't blow up the talks altogether. There were millions at stake and the start of the season was only three months away. If he tried to throw out ITV's new bid, he would have been out of a job before the league he had worked so hard to build had even kicked off. Besides, the owners had seen it now. They knew there was more cash kicking around.

So Parry did the only reasonable thing under the circumstances. He called Sam Chisholm and invited him to submit a counter-counterbid. 'Hell,' Chisholm replied, followed by a string of more agricultural expletives. 'Let me get back to you.'

Which is how Parry ended up standing in the middle of a hotel lobby waiting for a phone call with chaos brewing around him, and nothing to do but wait. 'We'll have to delay the start of the meeting,' he told Quinton.

This was not how Parry was used to doing business. He was an accountant by trade, having worked at Ernst & Young, and had always prided himself on being a details person, the sort of diligent worker who stayed up late reading the Football Association rule book – the English game's equivalent of the tax code – to immerse himself in the century-old intricacies of the sport's governance. He didn't appreciate surprises. But ever since he'd been persuaded to get involved in football by Graham Kelly, an old professional acquaintance now in charge of the Football Association, the surprises had barely stopped.

It had all begun with the first chat in 1990 when Kelly informed him that some of the country's top teams were plotting to form a new league and break away from the Football League, the antiquated institution that had overseen English football for more than one hundred years. What made this act of rebellion fraught with legal and logistical hurdles was that the top teams in England were bound to every other professional club in the country by a four-tiered structure consisting of ninety-two clubs, which sat on top of a broader hierarchy of dozens more semi-pro and amateur divisions that encompassed some seven thousand additional teams and stretched down almost as far as those eleven blokes from your local pub. It is possible, at least in theory, for any club in the football pyramid to reach the top with enough time and enough promotions. This is how English football's ecosystem had worked, more or less, since 1899, a monument to Victorian Britain's sense of order.

Until the early 1990s, no one could foresee any reason for this ever to change.

But as the top clubs grew their business ambitions, they came to see the rest of the English game as a burden. Anytime they tried to do anything, from putting names on the backs of shirts to lengthening the half-time break, there were the others digging in their heels for the sake of it. The big clubs were fed up. Why should the biggest potential football businesses in the country have their futures tethered to entities that moved at roughly the pace of tectonic plates? Their plan was to take the pyramid and lop the pointy bit off. The rest could fend for themselves.

That proposition alone was so explosive that Kelly had to go to extreme lengths to keep their meeting a secret, forbidding Parry from even travelling to London. Instead, Kelly told him, they would meet in Manchester at the Midland Hotel, an inconspicuous venue that would be ideal for their conspiratorial chat. And it was an ideal spot for a football meeting except for one minor detail: someone else thought so, too. As Kelly and Parry were shown to a table in the dining room, they realized that the Football League, the very people they were trying to undermine, had chosen the same place for their Christmas party.

Those sorts of surprises had become a feature of Parry's time working in football. At another highly confidential meeting, Irving Scholar, the owner of Tottenham Hotspur, was forced to sneak out through a kitchen window to avoid the British press who were waiting out front. Parry thought to himself that he should've seen the ITV manoeuvre coming.

In the hotel lobby, Parry checked his watch again. It was at times like these that he could barely explain how he'd wound up getting involved in this absurd enterprise, much less become its chief executive.

Parry had joined the Liverpool office of Arthur Young as an accountant in 1979, eventually rising to the position of senior management consultant. When the city of Manchester embarked on a quixotic mission to bring the 1996 Summer Olympics to the rainiest city in England, Parry, a native of the north-west, had been seconded to the city's bid team. Manchester's Olympic dream soon fizzled out, but Parry's work on the bid brought him into the orbit of some of the leading string-pullers in British sport. And in that world, he met a group of ambitious young businessmen who were on a quixotic mission of their own.

They wanted to make money from English football.

2

ENGLAND'S NATIONAL PASTIME in the 1980s was not an obvious investment for anyone looking to turn a profit. In fact, it was barely running as a for-profit business at all.

Corporate sponsorship and pitchside advertising didn't arrive until the late 1970s. And even then, that income barely covered the cost of keeping the grass green. Television wasn't merely an afterthought, it was considered a vile, pernicious influence on the game, a fiendish ploy designed to keep fans at home on their couches instead of standing on the terraces under grey skies and persistent drizzle watching their local team eke out another 0–0 draw.

What little money there was in football came almost exclusively from gate receipts, though those had been falling steadily since the 1960s. And it wasn't hard to see why. The experience of attending matches was about as comfortable as waiting for a bus. Stadiums were, by and large, crumbling husks. Many had barely been touched since they sprang up in the waning days of the nineteenth century in inner-city districts and working-class industrial towns across the country. Conditions inside them were primitive at best and often perilous to fans' personal safety, with leaking roofs and rusting fences. What passed for food and drink was usually worse.

With so little upside, it's easy to understand why football wasn't exactly teeming with the business world's best and brightest. Club chairmen were traditionally butchers and builders, unpaid and happy to donate a few grand when required – but happier to enjoy the networking, kudos and cigar-smogged bonhomie that came with boardroom life on a Saturday afternoon. They didn't spend a lot of time fretting over declining attendances and chronic underinvestment because they didn't feel they had to. They were big fish in little ponds and saw themselves as custodians of local concerns that didn't make any money anyway. It's not as if they were running British Airways.

But those problems didn't just solve themselves. By the 1980s, they had been allowed to spiral out of control. During a decade in which Britain was changed almost beyond recognition by a bruising recession, rising unemployment, urban riots, the Falklands conflict, and mass financial deregulation that transformed the country's politics and society, English football went through a mutation of its own: from national sport to national embarrassment.

Fighting and disorder in the stands were now as much a feature of Saturday afternoons as the linesmen and corner flags. This despite the clubs' deliberately segregating away fans from home fans by confining them to a roped-off or gated corner of the stadium since the 1960s – a practice that is still in place today. The subsequent advent of closed-circuit television to curb violence inside the stadiums merely pushed the skirmishes into the streets, where clashes between fans and police became commonplace. Hooligan gangs with names like the Chelsea Headhunters, the Cleethorpes Beach Patrol, and West Ham's Inter City Firm turned the neighbourhoods around stadiums into the settings for turf wars, and the business of football fandom became a test of self-preservation. No longer did the principal danger of attending a match lie in the decaying infrastructure of English football. Now the threat of physical violence hung in the air, too – along with the powerful smell of urine.

As conditions on the terraces got worse, the game on the field itself seemed to degenerate back towards something resembling its origins as a series of semi-organized riots pitting rival villages against one another with a ball somewhere in the middle. English football was a famously rough, direct sport, short on technical refinement and long on reckless tackles. In the 1980s, though, many of the country's top clubs became fixated with the 'long-ball game', launching speculative passes up the field at almost every opportunity. The best-case scenario then was a lucky bounce or a knockdown near the goal. Accuracy was sacrificed and possession given away cheaply. Any attempt at skilful play was liable to get you substituted. While there is no question that long-ball football could be effective, there is also no question that it made for an unbearably dull spectacle.

If all this gives the impression of a game in decline, 1985 marked the year that English football hit rock-bottom – the first time, at least. In May, a fire broke out mid match at Bradford's Valley Parade stadium when a cigarette butt allegedly ignited a pile of festering rubbish beneath the stands, which had no extinguishers, and led to fifty-six deaths. Later that month, clashes between Liverpool and fans of Italian football superpower Juventus resulted in thirty-nine fatalities and more than six hundred injuries at the European Cup final at Heysel Stadium in Belgium. And in between the two disasters, the *Sunday Times* published a leader that appeared to speak for the public at large – and the upper echelons of government – in which it branded football as a 'slum game played by slum people in slum stadiums'.

The very fabric of the professional game was coming apart.

By the end of the season, the league's title sponsor, Canon, had abandoned the sport. Attendance for the year was the lowest on record since the 1920s. It looked as if football was finally headed the same way as the classic Victorian pastimes of bearbaiting, bare-knuckle boxing, and colonizing far-flung territories in the name of the Crown. It was not, in other words, a business that people were clamouring to invest in.

All of which made it exactly the sort of opportunity that appealed to an enterprising young commodity trader named David Dein.

David Dein always liked to think of himself as a man who could sniff out a good investment where others didn't. And from the time he dropped out of university at twenty-one to embark on a career in business, his instincts had been proven right.

Dein started out importing tropical fruit in Shepherds Bush Market, hawking mangoes, yams, and other foreign produce to London's growing Caribbean community. At the age of thirty-six, he took his skill as a salesman and moved into commodity brokering, where his company, London and Overseas Co., had a turnover of £42 million by 1981. A natural raconteur with an easy charm and a permanent tan, Dein attributed his success to his ability to identify value, take positions, and, when all else fails, roll the dice. By 1983, however, Dein's run of luck in the trading business had started to turn. His company was the victim of a fraudulent scheme involving an Indian businessman, a half-dozen investment banks, and a single shipment of sugar bound for Nigeria that would take him years to untangle. In the short term, Dein found his business saddled overnight with debts of around $20 million. That was the push he needed to start looking for new investment opportunities. Without leaving London, Dein found exactly what he was looking for: a distressed asset in an underperforming market that he could smell was ripe for a turnaround.

In February 1983, he paid £292,000 for 16.6 per cent of Arsenal Football Club.

Even for someone who had made his fortune betting on risky propositions, Dein's investment in Arsenal looked like a reckless gamble. The club was a sleepy old institution in north London that hadn't won the league in more than a decade and whose home at Highbury was so quiet that it became known as the 'Library'. Dein's fellow traders were bemused. Friends looked aghast when he told them. Even Peter Hill-Wood, the club's majority owner and the man who had sold Dein his shares, called the investment 'crazy'.

'To all intents and purposes,' Hill-Wood said at the time, 'it's dead money.'

Dein didn't see it that way – which wouldn't be the only time he found that his vision for Arsenal was at odds with the rest of the board. The other directors were mostly men like Hill-Wood, a cigar-chomping Old Etonian whose grandfather had joined the Arsenal board in 1919. Like most English football executives at the time, Hill-Wood had inherited control of the club and viewed it much like being bequeathed a crumbling chateau in the south of France, less a business endeavour than a lifelong financial obligation. 'I have never looked at a football club as a financial asset,' he said. 'We used to buy shares at thirty bob each and, to be honest, viewed them as rather a waste of money.'

Dein was more than happy to squander his personal wealth on buying up shares. Over the next decade, he was relentless in building up his stake in Arsenal, though he insisted a story about an eight-hundred-mile round-trip to acquire two shares from an elderly woman in Scotland was apocryphal. By 1989, his shareholding had grown to 41 per cent, Arsenal were winning championships again and Dein was regarded as one of English football's most prominent executives. Though he was derided in some quarters with that most aristocratic of insults – a social climber; the best-known vice chairman in football, one critic called him – he had become a power broker in the small circle of executives who made it their business to drag English football out of the nineteenth century by the end of the twentieth.

Dein didn't have to travel far to find his accomplices. In 1982, Irving Scholar, a real estate tycoon, had tied up a deal for a property situated just four miles from Highbury – a stately pile of brick and mortar known as Tottenham Hotspur Football Club. Scholar had seen Dein rolling around town in a sports car with personalised number plates for years and was vaguely acquainted with his brother Arnold. But the two executives had never really crossed paths. Like Dein, Scholar was a self-made man. And, like Dein, he considered himself to be a savvier operator than most of the other owners in English football. His own acquisition of Tottenham had amounted to a corporate raid in which he scoured the club's original shareholder register, bought up shares cheaply and surreptitiously, and muscled his way onto the board of directors. In all, Scholar paid £600,000 for the 25 per cent stake that he used to seize control of his boyhood football club.

Up north, Martin Edwards had come to be in control of Manchester United through similar means. His father, a local butcher and wily businessman known as 'Champagne' Louis Edwards for his love of bubbly and fine cigars, had quietly amassed a 50 per cent stake in the club by similarly tracking down individual shareholders and snapping up their shares. When he died of a heart attack in 1980, Martin took over as Manchester United chairman. He soon became the third member of this group of modernizers after a 1983 pre-season tour to Swaziland, the tiny landlocked kingdom in southern Africa, which was chosen since political sanctions prevented British teams from playing in neighbouring South Africa because of apartheid. Tottenham also made the trip – a team called Tottman that was drawn from the two clubs defeated the Swaziland national team 6–1 in Lobamba's Somhlolo National Stadium – which is where

Edwards and Scholar shared their frustrations about the Football League, their resistance to change, the endless series of subcommittees, and their confounding lack of commercial know-how.

'It was a bit of a club – a club within a club,' Scholar said of the trio of forty-something young bucks. 'What we all had in common was that we loved football and we wanted football to do well. We knew that if football did well everything else would flow from that.'

Dein, Edwards, and Scholar weren't the only modernizers in English football at this time. Others would join their band of agitators, notably Everton chairman Phil Carter and Liverpool's Noel White, to round out what was then the Big Five group of the country's top clubs.

But in 1985, with English football mired in an existential crisis, absent from TV screens, and seemingly on the road to financial ruin, it was these three men whose casual conversations would kick-start the breakup of the game's old order. And it was their vision for the future that ultimately led to the lobby of the Lancaster Gate Hotel on a May morning in 1992. They pictured a modern, marketable, and media-friendly league, with safe, attractive stadiums fit for corporate hospitality that would harness the power of television and transform their teams into billion-dollar businesses.

As it happened, this vision had a name: the National Football League.

David Dein's tenure as a director of Arsenal, which began in 1983 and ended in 2007, will forever be defined by the Invincibles, the Gunners' side that went through all thirty-eight matches of the 2003–4 league campaign without losing a single one. It hadn't been done since the 1880s and it hasn't been matched since. Dein, as the club's vice chairman with a hand in every transfer, was one of the team's principal architects.

But it wasn't Dein's first brush with perfection in sports. That had come three decades earlier, shortly after Dein and his American wife, Barbara, were married and the newlyweds decided to spend some time in Miami. There, Dein was introduced to a different kind of football – 'Larry Csonka . . . He was about 200 kilos, a man mountain, a brick wall!' – courtesy of the 1972 Miami Dolphins.

The '72 Dolphins remain one of the most mythical teams in the annals of US professional sports and are still the NFL's only undefeated championship team. To this day, they convene once a season to pop champagne when the last remaining unbeaten team in the NFL finally loses a game, thereby preserving Miami's indelible mark on history. The Dolphins left a lasting impression on Dein, too, though not thanks to the exploits of quarterback Bob Griese or Larry Csonka, their Hall of Fame fullback. Dein was enamoured with the big screens at the Dolphins' stadium, the wide concourses, the gourmet food, and the cheerleaders. This, he realized, was what a top-class sporting event looked like.

'That was an eye-opener,' Dein said. 'I understood that was how a sport should be run. The way they marketed it – it was more than ninety minutes of football, it was an event. This was a family sport, good outlets, you could get a decent meal. Even the toilets were good.'

The toilets, it must be observed, were not merely a footnote. Dein would make the bathrooms in English football a personal crusade. To him, they embodied everything that was wrong with the sport.

Of all the potential hazards of attending an English football game in the 1980s – the dilapidated stadiums, the threat of fan violence, the damp chill of British weather – nothing was more fraught in Dein's mind than the experience of venturing inside the stadium toilets. They were not merely basic but downright squalid, often situated in the open air and comprising little more than a tin wall and a trench dug into the ground. (If you are even asking about the women's toilets, we have not made sufficiently clear the dire state of English football at this time.) Even worse, half-time lasted just ten minutes, an interlude so brief that many fans opted to forego the long queues for the bathroom by relieving themselves against a wall or into a sink instead.

'We're in the entertainment business,' Dein implored fellow owners at league meetings. 'It's got to be an enjoyable experience. You don't want to queue for ten minutes and still can't get to the loo. It's got to be pleasant.'

Much to his dismay, Dein found the other owners unmoved by

his bathroom predicament. It took him five years to convince them to extend half-time to fifteen minutes. Dein's mission to transform the toilet-going experience of English football would take a lot longer.

But with bathrooms remaining an ambition for the future, he made progress on other fronts. Indeed, not long after he bought into Arsenal, the club's stadium began to exhibit clear signs of his exposure to US sports. The Gunners added executive boxes and a roof to the Clock End stand in 1988. In the years that followed, the club would add a pair of jumbotrons, a supersize gift shop, a club museum, and, in 1994, its first mascot – an eight-foot green dinosaur in a baseball cap named Gunnersaurus, invented in a competition by an eleven-year-old.

The NFL influence would soon show up across north London, too, at Tottenham's White Hart Lane. Irving Scholar made his own pilgrimage to the US shortly after taking control of Spurs, searching for ideas to ramp up the club's marketing and commercial operations, an area where Tottenham had fallen behind. Spurs had only signed its first jersey sponsorship deal with the brewer Holsten in 1983, becoming one of the last top-flight teams in the league to splash a corporate logo across its famous white shirts.

Unlike Dein, who got to know the NFL as a spectator of the Miami Dolphins, Scholar had an insider's connection – to one of the all-time greats, no less, who changed the league and racked up accomplishments that are celebrated to this day.

His man was O. J. Simpson.

By coincidence, Scholar's trip to the States came at a time when the NFL was looking to broaden its global footprint. One suggestion making the rounds was the idea of staging a pre-season game in London between the previous season's Super Bowl participants. And Simpson had somehow involved himself as a middleman. Which is how Scholar wound up partying in New York City with a tuxedo-clad O. J. and a fur-coated Nicole Brown one night in 1983 – 'Serious VIP stuff,' Scholar recalled. The next day, Simpson introduced Scholar to NFL supremo Pete Rozelle upstairs at the league's Park Avenue headquarters. And even though the Super Bowl rematch never came off, Scholar returned to London with a new appreciation for the

NFL's way of doing business. 'In terms of the commercial attraction, it was amazing,' he remembered. 'You could see the future.'

Scholar would continue his NFL education in the following years, attending a New York Jets game in 1987 with Martin Edwards, who also became an enthusiastic disciple of the NFL's marketing playbook. Five years later, Manchester United would unveil a black jersey for away games that looked suspiciously like the black uniforms of the Los Angeles Raiders. Had Raiders owner Al Davis noticed, he probably would've sued.

In the decade before 1992, as the Premier League's new wave sought to upend English football and transform a game rooted in amateurism into an entertainment product for the twenty-first century, the NFL served as a kind of business case study for Dein, Scholar, and Edwards. It informed their thinking on everything from corporate branding to constitutional governance, from big-picture ideas to smaller details such as printing names on the backs of shirts. In their quest to infuse a century-old sport with the commercial expertise and razzle-dazzle of the NFL, no one was too shy to pilfer an idea.

But of all the things they learned from across the pond, one lesson stood out. If they were ever going to make any money from owning a football club, it was going to come from television.

3

MAKING A FORTUNE from television seemed an unlikely scenario when Irving Scholar, Martin Edwards, and a half-dozen other team owners convened in late December 1985 at the Posthouse Hotel, a monolithic grey block on the outskirts of Heathrow Airport. Back then, English football didn't look much like a dynamite TV product. Mostly because it wasn't technically a TV product at all.

Unable to reach a deal with the two major terrestrial channels, the BBC and ITV, for coverage of live games, the 1985–6 season kicked off in August with no domestic TV deal in place. That meant no live games on television and no highlights programmes either. ITN even refused to announce the results on their evening news bulletins.

The season was effectively invisible.

How the world's most popular sport was dropped from the TV schedule altogether in the country that invented the game was partly due to a breakdown in relations between team owners and the TV channels. Football executives had long been convinced that the BBC and ITV were colluding to keep the rights fees for matches artificially low, a suspicion that only hardened when negotiators for the two broadcasters pulled up to a critical meeting at White Hart Lane that summer and emerged from the same black cab.

But the blackout was also a legacy of English football's long-standing ambivalence towards television, an attitude borne out of the game's entrenched traditions, its time-honoured revenue-sharing model, and an overall power structure that by 1985 was teetering on the brink of collapse.

Football first appeared on British television screens in 1937, though it wasn't until 1960 that anyone made a concerted effort to show regular live games. That year, ITV agreed to a deal worth £150,000 with the Football League to air twenty-six live matches. There was just one catch: they couldn't show all ninety minutes of those matches. Terrified of the impact regular televised football would have on attendance, which remained their only real source of income, the clubs refused to allow ITV's cameras to start rolling until the second half. This compromise lasted a few weeks until Arsenal and Tottenham refused to allow ITV's cameras to roll at all, at which point English football's first major TV deal collapsed in a bout of mutual recrimination between clubs and broadcasters.

Over the next four decades, relations barely improved. By 1964, the BBC had debuted *Match of the Day*, its Saturday night highlights show, for which it paid a grand total of £5,000. The owners of the ninety-two Football League clubs split the money equally, which amounted to roughly £50 each, and congratulated themselves on expertly sidestepping the scourge of live television.

For the best part of two decades afterwards, that arrangement was allowed to persist. Football was shown on TV almost exclusively through highlights programmes. What little money the game commanded in rights fees was shared equally among the clubs in all four divisions, meaning Manchester United received the same payout as Millwall.

The players, for their part, had little inkling that any of this could ever change. They had been raised to believe that professional football was a trade, like carpentry or plumbing. You left school as a teenager to join a team as an 'apprentice' – which meant a lot of time spent cleaning the senior players' boots – and eventually graduated to a pro contract if you were good enough. Footballers earned decent wages – in the 1970s, the best players took home £12,000 to £15,000 a year, roughly double the average working man's salary – but by the time they retired from the game in their mid thirties, they needed to find something else to do. No one made enough to kick up their feet for the rest of their lives. So the players who didn't slide into coaching went back to their working-class roots and did working-class jobs – driving taxis or running pubs. Besides, if they did want to change the system, it's not like football gave them much of a voice.

By the 1980s, however, both clubs and broadcasters had had

enough and began to agitate for change. Eager for the mammoth ratings that live sport could deliver, the BBC and ITV were no longer content to show highlights and started to push for a package of live games. At the same time, the owners of the biggest clubs had come to realize that the terrifying impact of live television on attendance may have been a little overblown – people weren't abandoning the terraces for their sofas – and that their games were more than a little undervalued.

The nudge came from a familiar source. In 1982, the NFL inked a five-year, $2 billion TV deal that was widely hailed as a landmark in sport broadcasting history. 'The numbers were mind-boggling,' Scholar said. The following year, English football signed a TV deal of its own, this one a little more forgettable. The two-year deal was worth £5.2 million and allowed just ten live games to be aired each season. Within a few years, it would be eclipsed both in size and significance to English football. But in its own way, the 1983 contract stands apart as a triumph of deal-making. It was the rare negotiation that left everyone involved completely unhappy.

The truce didn't last long. Even before the contract expired, the BBC and ITV were railing against the ten-game limit and demanding more live matches. Rattled by dwindling attendance, which was in no way related to television coverage, the country's smaller clubs clamoured for a return to highlights-only programming. While the biggest clubs looked enviously across the Atlantic and saw cash piling up in the coffers of the NFL, NBA, and Major League Baseball owners, they realized that they were paupers by comparison – and they had a game that the whole world *actually played*. Now was the time, they decided, to get what they were owed from television. And if that meant cutting out their counterparts in the lower divisions, then that is what they were prepared to do.

Negotiations about renewing the 1983 deal had predictably imploded. The smaller clubs balked at increasing the number of live games, and the broadcasters laughed off a demand from Oxford United's owner, the cigar-inhaling media mogul Robert Maxwell, that they fork over £10 million for live rights. Their final offer of £4 million was summarily rejected, the meetings collapsed, and the 1985–6 season kicked off with no football on TV.

For the likes of Irving Scholar and Martin Edwards, who were trying to kick-start their clubs' commercial operations, the situation was abominable. Clubs were reduced to customizing their pitchside advertising hoardings to hawk products sold in Scandinavia, the one place on planet earth where it was still possible to watch live English football every weekend thanks to a £50,000 deal Scholar had forced through with Thames Television when the domestic contract fell apart. Edwards had even more reason to be infuriated by the blackout. Manchester United started the 1985–6 season with ten straight wins and topped the table for the first five months of the season. But without TV coverage, his team's achievements were barely noticed. (And by the time the television deal was restored, United had been leapfrogged by Liverpool.)

The blackout had been in effect for a matter of weeks when the Big Five met to discuss the most severe option available: ripping up their membership in the Football League and setting up a league of their own.

It wasn't the first time that the top clubs had threatened to abandon their association with the other seventy-odd teams that made up the four tiers of English football. Except this time it felt like more than grandstanding. The rebels invited representatives from Newcastle, Manchester City, and Southampton to the breakaway talks, and though nothing materialized on this occasion, the threat of what Edwards referred to as the 'nuclear option' hung in the air even as they began negotiations at the Posthouse Hotel.

The talks that followed were long, hostile, and full of obstinacy. But after six hours of back-and-forth, the club owners dispatched by each of the four divisions carved out an agreement on a ten-point plan that would give top-division clubs a greater share of TV and sponsorship revenues and a greater say in overall decision making. Within two days of the agreement, football was back on the air, albeit only after the clubs were forced to accept a collective sum of just £1.3 million for each of the next two seasons. The broadcasters were still sticking to absurd arguments that football could never be a premium TV property because ninety minutes was far too long for most people to spend sitting down.

The blackout crisis had been averted, but football's TV problem remained. As they left the Posthouse Hotel, Scholar, Edwards, and Dein resolved that next time they would take matters into their own hands. With satellite broadcasting finally set to arrive in Britain, the television landscape was changing. To unlock the game's potential, they needed to partner with someone who understood the magnetism of live sport and had a concrete vision for how satellite technology could transform English football beyond recognition.

Anthony Simonds-Gooding had exactly that vision.

He called it the 'squarial'.

Simonds-Gooding was the charismatic chairman of fledgling broadcaster BSB, one of two companies fighting for control of the nascent British satellite-TV market in the late 1980s. BSB was the country's only official satellite network, with a broadcast licence sanctioned by the government, a consortium of public-service broadcasting executives on its board, and state-of-the-art technology at its disposal. Its rival, Rupert Murdoch's Sky, had none of this. Sky relied on comparatively primitive technology and it lacked government backing, an inconvenience it planned to sidestep by beaming a signal to the UK from Luxembourg.

Leaning on his marketing know-how from his days at Saatchi & Saatchi, Simonds-Gooding cooked up a plan to outwit Sky and win the satellite wars by focusing on branding. He was going to sell BSB on the backs of two unique features. One was the squarial, a ten-inch-square aerial conceived as a stylish alternative to the traditional round satellite dish. The other was live football.

Simonds-Gooding was convinced that live sport was the key to making satellite TV a success in Britain, and in March 1988 he made his pitch to David Dein, Everton's Philip Carter, and the remaining members of the Football League's management committee, outlining a future in which satellite TV beamed hundreds of matches to armchair sports fans, broke terrestrial TV's chokehold on the game, and sent club revenues skyrocketing. The presentation got the audience sitting up straight, but what came next had them falling out of their chairs. BSB's initial bid of £11 million was already three times the value of the league's current contract – and that figure was projected to rise to £25 million a year if certain subscription targets were met.

What's more, BSB proposed forming a joint venture with the league, giving clubs a piece of future subscription income and advertising revenue from live football, plus a piece of whatever it made from boxing and other sport.

When the details of BSB's offer were put to all ninety-two Football League clubs in June, it proved to be one of the few occasions in more than a century of professional football in England when the clubs were in (almost) universal agreement. The clubs voted 91–1 to open negotiations with BSB, paving the way for subscription TV to shake up the stuffy world of English football.

Then, while owners began plotting ways to squander their new-found riches on new players and their increasing wages, doubt set in. Dein, Scholar, and the rest of the Big Five began to have second thoughts. For all of BSB's obvious advantages, one thing was missing: two years after the company's launch and mere months before it was due to hit the airwaves, the company hadn't actually shot a satellite into orbit. 'The whole thing was literally pie in the sky,' Dein said. Then there was the fact that BSB seemed rather extravagant for a start-up. The way they burned through money made the Big Five nervous. They were headquartered in a gleaming glass building in the chic Battersea neighbourhood where, a rival TV executive observed, 'everyone had a BMW and a chauffeur'. At one of the many corporate parties BSB laid on for investors, the company spent £80,000 on designer peppermints.

Spooked by the possibility that BSB might not survive to the end of their contract and leave football off British TV screens again, the Big Five began to cast around for an alternative. As tantalizing as the prospect of satellite TV was, they felt more comfortable with something a little more down to earth. What they were looking for was a proven broadcast executive, someone with their finger on the pulse of the British public. What they wanted more than anything was a pragmatist.

They settled on a man whose most famous contribution to British broadcasting was a puppet rat with dark glasses, a Hawaiian shirt, and a thick Black Country accent. The executive's name was Greg Dyke, an up-and-comer at ITV, who had revived the flagging morning show *TV-am* by adding Roland Rat to the line-up during school holidays. Within a month, the show's audience had doubled.

Dyke, a jaded former print journalist from the London suburbs with a horseshoe of silver hair, was an outsider in the clubby world of British broadcasting. The archetypal barrow boy made good, Dyke had once been mistaken for his own chauffeur. More than anything, he was a realist. (Years later, during a peripatetic career that would take in stops as a Manchester United board member, as chairman of Brentford Football Club, and as director general of the BBC, Dyke would attend the 2014 World Cup draw as head of the FA. When England were placed in a group alongside Italy and Uruguay, Dyke responded by pretending to slit his own throat. The gesture proved prophetic. That summer, England were eliminated without winning a single game, their worst World Cup performance in six decades.)

But back in 1988, Dyke was also realistic about the value of live football and the threat subscription TV posed to the terrestrial channels. With the Big Five dithering over BSB's offer for live rights, Dyke sensed an opening. 'I decided my job was to pinch those rights,' Dyke wrote in his autobiography. So he enlisted Trevor East at ITV to set up a meeting with one of the team owners, preferably from one of the big clubs and ideally someone forward-thinking who would be open to Dyke's direct approach to doing business.

That man could be none other than David Dein. Greg Dyke met him at Suntory, a ritzy Japanese restaurant just around the corner from St James's Palace in the West End, in the summer of 1988. It turned out to be a perfect match. Dein's frustration with English football's blazer culture and its endless committees and subcommittees mirrored Dyke's own experience in the world of broadcasting. Recalling their meeting later, Dyke described Dein rather dreamily as the 'most revolutionary bloke I'd met in football'. Dein, for his part, admired Dyke's plain-spoken style and anti-establishment ethos. 'Greg is a swashbuckler; he shoots the lights out,' as Dein put it. 'We were kindred spirits.' By the end of the meal, the two had cooked up a plan for a TV offer to rival BSB's.

Unlike the majority of TV executives at the time, Dyke wasn't interested in the redeeming social importance of his programming. He was interested in ratings. Dyke was after the mass audience that he knew would attach itself to live top-division football. The lower divisions were far less interesting. So Dyke and Dein decided to cut them out of the deal. Dyke would offer each of the Big Five clubs – Liverpool, Arsenal, Manchester United, Everton, and Tottenham – a minimum of £1 million for the rights to their home matches provided they could extract themselves. The remaining eighty-seven clubs in the Football League, Dyke reasoned, could figure out a deal of their own.

Dyke's proposal was clear-eyed, uncompromising, and unscrupulous. He was speaking the Big Five's language. When he met their representatives in a Knightsbridge restaurant to discuss his offer, Dyke sealed the deal by admitting that he thought the BBC and ITV had been colluding over football rights. 'He was the first person ever to tell us the truth,' said Irving Scholar. 'It was at that moment, for me, that Greg Dyke won the contract.' The exact details of the ITV offer were fleshed out later with the inclusion of five more teams – Aston Villa, Newcastle, Nottingham Forest, Sheffield Wednesday, and West Ham – which would receive a lesser sum. But by the end of the evening, the teams were on board, handshakes were exchanged, and champagne corks were popped.

The Football League and the rest of its member clubs weren't quite so cock-a-hoop. When they discovered that the Big Five had been unilaterally negotiating a TV deal for themselves, they interpreted it as an act of betrayal and swiftly retaliated. Philip Carter was fired from his position as Football League chairman, David Dein was made to step down from the league's management committee, and Bill Fox, a former corporal in the British army and chairman of the struggling second-division Blackburn Rovers, was elected as the league's new president. This riposte succeeded in widening the divide between the Big Five and the rest of the Football League. But it came too late to salvage BSB's deal for football. To stave off a rebellion by the top clubs – Edwards's so-called nuclear option – the Football League folded and opened negotiations with ITV. They ultimately agreed to a deal worth £11 million a year for twenty-one live games. ITV also undercut the BBC by including highlights in its rights package and choosing not to use them – all in a ploy to knock *Match of the Day* off the air.

The marriage between English football and ITV was not a perfect love story, but by the end of the first season it looked like a lasting relationship. Football succeeded in delivering the huge audiences Dyke had been banking on – the final game of the 1988–9 season, which saw Arsenal snatch the title from Liverpool with a last-gasp goal at Anfield, drew an audience of more than 10 million, the largest ever for a league match. And the bumper payday that the First Division clubs received from the ITV deal helped them forget about the underhanded way it had come about. 'These club chairmen had eyes bulging, they couldn't believe it,' Dyke remembered.

Things didn't work out quite so well for BSB. Without regular live football to help sell subscriptions, the star-crossed satellite network haemorrhaged money until it was forced into a merger with its rival, Sky.

The new company, now known as BSkyB, would be under Rupert Murdoch's control. Though Dyke remained anxious about the power of satellite TV, he wasn't unduly worried. After all, he had the Big Five in his corner. What Dyke couldn't have anticipated was the crisis that started at a single Liverpool match and would shake English football to its foundations.

4

THE DISASTER THAT unfolded on the afternoon of 15 April 1989, at Hillsborough Stadium in Sheffield, was a sporting tragedy that immediately transcended sport.

When ninety-six Liverpool fans were killed – and more than seven hundred injured – in a crush on the terraces caused by a combination of severe overcrowding and negligent policing, it was more than the deadliest stadium catastrophe in British history. It was a calamity that has blighted the lives of thousands; led to more than two decades of smears, cover-ups, and outright lies by culpable authorities; and raised a series of deeply troubling social, political, and economic questions. To this day, the country is still grappling with the fallout.

But in the narrow world of football, once the shock and grief began to subside, it brought about a ground-shaking business crisis. The catalyst was Lord Justice Peter Taylor, who was appointed to conduct an official inquiry into the Hillsborough disaster. His findings, which were published in January 1990, laid bare the parlous state of the national game, from crowd disorder to derelict stadiums. It also recommended solutions to these problems, including the removal of crowd fencing, the reduction of standing-only areas, and a gradual transition to all-seater venues. (To the delight of Arsenal's David Dein, who continued to wage a holy war on stadium bathrooms, it even addressed the toilets, which it described as 'primitive in design, poorly maintained and inadequate in number'.)

'He got everything 100 per cent right – right down to the loos!' Dein said. 'He saw that the stadiums needed to be modernized, that you need to give people a better experience. When I read that report, I thought, *Gosh, this guy has got it*. Something had to be done.'

The government duly implemented a ban on standing in stadiums, requiring every club in the top division to have all-seater grounds by the start of the 1994–5 season. In doing so, officials dropped an economic dilemma in the lap of every club in the league. Teams were expected to stump up for the refurbishment, remodelling, or wholesale rebuilding of their home stadiums even though those same renovations would inevitably result in reduced capacity and cut into their primary revenue stream.

'We went from 55,000 at the time to 36,000 overnight with the stroke of a pen,' Dein recalled, speaking about the capacity at Highbury – though the Gunners were among the lucky ones. Many clubs found themselves threatened with bankruptcy.

The government agreed to subsidize a portion of any stadium conversions, but the First Division teams still needed a source of income to cover this sudden shortfall. It didn't take the Big Five long to settle on a solution: they resurrected the possibility they'd been kicking around for years. If they were free to negotiate TV deals on their own – and if they could keep the money for themselves rather than being forced to share it with the lower divisions – this would go a long way towards plugging this new funding gap.

English football had been edging towards a breakaway by the biggest clubs for the better part of a decade. Now, in the aftermath of the Taylor Report, they could finally argue it had become a necessity.

When the Big Five and Greg Dyke met at a chichi Soho restaurant to discuss the renewal of ITV's broadcast contract in the autumn of 1991, the decision was made. Over prime cuts of steak, David Dein, Martin Edwards, Philip Carter, Irving Scholar, and newly appointed Liverpool chairman Noel White agreed to renounce their memberships of the Football League and establish a league of their own, an enterprise that would be run by its twenty member clubs for those twenty member clubs, with the proceeds from television, advertising, corporate sponsorship, and commercial activity going directly to them. There was no going back now.

To achieve their vision, they would be forced to rip up a century of *this is how we do things*, incur millions in legal expenses, and oversee one of the wildest battles for television rights in broadcast history. But within twelve months of that autumn night, the Premier League would be up and running. They were on their way to founding the most popular professional league on earth.

If the decision to renounce membership of the Football League and form a new, more advantageous league sounds straightforward, the reality was a little more complex. The only thing binding the ninety-two Football League teams together was a dusty agreement to operate as a sort of loose association. The issue was that everyone inside that loose association treated it as iron-clad.

For starters, the Big Five were staring at a public-relations nightmare. While it was true that the impetus behind the Premier League was a desire for greater control – of their finances, their commercial arrangements, and the entire business of English football – they couldn't possibly share that with the general public. It sounded a little too much like naked self-interest. Plus, they were still linked to the divisions below them by the annual ritual of promotion and relegation. They would have to find a more palatable solution, something that England's football-going public could understand, even support.

Then there were the practical hurdles. Some years earlier, the Football League had introduced a piece of legislation dictating that any club wishing to quit the league would have to serve a notice period of three years. The move was specifically designed to head off the sort of breakaway the Big Five were now proposing. The Big Five answered by hiring a cadre of high-priced lawyers to find a work-around, but they all came back with the same bad news. 'The legal advice was that it's watertight,' said Rick Parry, who was now working full time as a consultant to the new league. 'The lawyers said you can't ignore it; if this goes to court, it will be very messy.'

As it turned out, all of these thorny problems had the same exact solution: a venerable institution known as the Football Association.

Formed in 1863 as the national governing body for English football, the FA had never concerned itself with the day-to-day running of the pro game. That was the remit of the Football League. The FA's chief responsibilities were safeguarding the game's rules and overseeing the perennially hapless England national team. Predictably, the two organizations had spent the best part of a century at logger-heads, which helps explain why the FA was all too happy to back the Big Five's breakaway – the Football League would go ballistic.

The FA's support would prove crucial. The governing body's blessing allowed the clubs to justify their breakaway on the grounds that it would raise the standard of the national team. The FA, which was in the midst of producing its latest inquest into England's failure to win the World Cup since 1966, hastily rewrote the document to include a hearty endorsement of the Premier League even though the specific benefits they outlined – an eighteen-team league operated in partnership with the FA – were later abandoned when the Premier League formed as a twenty-two-team league run independently from the FA. The only real concession the FA received in exchange for their support was that the new league would be known as the FA Premier League. And even then, the 'FA' part was left out of the Premier League's Founder Members Agreement until Graham Kelly, the FA's chief executive, added it to the document by hand.

The other benefit of the FA's support wasn't obvious until several months later when Rick Parry unearthed it in the yellowing pages of the Football Association's rule book. Holed up in a room at Whites Hotel before a meeting at FA headquarters, he was killing time by leafing through a copy of the century-old text. It was there, roughly ninety pages in, that Parry uncovered an obscure stipulation stating that no league could require 'A Full Member Club or an Associate Member Club' to give notice of its intention to withdraw before 31 December of the current playing season. Which, in plain English, meant the Football League's three-year rule was in direct contravention of FA rules. Parry had found himself a loophole. If he read this correctly, then the Premier League clubs were free to resign from the Football League and begin playing the following year.

'That was pretty much the eureka moment,' Parry said.

With the legal hurdle cleared, all that was left was the small matter of crafting a constitution for the new league, a charter that would govern a pro-sports start-up from its initial launch through a twenty-five-year transformation into a global media and entertainment behemoth. The document in question took precisely forty-five minutes to cobble together. It was produced on 13 June 1990, after a meeting to iron out some final details, including how the new league would divide its TV revenue. Here, the Premier League again looked across the Atlantic for inspiration.

Parry, now installed as the league's inaugural chairman, had travelled to the United States to spend time with long-time NFL executive director Don Weiss, a member of league supremo Pete Rozelle's inner circle, who had helped build the NFL empire. Parry returned with a raft of ideas that the Premier League lifted almost wholesale, including a *Monday Night Football* package to sell to broadcasters, the need for an independent chairman, and – crucially – a one-club, one-vote system for making decisions, with a two-thirds majority needed to enact new rules.

In anticipation of a tense meeting, Parry had booked a conference room inside FA headquarters for two hours. But when he summarized the key points and unveiled the proposed formula for TV revenue sharing – a 50:25:25 split, in which 50 per cent were shared equally, 25 per cent were based on television appearances (with each club guaranteed a certain minimum), and the remaining 25 per cent were based on a team's position in the final table – he found that he was staring at a consensus. So with an hour left in the meeting room, and mindful that the consensus might soon evaporate, Parry jotted the details down on his own Ernst & Young scratch pad. Those handwritten notes, which were immediately sent upstairs to be typed up on FA stationery, were titled the Founder Members Agreement, the document that governed the Premier League for a quarter-century and came to be viewed as a sort of sacred text in the world of professional sport.

For all that drama, the irony was that the breakaway left the day-to-day ecosystem of English football largely intact. The real consequences would take longer to blossom as the game moved from a doomed socialist model to a nakedly capitalistic one. Graham Taylor, then England manager, was one of the few football insiders who could see where the game was headed, proving that he had a keener understanding of microeconomics than of how to unlock an opposing defence. 'People think there must be a lot of thinking in this Premier League,' Taylor said of the planned breakaway. 'There is none, and I'm not totally convinced this is for the betterment of the England team. I think a lot of this is based on greed.'

But for now, with the particulars ironed out and the league not due to launch for another fourteen months, Parry looked to have it easy. The only thing left to resolve was selecting a broadcaster for the Premier League's inaugural season. It would be a straight head-to-head showdown between Greg Dyke's ITV and Rupert Murdoch's Sky.

How hard could it be? Parry thought.

Back at the Lancaster Gate Hotel, Parry couldn't believe that he'd ever thought this thing would run smoothly. Hours past the deadline, ITV's offer of £262 million over five years had trumped Sky's final offer and thrown Parry's meticulous bidding process into disarray. Instead of calmly heading into the conference room for his presentation to the twenty-two club owners, he looked around at the hysteria in the hotel lobby.

Over by the main entrance, he saw Dein engaged in a furious display of backslapping along with Philip Carter, Martin Edwards, and Noel White. This was exactly the outcome they had wanted all along, of course. It had been four years since Dein and Dyke first discussed a deal for ITV to acquire the rights to the Big Five's games. Now it looked as if they would get an entire twenty-two-team league for good measure.

Irving Scholar was the only one missing. The final member of the Big Five club had sold his stake in Tottenham just a few months earlier, amid mounting losses and a threat from FC Barcelona to repossess Spurs striker Gary Lineker over unpaid debts. He was replaced at the table by Alan Sugar, the irascible wheeler-dealer with a tendency towards pinstripes, gold jewellery, and alarmingly wide ties.

Sugar was less than thrilled with how the morning was going. He'd caught wind of the ITV offer minutes earlier and was now shrieking into a public payphone on the other side of the hallway.

Parry rolled his eyes. He could guess what was going on. Everyone knew Sugar's company, Amstrad, was the principal satellite-dish manufacturer for Sky. He stood to benefit more than anyone if Murdoch won the Premier League rights. Which is why he was now bellowing at some poor sap at Sky's Isleworth headquarters to put together a new bid and 'blow them out of the water'. It was a waste of time, of course. Parry had called Sam Chisholm with the details of ITV's offer an hour earlier. Chisholm had told him to sit tight.

But with the whole morning going to hell, Parry was still waiting for word from Chisholm. He checked the mobile telephone in his briefcase for what felt like the hundredth time. *Why hadn't Chisholm called back?*

Parry cast his eyes around the room again. Among the familiar faces of the club chairmen he'd been used to working with were some unexpected newcomers. It appeared that Nottingham Forest chairman Fred Reacher had sent Paul White, the club's commercial director, in his place. And unless Parry was very much mistaken, it looked as though West Ham's Len Cearns had delegated the responsibility to his son, Martin, until recently a local bank manager. *Didn't these people realize what was at stake?* Parry wondered.

John Quinton, the Premier League chairman, reappeared by his side. The start of the meeting had been successfully delayed, but he wasn't sure how long they could stall. Everyone was there and the ITV offer was on everyone's lips.

At that moment, Parry began to believe for the first time that ITV were going to pull this thing off. Dyke had always told him that ITV would win because only he could deliver the Big Five. But Parry had dismissed that as typical bluster. For one thing, Parry had deliberately set up the Premier League to be a paragon of corporate governance – and it would take a lot more than the Big Five to make something happen. Under Parry's one-club, one-vote system, it would take a fourteen-club majority to pick a TV contract, nothing less.

Sky knew this, too. Now they needed to pull the trigger. Parry had been impressed by their determination to secure the Premier League rights and their commitment to making live football a keystone of their operation. They had promised to show more matches, feature more teams in more time slots, and help to turn run-of-the-mill midweek games into major television events. They had pledged to air hours of analysis before and after each game. They would grow the game, promote it. 'We're going to teach your grandma to watch footy on telly,' Chisholm had told him. Parry had felt sure it was the right offer. But he couldn't rightly look the twenty-two owners in the eyes and tell them to take the cheaper one now.

He hoped Rupert Murdoch had one more ace up his sleeve. Right from the start, Murdoch had gone to work on the club chairmen, wooing the likes of Dein and Chelsea's Ken Bates over smoked salmon and champagne at his penthouse apartment in St James's. He had met with Parry at Sky's Scotland headquarters in Livingston. At all times, he had given the impression of a man ready to do whatever it took to own the Premier League. Would he really allow ITV to get away with this?

That's when Parry's phone rang. He snatched the clunky handset from his briefcase, pulled out the antenna, and hoped the reception would hold out.

'Rick,' uttered a familiar voice on the other end of the line. 'It's Sam Chisholm. Have you got a pen?'

PART II

Rise and Rise

'Just make it fucking good.'
Dave Hill, Sky Sports

5

THEY MARCHED ONTO the pitch in August 1992 wearing the season's new kits for the first time, a dozen Sky cameras trained squarely on them from the touchline, the centre circle, and the sky above Manchester City's Maine Road stadium. Every member of the squad knew that by simply doing their jobs they were taking part in a radical new sport and entertainment experiment. They were in the Premier League now. And they had been selected for the debut of Sky's brand-new Premier League product, a gimmick imported straight from the States: *Monday Night Football*. Sky hadn't even bothered to change the name.

Between the shirts on the team's backs and their formation on the pitch, English football had never seen anything quite like what this bunch was about to deploy. They smiled nervously until it was time for their cue. Then, in homes and pubs around Britain, the broadcast went live. Over the stadium, an advertising plane buzzed past pulling a banner that said, A WHOLE NEW BALLGAME. And on the pitch, the team kicked off in pristine white shirts, navy shorts, and white socks.

And also bright-yellow skirts.

These were the Sky Strikers, fifteen cheerleaders hired by the broadcaster to warm up the audience and guarantee that everyone remembered the moment English football dived headlong into showbiz.

'Mondays. Are. Changing,' announced the black-jacketed, garishly tied Richard Keys, a veteran of breakfast television, in the Sky studio above the stands. 'No longer that start-of-the-week depression, we're into a whole new ballgame on Sky Sports. Monday night is now officially part of the weekend. That means a few smiles, some family fun.'

Family fun now apparently included a cheerleading squad, pyro-technics, and a platoon of parachutists swooping in from the heavens to deliver the match ball. Never one to miss a chance for synergy, Rupert Murdoch's underlings had giant logos of the *Sun* printed on the canopies.

The model for *Monday Night Football* was explicitly and shamelessly the NFL. The boxy computer animations with giant team crests, the electric-guitar power riffs . . . You'd have been forgiven for thinking Manchester City and Queens Park Rangers were about to roll out in helmets and shoulder pads.

In the studio, Keys turned to the two ex-players alongside him, Chris Waddle and Andy Gray, as they all stared out the window. 'Impressed with what was in the centre circle, boys?'

'Yeah, I forgot the game was on,' Waddle guffawed, with one eye on the Sky Strikers. 'I just watched them.'

(That kind of casual sexism would catch up to Keys and Gray nineteen years later, ending their Sky careers when they failed to realize a live microphone had picked them up mocking a female assistant referee on air. 'It was just banter' was Keys's lame defence at the time.)

On that Monday night in 1992, however, banter was turning into Sky's hallmark. Stirred in with exhaustive analysis from Gray and the timeless model of three guys in suits talking, the chatter continued right through to kick-off. 'It was never like this at Halifax Town,' chuckled Sky's commentator, Ian Darke, when the broadcast kicked to him with a live feed from the gantry.

But even from their prehistoric perch, Darke and Gray had access to one revolutionary piece of technology: the replay monitor. Though Americans had used it for years, it was a relatively recent arrival in creaking English football stadiums. Under Sky's new broadcasting formula, the instructions were for the main commentator to handle 'names and numbers' while the colour man – Gray and his excitable Scottish brogue – chimed in over the first replay in real time. The recipe has remained pretty much the same ever since. On that first Monday night, QPR's Andy Sinton gave the gantry plenty to coo over when he equalized with a left-footed thunderbolt from twenty-five yards. The Premier League might not have felt any different to the players on the field, but one moment of magic under the Maine Road lights, properly dissected from every angle, could now produce endless minutes of premium satellite television. 'Gets a little bit too much space, you can't allow that!' was Gray's first take on the goal. 'But look at that for a finish.'

Goals, cheerleaders, and fireworks were precisely what Sky had dreamed of when they beat ITV to the Premier League rights three months earlier.

Sky's final bid back in the spring, phoned into Rick Parry by Sam Chisholm with Murdoch's green light from New York, was a blow-them-out-of-the-water £304 million for a total of five seasons – enough to convince a majority of the Premier League clubs to choose Sky over ITV's rival offer. But only just.

The Big Five had stuck with their preference for Greg Dyke's network, voting *en bloc* for ITV's bid with the lone exception of Alan Sugar. His loyalty wasn't to Dyke, ITV, or the rest of the Big Five. It was to Alan Sugar, and Sky's offer meant selling more satellite dishes. He duly backed Sky's offer after surviving a motion by David Dein to have him blocked from the final vote over this conflict of interest, and it was Sugar's ballot that proved decisive. The vote went 14–6, with two clubs deciding to abstain from the biggest business decision in the modern history of English football. Sky's astronomical offer, complete with an early morning premium, had won it exactly the two-thirds majority required.

The £304 million bought Murdoch's upstarts sixty live matches a year, and for that price, they were determined to milk every one of them. Instead of the roughly two hours that broadcasters used to budget for a match – a few minutes of chitchat before kick-off, ninety minutes of action plus half-time – Sky decided the Premier League should be consumed in five-hour marathons. After all, it had nothing but empty airtime to fill. And in Keys, it had a host who knew all about how to keep people chatting and chuckling endlessly from his days hosting the breakfast show *TV-am*. Sky dressed him in all kinds of garish jackets and ties that were more than just fashion crimes of the 1990s. They were deliberate. 'Do you think I really wanted to sit in green, pink, yellow, purple, blue, orange, white jackets? No!' Keys said. 'The idea was we had to make a statement.'

To the Sky team, guided by producers Dave Hill and Andy Melvin, no innovation was off limits. Hill, a gruff Australian, had taught an old sport new tricks on TV before. He'd been responsible for bringing some razzmatazz to cricket when the Aussie media mogul Kerry Packer overhauled the sport into a loud, high-paying televised road show Down Under. Later in his career, Hill would produce coverage of the NFL on Fox and major events including Hollywood's Academy Awards. In 1992, though, his job was to get Sky's Premier League programming off the ground. His instructions to Melvin were straightforward: 'Just make it fucking good.'

Melvin started by giving Andy Gray licence to develop an idea they'd come up with one boozy afternoon when Gray started moving bottles and salt-and-pepper shakers around a bar table to explain football tactics. That morphed into long on-air segments with a large green table and coloured discs where he was free to educate a generation of viewers on the finer points of a 4-4-2 formation. The best part: it ate up as much as ninety minutes of the broadcast.

'In some ways, the sport programme became more important than the live game,' Keys said.

Sky also included time for a phone-in, where viewers could ask questions of the endless parade of ex-player guests. Except, in the early days, what most of those fans really wanted to do on the phone was complain about another of Sky's newfangled ideas. At Hill's insistence, they had created a score box and live clock that lived in the top corner of the screen throughout the match. And people hated it. For some reason – probably the English aversion to any sort of change – viewers refused to concede that it might be useful to know the state of play in the sporting event they were watching. But Hill and Melvin wouldn't hear any criticism. The clock and the score had to stay.

One idea they were less committed to was their hare-brained scheme to bring in a comedian to kill time with football-themed jokes. He bombed every time. The Sky producers knew they had to scrap him for good after the comic tried a bit about Paul Gascoigne's recent transfer to Lazio in Rome.

'He's learning some Italian, you know.'

'Oh?' asked Keys, playing the straight man. 'What does he know how to say?'

'*Pizza.*'

Nope. Cancelled.

In the end, the Sky boys realized that the improvements that stuck weren't the ones that were new just for the sake of it. They were the changes designed to teach people the game they thought they had already mastered – Sam Chisholm's old promise to make your granny like footy. Now they had instant replays from multiple angles, live interviews, and more airtime than anyone else knew what to do with, all to feed a never-before-seen, never-ending conversation.

Sky had managed to pad out ninety minutes of live action with the one thing they sensed football fans had always been missing from the TV experience: a long chat at the pub.

6

ONLY IN THE latter part of English football's 150-year history did the idea occur to anyone that a football club should be run like a business. Until the 1980s, the game's origins as a loosely affiliated collection of working men full of amateur ideals had taught most club directors to abhor the idea of operating a team for profit. And, indeed, to reject the very idea that the running of a football team might in any way mirror the operation of the factories, mines, and foundries where the original players spent their weeks slaving away. This sentiment was enshrined by the Football Association in the nineteenth century in what came to be widely known as Rule 34, a regulation that prevented directors from drawing salaries and limited any dividends paid out to shareholders. Owners were supposed to be custodians above all.

Anyway, it's not like many of them could see how their clubs could be profitable in the late 1970s or early 1980s.

Martin Edwards was one of the few who smelled the potential for more.

Edwards was thirty-four years old when he became Manchester United chairman in 1980, the second-youngest chairman in the entire Football League behind some guy who was running Watford as a hobby: a flamboyant pop star named Elton John.

At the time, Manchester United had once been – but were not currently – a great club. The team Edwards took over hadn't won the league since 1967 and were twelve years removed from their European Cup triumph against Benfica. Since then, they had lifted just one trophy and even spent a season in the second division in the mid 1970s. The larger context of English football was equally bleak. In the first five years of Edwards's tenure, the game was racked by hooliganism, declining attendance, and the 1985 ban on English clubs in European competitions.

His timing was perfect.

During the next decade, a series of interconnected, often unpopular decisions inside the United boardroom combined to build the Premier League's first dynasty. That work, obscure as it might have seemed, would give Manchester United a financial advantage over their rivals that would last well into the twenty-first century.

Even as he banded together with David Dein and Irving Scholar off the pitch to increase television revenues, Edwards was plotting to beat both of them on it. And that began with the appointment of a promising Scottish manager Edwards had secretly courted one evening in a motorway service station south-east of Glasgow, one Alexander Chapman Ferguson.

A former forward for six Scottish clubs with a gruff manner, a mumbling accent, and a fascination with the assassination of John F. Kennedy, Ferguson had impressed the United brass by beating Real Madrid in the 1983 Cup Winners' Cup final with Aberdeen. Other clubs, including Rangers and Arsenal, were already circling him. But Edwards moved quickly. Within seventy-two hours of their clandestine meeting off the M74, Ferguson was installed as United manager.

Ferguson, it hardly needs pointing out, would leave Manchester United in 2013 as, arguably, the greatest manager in English football history. But among all the trophies, all the glory, and even the knighthood that came later, Fergie's first three seasons at Old Trafford are easily forgotten: one second-place finish sandwiched between two years in eleventh position. They don't make you 'Sir Alex' for that. The ugliness culminated in a December 1989 loss to Crystal Palace when one supporter famously unfurled a sign that read: 3 YEARS OF EXCUSES AND IT'S STILL CRAP. TA'RA FERGIE.

It was grim for most of the next season, too, as United slumped to thirteenth. Edwards knew that the knives were being sharpened around Manchester. He had personally hired two managers, and neither one was able to bring home a league title before the 1980s were up. Yet Edwards was inclined to give Fergie a little longer. Luckily for him, United's narrow victory over Palace in the 1990

FA Cup final earned Ferguson just enough cause to keep him in the dugout without sparking an Old Trafford mutiny.

But if sticking with Ferguson was Edwards's public risk, his private gamble stood to be far more expensive. He'd mortgaged his home and willingly plunged into debt to sweep up as much Manchester United stock as he could get his hands on even after becoming chairman. He wanted as much control of the club as he could afford. Quietly buying shares from anyone he found on the registry, he was in the hole to the tune of £950,000 by the early 1990s. Not by coincidence, Edwards was now a heavy smoker, too.

For ten years, he'd sought new ways to boost the club's revenues. In 1982, he followed Liverpool's lead and found a sponsor whose name he could splash across the front of United's shirts for a fee. That turned out to be Sharp, the Japanese electronics company with a large campus in Manchester. Edwards charged them £500,000 a season, which wasn't bad in an era when United might be lucky to get on television ten times in a year. As for the people making those shirts, Edwards was aghast to discover that the club's manufacturing deal was being negotiated by United's coaches, who had no business experience or commercial knowledge. Whatever money these men happened to recoup went straight into a pool for the players. Edwards ended that immediately. He cut a deal with a company called Admiral, which had also made England's national kits, for the princely sum of £15,000 a year. When Edwards quit the club twenty years later, he would leave behind the groundwork for a ten-year agreement with Nike worth £303 million.

The Admiral deal wasn't much, but it was a start, something to put money in the club kitty beyond gate receipts. After all, United could collect gate receipts on only about thirty days out of the whole year and that relied on the team's making a run in multiple tournaments. The rest of the time, United were just sitting on one of the biggest outdoor collections of folding seats in England without a reason to fill them. So it dawned on Edwards that Old Trafford would make an ideal concert venue. In 1982, Manchester United tried to host a Queen show until the club realized that they had no idea how to organize anything other than football matches. They were caught completely off guard by all of the details the local council wanted to know about, sticking points such as what time the concert would end, how loud it might be, and whether they had planned for enough outdoor toilets. Edwards had none of those answers. The concerts would have to wait. (United eventually hosted one when Rod Stewart played Old Trafford in 1991.)

This being the 1980s, however, there was another way of raising cash that was all the rage in the world of corporate Britain. Edwards could float the club on the London Stock Exchange. When he finally listed the company in 1991, supporters were unwittingly transformed into fans of Manchester United Football Club, a subsidiary company of Manchester United PLC.

The plan was to raise cash quickly for a renovation of the section of the stands at Old Trafford. Making any kind of tweak to Old Trafford, the redbrick stadium that had owned its corner of south-west Manchester since the 1900s and survived German air strikes during the Second World War, was already a tricky proposition. Radically altering the raucous Stretford End, which housed United's most vocal fans, would be about as popular as offering to play without a goalkeeper. But Edwards knew it had to be done. And he knew the scheme was viable, too. He had seen his buddy Irving Scholar do the same at Tottenham eight years earlier. Scholar, having staged what was effectively a corporate raid of the club, had figured out that he could circumvent any football-specific restrictions on how the club handled their business by forming a holding company for the team. That allowed Scholar to make Tottenham Hotspur PLC the first sporting entity on the stock exchange and leave Rule 34 in the dust. It also opened the gates for directors to start drawing salaries. Doug Ellis at Aston Villa was one of the first to write himself a lavish pay cheque in 1983, because he felt he'd earned it. 'Only women and horses work for nothing,' he said at the time. 'Deadly Doug', as he was known to Villa fans, was always a charmer.

Scholar never took a salary from Spurs. He was already taking enough flak from fans who didn't understand why their football team should be publicly traded. But he knew that a public share offering was the fastest and easiest way to raise cash and reduce the club's debt.

'Why shouldn't it be done?' Scholar said. 'Every other company does it.'

At United, the scheme was useful insofar as it boosted the club's liquidity. But around half of the 1.2 million shares went unsold. No matter. Edwards had other tricks up his sleeve that he could sell to fans — T-shirts, hats, scarves, and basically anything else that a Manchester United logo could be printed on.

The inspiration for the club's commercial empire once again came from the United States. When Edwards and Scholar had travelled to New York to visit the Jets as guests of the owner in 1987, they realized that the NFL's full-blown marketing operations were the future of professional sports. And when he returned to Manchester, Edwards set about making the future happen.

That meant transforming United's merchandising business, which in those days consisted of a mail-order operation with precisely one person manning a phone. The situation with the club's gift shop was even more absurd. It turned out that Manchester United didn't even own it.

As a parting gift to its legendary former manager, Matt Busby, who had won United the 1968 European Cup, the club had awarded him a twenty-one-year lease on the stadium shop. In 1991, nineteen years into the arrangement, Edwards realized that United badly needed it back. With two years left on the lease, he wrote out a cheque to the Busby family for £146,500.

Perhaps United's shrewdest move during this period, however, was the transfer coup it pulled off with Tottenham in 1992 for a guy named Edward Freedman.

Freedman had never played a single professional game for Spurs, but Edwards knew what he could bring to a club. He'd been Irving Scholar's commercial guru. Freedman immediately saw what United was doing wrong. The club was licensing its name to anyone who paid a fee and then recouping only a fraction of the royalties, not to mention being constantly pestered by charlatans with moronic merchandise ideas — one of them pitched the club women's knickers emblazoned with the words, I SCORED IN THE STRETFORD END. (United declined that particular opportunity.) Freedman decided to bring everything in-house. By 1994, United were pulling in £44 million from brand-name products, up 180 per cent from the previous year, and rival supporters had taken to deriding the club as Merchandise United. By 1998, United's total turnover was more than Arsenal and Liverpool's combined.

This particularly grated Liverpool, the club that by all accounts should have been the Premier League's first commercial power. They were the country's most recent dynasty, having racked up ten league titles between 1975 and 1990, and were uniquely positioned to export their brand all over Europe, since fans abroad had been mesmerized by Liverpool's four European Cup wins. As the former defender Phil Thompson put it, 'You'd have had to be living on the moon' not to have heard of Liverpool Football Club. The problem, it seemed, was that Liverpool's marketing department might as well have been in outer space.

Alex Ferguson had said early on in his Manchester United tenure that his mission was to knock Liverpool 'right off their fucking perch'. But he had no idea that his club would do it on the field and in the year-end accounts. Or that the latter would be a big reason for the former.

The influx of cash into Old Trafford allowed United to do two things that few others around the country could afford. First, they could invest massively in redeveloping their stadium. After the Stretford End transformation into a Taylor Report-compliant all-seater stand, United spent another £30 million to expand the North Stand, which brought the stadium capacity to a league-leading 55,000 when it opened in 1996. With more luxury boxes and hospitality facilities than ever before, the club could rake in £1.2 million on every match day.

United's dabbling in the construction business worked so well, in fact, that the club spent the rest of the 1990s cooking up new projects. Edwards shelled out another £30 million to increase Old Trafford to 67,000 seats before the year 2000. And in 1999, he bought the club a new training facility at Carrington, whose cost would swell to £60 million. There was nothing United couldn't afford any more. Its books hadn't shown a loss since 1990.

The second advantage of United's financial might came from the virtuous circle that Ferguson helped create on the field. With Ferguson hitting his stride in the dugout, the club were able to build a deep squad of high-quality (read: highly paid) talent. That meant Ferguson could rotate his squad at will to keep his best players fresh and carefully tailor his tactics. During the 1992–3 title run, for instance, Ferguson used the same starting eleven in seventeen different league games. Three seasons later, he named the same line-up only four times. And on United's way to the 1996–7 Premier League title, Ferguson rotated his way through thirty-eight different line-ups in thirty-eight league games while also contending for the FA Cup and in Europe. When the season entered its final stretch, United's carefully tended players simply galloped past their leg-weary rivals.

By the turn of the millennium, United's finances were a runaway train. In 1998, Rupert Murdoch's BSkyB made an abortive attempt to buy the club itself for some £623 million only to be undone by the government's Monopolies and Mergers Commission. The commission didn't much like the look of Murdoch's controlling both the richest competition in the country and its biggest club, fearing that a takeover would only deepen the inequality in an already unequal league. The following year, United's valuation crossed the billion-pound mark for the first time – and the company had only slightly more than five hundred employees. Everything they touched turned to gold. Fergie kept picking up trophies, United launched their own TV channel and a global website, and the club shop evolved into a 'Megastore'. With Peter Kenyon, a former Umbro executive, installed as CEO, United went on to shatter the British transfer record three times in the space of thirteen months by acquiring Ruud van Nistelrooy, Juan Sebastián Verón, and Rio Ferdinand for a combined £77 million.

In the middle of this frenzy, Edwards quietly made a subtle but significant change to his grand old institution: he had the words 'Football Club' removed from the Manchester United crest. When you're the most famous team on the planet, you don't have to remind anyone which sport you happen to play. The world already knows. As Edwards likes to say, the Harlem Globetrotters never needed the words 'Basketball Team'.

United's knack for developing their stadium and commercial operations in the 1980s and early 1990s – not to mention the team's on-pitch progress under Ferguson – gave them a first-mover advantage that no other club was in a position to catch. By all rights, United should have been winning the title every year almost from the beginning of the Premier League era.

In this new reality, there seemed to be only one way to fight Man United. And that was to follow a blueprint developed in 1995 by a semi-retired tax exile who went by the nickname 'Uncle Jack'.

7

SIMPLY BEATING MANCHESTER United was never going to satisfy Jack Walker. What he really wanted, deep in his heart and in his wallet, was to make Manchester United look downright cheap.

The crazy thing was that Uncle Jack had the money to do it. Selling the family steel business he had run for four decades for more than £300 million turned Walker into one of Britain's twenty-five richest men. But the club he supported as a boy, Blackburn Rovers, weren't quite ready for his vision when he took them over in 1991 as a retirement hobby. For starters, they weren't even in the top division. While decisions that would reshape football in England were being made thirty miles away at Old Trafford, the sixty-one-year-old magnate watched his beloved club drift further and further away from football's brave new world. The season he assumed control of Blackburn, they finished in nineteenth place in the second division. Any worse, and they would've plummeted straight into the third tier – which, as far he was concerned, amounted to slipping off the face of the earth. Putting Blackburn back where they belonged was about to become even more of a chore with the advent of the Premier League since the voices defending everyone below the top tier had gone conspicuously quiet. The big boys were now free to screw him and other clubs Blackburn's size out of gate receipts, television money, and, if the pessimists were to be believed, a meaningful future in English football.

Uncle Jack decided he wasn't just going to save Blackburn. And he wasn't just going to haul them back into the Premier League. He was going to spend enough of that steel money to win the whole bloody thing.

Which was pretty rich for a club that hadn't lifted a major trophy of any kind in more than sixty years and a town that was easily confused with any number of other northern English industrial towns in the greater orbit of Manchester. They all looked the same – terraced houses and empty factories – and they even sounded similar: Blackburn, Burnley, Bolton. In fact, the football team, with their half-blue and half-white shirts, were the only reason that most people in England had even heard of this former industrial outpost. For a man who loved the club and loved the town of Blackburn as Walker did – even though he'd been a tax exile in the Channel Islands since the early 1970s – here was a chance to put both back on the map.

In the hidebound world of English football, what Walker was planning amounted to heresy. In the 1990s, teams were still steeped in the legend of growing a title-winning team in their youth academies and on their training pitches. There was an English sense of propriety to the whole thing, of earning one's accomplishments (however modest they might be) amid the larger injustices of life. Above all, one needed to know one's station. And to most observers, Blackburn's station was right around nineteenth place in the second division. But to Walker, a self-made man who left school at fourteen to work in his father's sheet-metal factory and later served in the army's Corps of Royal Electrical and Mechanical Engineers, that was a small-time attitude. Easy prey for a big fish like him. He planned to splash so much cash on the country's finest players that he would turn the established order on its head.

His millions might have seemed vulgar to some fans, but Walker's story wasn't too different from those of most other team owners. His bank balance just had a lot more zeros on the end.

Walker and his brother had taken over C. Walker & Sons at the time their father died in 1951, turned it into Walkersteel, and, over the next thirty-seven years, grown the company to employ 3,400 people at more than fifty sites while earning eight-figure profits. When they finally cashed out in 1989, for more than £330 million, their sale to British Steel was a record at the time for a privately held company in the UK.

The way Walker had patiently built up his business was exactly the way building a football team was supposed to work. But when it came to turning around Blackburn, Walker didn't have another thirty-seven years to work his magic. Luckily, this didn't look like a thirty-seven-year operation to him. Forging Blackburn Rovers into a competitor struck Walker as a more straightforward exercise.

Uncle Jack's first coup was luring Kenny Dalglish out of retirement to rivet second-division Blackburn together. For an instant injection of football pedigree, there was no one better. Over the previous fourteen years, Dalglish had established himself as the classiest player at what everyone viewed as England's classiest club, the red-shirted dynasty of the 1970s. He *was* Liverpool FC: first as a silky forward, then as a player-manager, and finally as one of the most visible faces of mourning in the wake of the Hillsborough disaster – he once attended four different funerals in the same day. As far as adoring Liverpudlians were concerned, the city's adopted son from Glasgow might as well have been one of the Beatles.

But by 1991, the forty-year-old Dalglish was shattered, exhausted by the pressure. After a 4–4 draw with Everton in February, he announced out of the blue that he was quitting the Liverpool bench. For the first time in twenty-four years, he felt he could no longer be around football.

Uncle Jack's chequebook made a compelling argument to the contrary. 'I was doing nothing, so it seemed like a good idea at the time,' Dalglish said. Over the next three years, Walker allowed him to break the British transfer record twice in quick succession, first for Alan Shearer, poached away from Southampton before Manchester United could reach a deal of its own, and then by dropping £5 million on Chris Sutton. Pulling off the Shearer transfer, in particular, was a highly targeted statement of intent to the Premier League's powers. Though he had yet to prove himself as a truly elite marksman, Shearer was already England's record scorer at the Under-21 level. Anyone in the business of predicting football's future could sense the boy was about to catch fire. And that included Alex Ferguson, who had taken more than a passing interest in Shearer before missing out on him. In a career that saw Shearer become the Premier League's record goal scorer, he would prove Blackburn right many times over.

Not that Dalglish needed to be emboldened. As talented players from around the country bought into what he and Walker were building, he learned never to take no for an answer on his shopping spree. When Ireland's Roy Keane declined to join him at Blackburn and went to United despite a then-galactic salary offer of £400,000 a year, Dalglish threatened to hunt him down on holiday – even if it meant barging into every bar in Cyprus.

Of course, Walker knew it would take more than spending on the playing squad to turn Blackburn into a winning machine. The club's training ground wasn't even a training ground, it was a public park in a corner of the town misleadingly called Pleasington. Every morning, the players and staff would meet at the stadium with the training gear they had laundered themselves, pile into a fleet of their own cars, and haul out to a muddy pitch down the hill from a crematorium. The scattered dog turds were not the only occupational hazard. There was also the occasional interruption of a funeral cortège wending past the field – the players were never quite sure whether they should carry on training or stand at attention. Either way, it didn't matter much when the same group of mourners, having sent their loved one off to the great beyond, would proceed back down the hill, hanging out of car windows shouting, 'Good luck Saturday, lads! Go on Rovers!'

The stadium, Ewood Park, wasn't much better off. Years before taking full control of the club, Walker donated the steel to refurbish one of the stands. Then, once he was in charge, he took on the rest in short order at a cost of more than £15 million. Bits of the stadium would disappear for months at a time while they were razed and built back up. Blackburn even spent some of their early days in the Premier League without the main stand, which ran the length of the pitch and contained the dressing rooms. For this, as with everything else, Uncle Jack had a work-around. The teams and referees dressed in temporary structures down the street where three local buses would pick them up before kick-off and drive them five to ten minutes through the crowds around the stadium. Inside a pair of tiny improvised dressing rooms with no showers, separated only by plasterboard, Blackburn and the utterly appalled visiting team would pull on their kits, lace up their boots, and run out onto the pitch. 'We absolutely psychologically destroyed opponents before we even played,' defender Graeme Le Saux said.

Walker's plan was working. In the first season of the Premier League,

Blackburn finished fourth. After another influx of cash in 1993–4, which included finally investing in an actual training facility of their own, they ran Manchester United close and came second. Blackburn were now just a big-money signing or two short of a title-winning squad. But for a man who spent money as if he were printing it, Walker knew the value of a pound. He had long ago established residency in the Channel Island of Jersey for tax purposes, which is why his formal title had to remain vice president of the club. And every other weekend, he flew in on a rented private jet to attend Blackburn games. Yet, through all those flights over all those weekends, he never considered buying a plane of his own even though he also owned a small regional airline. 'Waste of money,' he said.

Off the books, Walker also ran a one-man mission to claw back some of the lavish salaries he was paying into his own pocket – twenty pounds at a time. In addition to being cheap, Uncle Jack was also a gambler. His game was pitching pennies. The challenge could drop anywhere at any time. Walker would go up to a player or a coach with a couple of coins in his hand and point at a wall. The rules were simple. Flick the penny at the wall so it hits and bounces back. Whoever lands his coin closest to the wall is the winner. Everyone knew Walker was a shark, but they played along anyway. 'He'd take anyone on,' Le Saux remembered. 'And he'd win.'

Walker approached the 1994–5 season with the same mentality. He had thrown more than £50 million at the wall. Now was the time for his investment to pay one massive dividend.

On the morning of 14 May, the last day of the season, Walker rolled into Liverpool with his dream close enough to touch. If Blackburn could simply avoid defeat, then he and his team would beat Manchester United to the title by a nose. But if Blackburn slipped up and United snatched a victory on the road at West Ham, then Walker's self-made fairy tale would fall apart.

There had already been plenty of hints that it might. Only one player in the entire Blackburn squad had ever won the championship before, and the nerves in the rest of the team were showing. In the final weeks of the campaign, Rovers' advantage at the top eroded from eight points to just two. And United manager Alex Ferguson smelled blood.

With his own brand of psychological warfare, he began needling Blackburn every chance he got – an early version of Fergie's 'mind games'.

Those would famously send Newcastle manager Kevin Keegan into an on-air meltdown at the tail end of the 1995–6 season and later prompt Liverpool manager Rafa Benítez to launch into a five-minute diatribe punctuated by the word 'fact!' that detailed each of his objections to Ferguson and Manchester United. On both occasions, Ferguson's team came from behind to win the championship, cementing his legacy as a master manipulator. But his attempts at psychological voodoo often succeeded in only breeding resentment among neutral supporters.

On this occasion, as he attempted to unsettle Blackburn, Ferguson fell back on his other passion: horse racing. His weapon of choice was a reference to the 1956 Grand National, when a gelding named Devon Loch that belonged to the Queen Mother collapsed in the lead on its way to certain victory.

'Blackburn can only throw the league away now,' he said, in the kind of feisty interview that Sky was now tacking on to the end of its match coverage. 'We must hope they do a Devon Loch.'

Dalglish claimed not to know what Ferguson was on about.

'Is that a lake in Scotland?'

For Sky, the scenario going into that May afternoon was better than any soap script it could have commissioned. The Premier League era hadn't yet experienced a final-day finish. There had been thrilling conclusions as recently as 1989, but the Whole New Ballgame hadn't been around back then, so as far as Sky was concerned, it had never existed. The extra cameras were trained on the managers, the multi-hour studio show, and the legion of analysts; everything the producers had cooked up during their first three years of experimentation was about to pay off. For the first time, Sky was going to give a football season a Hollywood ending.

Could Blackburn hold their nerve? Would Liverpool, acting out the wishes of the Anyone-But-United crowd, roll over to keep the title away from Manchester? Or would Ferguson's mind games help United pip Blackburn in the final furlong? And what about Dalglish, the Liverpool hero – was he about to win a championship for a different club in the stadium where he'd become a god?

For once, Sky would have no problem filling five hours of coverage. 'It was made for us,' said Richard Keys, who hosted the broadcast from a studio in west London.

Inside Blackburn's dressing room in Liverpool, the players did their best to ignore the profound weirdness of the occasion. But they couldn't ignore the fact that they had never seen Kenny Dalglish so anxious. Wearing a wide black tie with yellow polka dots, he emerged onto the touchline with his teeth clenched and his jaw set, not speaking to anyone. He relaxed imperceptibly when Alan Shearer gave Blackburn a 1–0 lead. But Dalglish, 'King Kenny' to the Anfield locals, knew deep down what he was looking at: his side were playing like rubbish.

The players filing into Anfield's away dressing room at half-time had sensed it, too. Consumed by nerves, midfielder Stuart Ripley announced to no one in particular, 'I can't feel my bloody legs!'

Judging by how the second half played out, he wasn't the only one. Liverpool equalized in the sixty-fourth minute. At which point the Sky cameras began cutting over and over to close-ups of Blackburn fans biting their fingernails. When stoppage time rolled around, they were down to their knuckles. And in the ninety-third minute, Blackburn presented Liverpool with a chance to finish them off, a free kick twenty-five yards out.

Jamie Redknapp stepped up. No one was thinking about Liverpool rolling over any more. He hit it with his right foot, bending it just over the head of Le Saux in Blackburn's three-man wall. 'As soon as he struck the ball, I knew it was in,' Le Saux said. 'I didn't need to look.'

As the net billowed, the Blackburn players froze. In that moment, every one of them knew they had lost the championship. Three years' worth of progress undone by one brilliant shot in a game Liverpool didn't care about. The home fans barely celebrated – if Liverpool had helped bitter rival United become champion, it was better just to forget about this season and move on. And in the strange half applause that greeted Redknapp's goal, Blackburn Rovers started the slow trudge back to the centre circle, looking to Dalglish for help. They needed a plan, one more throw of the dice. What they got was resigned silence. Until, that is, the players saw a conversation bubbling up behind Dalglish. Then some hugs. Now the dour Scotsman was actually smiling. The players looked at one another in disbelief.

Had West Ham done them the ultimate favour?

Word spread to the field that the whistle had blown at Upton Park. Final score: West Ham 1, Manchester United 1. As for the final score at Anfield: who cared? From the gantry, Andy Gray spotted the reaction on the bench, too. 'Blackburn have won it!' he cut in. 'Blackburn have won it!' Four years after Walker had laid out his vision and opened up his chequebook, Blackburn Rovers were champions.

There was only one problem. Walker's careful provisions for the club extended only to the precise moment when he pushed through his players and lifted the trophy.

Blackburn had no idea what they were supposed to do next.

The only celebration they had planned was a couple of cases of champagne that the players chugged so fast in the locker room that it dribbled out of their noses. The fiercely superstitious Dalglish hadn't allowed the club to prepare any kind of formal party, which is how the newly crowned Premier League champions wound up that night in a theme restaurant in Preston. There was nowhere to live it up in Blackburn, and on this particular evening, Manchester's nightlife was out of the question – too many United fans running around without a championship. So they fell back on the restaurant they already knew as a regular post-match hangout, where the staff were famous for putting on a funk-and-soul floor show after dinner.

But Blackburn had longer-term issues than an awkward after-party and some soul hits from the seventies. Walker's dream had come true and decisions had to be made. RULE ONE, I AM ALWAYS RIGHT read the sign he kept on his office wall. RULE TWO, WHEN I AM WRONG, READ RULE ONE.

In 1995, no one could argue with those rules although people did sneer that Blackburn's meteoric rise didn't live up to English football's strict standards of authenticity. Title contenders had an inherent quality, an entitlement bred into them over decades. They were meant to be tended like rare plants raised from the local soil – not hastily imported and assembled with cash. Nevertheless, Walker had beaten United and chalked one up for rich outsiders and their plaything football teams. Or, as one former player called Walker's Blackburn, 'his train set'.

He had built a training ground, a stadium, and a title-winning team. There was nothing left to do. While other top clubs built for the future, rearming their squads and clearing out the chaff, Walker the gambler felt about ready to cash out. That summer, the club made no meaningful signings, spending only slightly more than £2 million on four players, one-third of what Walker had shelled out twelve months earlier. When Dalglish moved upstairs into a director-of-football role, Blackburn's board didn't exactly cast a wide net to find his successor: they promoted his assistant, Ray Harford. And almost from the moment the season began, it became clear that Blackburn's title was a once-in-a-lifetime deal. Injury cost record-signing Chris Sutton nearly two-thirds of the campaign. The club's first foray into the Champions League saw them fail to win any of their first five games because the coaching staff had barely bothered to watch video of any of their new European opponents. If they had, they might have realized that the direct, cross-heavy English game wasn't going to worry anybody on their trips to Moscow, Warsaw, and Norway. Especially not when two Blackburn players ended up fighting each other on the field during a defeat in Russia.

It became painfully obvious to Blackburn's board that the club hadn't been prepared for success. The league title, one member said publicly, had come a year too early. That perfectly stupid remark served only to annoy the players even further. How had Rovers' brass failed to recognize that a championship was possible when the club finished second the previous season? The directors' ultimate crime was a lack of ambition and a failure of imagination. In the eyes of the Liverpools, Uniteds, and Newcastles, the title hadn't changed Rovers' station in football's class system. And Blackburn weren't prepared to keep pushing through the ceiling.

One by one, the players the club had paid for so handsomely were picked off by bigger teams. David Batty left for Newcastle for

£3.75 million. In 1996, Shearer followed him there for a then-world-record £15 million. And in 1997, Le Saux shipped out for a price of £7 million, the highest price to date for an English defender. All told, the title-winning squad were sold off at a profit of more than £40 million. At Walkersteel, those were numbers the accountants dreamed of. At Blackburn Rovers, they simply formed the ledger for a collapse.

In the space of four years, Walker's monument to himself eroded just as quickly as he had built it. It turns out that there is something to the art of curating a perennial winner. By 1999, what had so recently seemed unthinkable caught up to Uncle Jack. Blackburn slumped to nineteenth place and were relegated.

The Premier League would motor on without Walker. Blackburn's legacy was being a one-off – a provincial club that interrupted a long stretch of dominance by big-city clubs thanks to one wealthy benefactor. He didn't realize it at the time, but Walker had given life to a new model of club stewardship: pour in cash, buy the best players, and don't sweat the losses. The only thing that matters is winning. Except the league's expanding bubble pushed the sums of money involved to such ridiculous heights within a decade that Walker's spending looked like bargain-hunting. Before long, £100 million would no longer put you in a position to win a title the way Blackburn did; it was merely the cost of doing business in the Premier League. And owning a family steel business, no matter how successful, would look positively quaint up against the later riches of Russian plutocrats and oil empires in the Gulf. One season at the pinnacle of English football was all Blackburn could afford.

Manchester United might even have called it cheap.

8

THE COLLAPSE OF Blackburn Rovers reads like a classic tale of boom and bust. But it wasn't misplaced ambition that toppled Jack Walker's empire, it was a fundamental miscalculation.

Walker's mistake was thinking that winning the Premier League title was the only prize that mattered. In fact, the real prize was about to become membership in the Premier League itself.

English football wasn't always so elitist. In the past, teams would shuttle up and down the divisions as their fortunes fluctuated, with no lasting damage to their reputations – or their balance sheets. Relegation was a sporting frustration and not much more because everyone understood it could happen to anyone. Only Arsenal have avoided relegation completely since reaching the top flight in 1919. And fans and owners could always find solace away from the league table. A cup run, for instance, could save even the gloomiest season. (The maligned League Cup was essentially invented for precisely this purpose – giving teams with no other hope for silverware a chance to rise above their station for once and lift some kind of trophy.) Even the heartache of missing out on the title could be soothed to some degree by earning entry into Europe.

The arrival of the Premier League scrambled everyone's priorities. With each passing season, teams realized that the real prize wasn't winning the league since only a handful of clubs could aspire to that. It was staying in it. In the season before the Premier League launched, 1991–2, the collective revenue of the twenty-two old First Division clubs was £170 million while the twenty-four teams in the Second Division posted total revenues of £58 million, for a difference of £112 million. Within fifteen years, that gap would multiply by a factor of ten. The twenty top-flight teams would achieve collective revenues of £1.53 billion while the twenty-four Championship clubs would post a total of £318 million. And by 2015–16, that chasm would grow to more than £3 billion.

What did that mean for individual Premier League clubs? It meant: do every last thing in your power to keep turning up. (Sunderland finished bottom of the table in 2017 and still collected exactly £93,471,118 from the Premier League, more money than Ligue 1 paid the champions of France that season and roughly the same amount that Real Madrid earned from UEFA for winning the Champions League. You can understand why Premier League clubs might have a hard time getting excited about anything else any more.)

Yet even while that wave of cash washed over English football in the years that followed, the league never forgot its original formula, written down on that solitary sheet of Ernst & Young stationery by Rick Parry. The result was that no matter how much money flowed in, the ratio between the payments to the league's top earner and those to its twentieth-place team would always remain around 1.6 to 1. The equivalent ratio in Spain's La Liga or Germany's Bundesliga, meanwhile, was around 3 to 1. Those leagues had relegation, too, unlike the protectionist US sports, but dropping into a lower division didn't spell doom for smaller clubs the way it did for English teams. Therein lay the secret ingredient to the Premier League's competitive recipe – provided you could stay in it.

The founders of the early 1990s had created a framework to keep the smaller clubs comparatively rich and make relegation a financial catastrophe. Every game mattered now. Whether a club was chasing the title or battling to avoid the drop, the stakes for thirty-eight weekends a year were measured in millions. On the pitch, that manifested itself by making every match extra competitive. No one rolled over any more, not even when trailing by two or three goals – a fact that foreign players and managers all seem to notice immediately when they land in the Premier League.

There was just one other unintended consequence of the Premier League's financial explosion. People in the business of making money with money were going to take notice. The Premier League was quietly turning English clubs into investable assets.

And in a post-Uncle Jack world, you'd also be forgiven for thinking that all of your wildest dreams were never more than ten or twenty million pounds away. It wasn't quite that simple.

Just ask Bradford City.

The seven-bedroom, five-bathroom, half-million-pound house probably wasn't Bradford's biggest mistake. But it was close. In the summer of 2000, after their improbable survival in the Premier League, the tiny Bantams convinced themselves that they suddenly belonged with the big boys. So, despite having a wage bill of just £12 million the season before, they started spending like them. Club chairman Geoffrey Richmond, a loud, bushy-eyebrowed Yorkshireman, signed Italian forward Benito Carbone on a deal that paid him £40,000 a week, then sweetened it by throwing in a palatial house in nearby Leeds. Richmond also blew £5 million on three players who were all twenty-nine years old or above and looking backward at their primes. He promised them lavish salaries while he was at it, too. Why not? To the flightless Bantams, the sky was the limit.

Which was strange because Richmond had, until that point, been quite tight with money. He'd made his fortune first as a salesman hawking stickers and light bulbs for cars, then by turning around the Ronson lighter company – he bought it for around £250,000 when it went into receivership and sold it for £10 million in 1994, the same year he acquired Bradford City. His partners in the football venture were a father and son, David and Julian Rhodes, who ran a successful tech company. As far as they were concerned, Richmond had free rein to run the club. The Rhodeses were happy to sit quietly on their 49 per cent stake and watch Bradford claw their way up from the lower divisions to the upper reaches of English football.

Just getting there was something of a miracle, because nothing about Bradford City screamed Premier League. Hailing from a West Yorkshire textile town that had been in steady decline for eighty years, the club played at Valley Parade, a 25,000-seat stadium that hadn't sniffed top-tier action since the early 1920s. In the 1980s, it had also become synonymous with the nadir of English football after the Bradford stadium fire. But at the start of the 1999–2000 season, there were Bradford City, ready to rub elbows with the likes of Manchester United, Arsenal, and Liverpool.

The wildest part of Bradford's adventure was that once they reached the Premier League they managed to stay there. Five games from the end of that first campaign, the Bantams were dead and buried on only twenty-six points. That is until they managed to scrape together ten more, capped by a stunning 1–0 home victory over Liverpool. David Wetherall's goal gave the Bantams the lead after twelve minutes, and Bradford somehow held on for another seventy-eight. As if to underline how far the new league had shifted priorities, the home supporters invaded the pitch at the final whistle as if they'd won a title. The city of Bradford even threw the team an open-top-bus parade – for finishing seventeenth.

'They said it would be a miracle if Bradford City survived in the world's toughest football league,' the *Bradford Telegraph & Argus* wrote, 'but the band of players dubbed Dad's Army yesterday pulled off that miracle in sensational style.'

They say a near-death experience can teach you to live life more fully. If that's true, then Richmond's wave of spending and borrowing after his brush with relegation was like surviving a car crash and taking up bungee jumping. The way he saw it, his seventeenth-place side could be good enough to compete for European places if only he could add a few more pieces. He just needed a little cash on hand, something short-term. Then it dawned on him. When he looked around the club, he was surrounded by collateral. So Richmond borrowed against the stadium, he borrowed against nearly everything inside it, and he borrowed against some of the most valuable things on Bradford City's balance sheet, the playing squad.

'Our chairman went ballistic,' Julian Rhodes said. 'He thought we were the next Manchester United.'

Benito Carbone, the seven-bedroom house, and nine more players all landed on the club's books over the course of the following season, creating a mountain of debt. And what did all of Richmond's deficit spending buy? Nothing but misery.

Bradford finished rock bottom. The club was relegated with four games to spare.

Twelve months later, the situation was still spiralling out of control. After a chaotic season in the second tier, Bradford's finances became untenable. The bottom had briefly fallen out of the transfer market just as the club tried to sell off its more expensive players. Carbone's proposed move to Middlesbrough crumbled. Making matters worse was the collapse of ITV Digital, which held the television rights for a chunk of lower-league football. The seven-figure TV revenue stream the club was so desperately counting on had suddenly run dry.

Bradford, stuck in a mess of high salaries and crushing debt, had no choice but to enter administration. On the first day, the club shuttered its shops and laid off the staff.

The bankruptcy proceedings showed just how far the financial rot had penetrated. Bradford City were in hock to twenty-six different leasing companies. It turned out that almost nothing around Valley Parade actually belonged to the club. The floodlights were rented. Many of the seats were rented. Even the carpets and the kitchen fittings in the offices were rented. Everyone around Bradford knew there was only one man to blame.

'I will never, ever forgive myself for spending the money we did,' Richmond told the local papers. 'Looking back now, it was six weeks of madness and I hold my hands up.'

Within six years, Bradford were relegated twice more and languished in the fourth tier, struggling to remember that they had ever tasted the promised land at all.

Today, the Bantams sit in the third tier of English football in relatively stable financial shape, and Rhodes can finally laugh about his club's legacy: Bradford City were the rare case where staying in the league was the worst possible outcome.

'Without a shadow of a doubt, we'd have been better off losing that game and going down,' Rhodes said. 'Had we gone down, I think we'd have been strong in [the second tier]. Unfortunately, because we stayed up, we got too big for our boots.'

The consequences of Wetherall's goal against Liverpool on the last day of the 1999–2000 season didn't stop at Valley Parade. They rippled around the league far beyond one club and its six weeks of madness. Bradford's salvation meant that Wimbledon had to be relegated, triggering the club's own decade-long crisis. It also cost Liverpool a spot in the Champions League – and the eight-figure windfall that went with it – while sending Leeds United into Europe, where their short-lived success prompted the club to start spending money like a drunken sailor – or the chairman of Bradford City. Within seven years, their own extravagance and mismanagement would send Leeds into administration and down to the third tier.

So when Julian Rhodes ran into David Wetherall after Bradford's stint in the Premier League, he reminded him, 'Well done, David. You've managed to ruin four clubs with that goal.'

'Boss, it wasn't my fault,' Wetherall replied. 'We'd have stayed up with a 0–0.'

9

THE DEMISE OF Bradford City became a cautionary tale for the Premier League. But it would take more than relegation and a little financial oblivion to scare away investors. Wealthy businessmen were still more than willing to drop fortunes on running a football club without ever viewing it as a gamble. That was partly because Manchester United had made the business of making money in English football look as simple as switching on the floodlights.

Backed by the most sophisticated corporate department in the league, United were in the process of building an empire. Their commercial advantage over the rest of the league had turned the club into perennial title contenders. Now Alex Ferguson was turning them into perennial title winners. In the six seasons following the Blackburn anomaly, United lifted the Premier League trophy five times.

Ferguson's recipe was to build the United squad around a certain moody French striker named Eric Cantona and a core of home-grown players who had graduated together from United's youth academy, the Cliff, and won the FA Youth Cup in 1992. *Match of the Day* pundit and former Liverpool great Alan Hansen had famously proclaimed, 'You can't win anything with kids', but these kids, the Class of '92, happened to be the most absurdly talented collection of footballers produced by a single English club in more than a generation. Their names were Ryan Giggs, Paul Scholes, Nicky Butt, Gary Neville, and the one simply known as Becks.

That group had been maturing nicely for years even if Ferguson once had to bust up a party at Giggs's house two nights before a game – as if he were an exasperated teacher on a school trip to France. Unlike exasperated teachers, however, Ferguson had licence to personally cuff Giggs and the other players in attendance around the backs of their heads. 'I know the guardians of political correctness wouldn't approve,' Ferguson wrote later, 'but I think the lads' parents would have supported me.' Ferguson had made his point. Luckily for Giggs and the rest, he also discovered around that time that there was a far more useful tool to teach the kids professionalism than a smack in the ear. It went by the name Cantona.

King Eric planted the flag for French players in England when he arrived at Leeds United in 1992 and moved to Manchester United later that year. A barrel-chested six-foot-two forward, his style, stubble, and unflinching swagger made him more French than a pack of Gauloises and a bottle of Bordeaux for lunch. His signature was a turned-up jersey collar and a propensity to volley the ball into the goal from twenty-five yards. And from his earliest days at United, Cantona would go up to Ferguson after practice ended and requisition two players: a goalkeeper and someone to whip in crosses. Training might have been over and his teammates back in the showers, but Cantona wasn't done. Even Ferguson was taken aback. For half an hour or more, Ferguson would watch Cantona out in the cold, honing his finishing. It didn't take the youngsters or Ferguson long to understand that this was how the greats handled their business away from the crowds – with a kind of unstructured perfectionism that no manager could instil. Cantona, for all of his eccentricity, had it in spades. 'Nothing he did in matches meant more than the way he opened my eyes to the indispensability of practice,' Ferguson wrote. 'Practise makes players.'

United's model of a young British core complemented by a stylish veteran from Europe was so effective that they went on to win the 1995–6 title with six kids under the age of twenty-three making at least ten appearances, a number that hasn't been matched since. Their success also spawned imitators all over English football.

For most of their century-long history, West Ham had never struck anyone as a likely candidate to emulate Manchester United. While other London clubs in more upscale areas – like Arsenal and Chelsea – have all enjoyed long periods as the capital's pre-eminent team with championships and trophies to their name, glory has always remained tantalizingly out of West Ham's grasp. Not that their fans are unduly concerned; they embrace their status as the city's gruff, working-class underdogs with a healthy slice of gallows humour. When Harry Redknapp went to inspect the club's trophy cabinet after taking over as manager, 'Lord Lucan, Shergar, and two Japanese prisoners of war fell out,' he wrote. Even the club's anthem, 'I'm Forever Blowing Bubbles', is about shattered dreams and disappointment.

However, West Ham soon found that they had a crop of budding young stars to rival United's Class of '92. This group of pimply teenagers included Rio Ferdinand, Frank Lampard, Michael Carrick, and Joe Cole – those four would post a combined 277 appearances for England over the course of a decade. Redknapp – a red-faced east London native with the manner and accent of a second-hand car salesman – even signed a maverick talent from the Continent to pair with them in the mould of Cantona. His name was Paolo Di Canio. Like Cantona, he was a talismanic presence on the pitch – one whom Alex Ferguson would try to sign as a replacement for the Frenchman in 2001. Also like Cantona, he was a maniac. The season before he signed for West Ham, Di Canio had served an eleven-match ban for shoving a referee.

West Ham appeared to have copied Manchester United's blueprint for building a dynasty almost to the letter. But it hardly needs saying that West Ham's class of academy graduates never did challenge for a Premier League title. The club has a pair of crossed hammers on its badge, but its capacity for face-planting is such that they might as well be banana skins. The Hammers finished ninth in 2000 and fifteenth in 2001. Two years later, West Ham were relegated and their precocious youngsters sold off. There was more to winning than mimicking the United model. At West Ham, it got Redknapp sacked. At United, Ferguson used it to carry the club to untold heights.

In the second half of the 1990s, those heights began to extend beyond England's shores. In the Champions League, Manchester United began to show signs of real mettle: semi-finalists in 1997, quarter-finalists in 1998, and then . . . the miracle of 1999.

Manchester United, already champions of England and winners of the FA Cup, travelled to the Champions League final in Barcelona to stare down Bayern Munich, the big bad Panzer tank from Germany. Within six minutes, Bayern took a 1–0 lead and looked set to roll right over United. What transpired during the rest of that evening has been told so many times from so many angles that it's easy to get caught up in the haze and sweat and noise of the tale. So here are the two most important things to know from one of the most extraordinary conclusions to a final in European history.

Ninety-first minute: Teddy Sheringham bundles home the equalizing goal after a Manchester United corner. 1–1.

Ninety-third minute: seconds from extra time, Sheringham heads a David Beckham corner kick across the face of the Bayern goal and Ole Gunnar Solskjaer pokes it in. Solskjaer had been on the field for only twelve minutes. 2–1.

It was time for Europe to pay attention to English football again.

None of it was an accident.

Manchester United were simply the best-positioned club to capitalize on a perfect storm that swept across European football in the 1990s and allowed the Premier League to turn itself into the Continent's pre-eminent domestic competition.

In London, there was Rick Parry's successful negotiation of a second television deal with Sky, which was ratified by the clubs in 1997, unanimously this time, for £670 million over the next four years. Just as it did under the previous deal, Sky would air sixty games a season. But instead of paying £640,000 per game, they would now shell out £2.79 million, a fourfold increase. Overnight, every club in the Premier League could afford to pay higher wages and transfer fees than nearly everyone else in the game.

And in Luxembourg, the European Court of Justice ruled in favour of an obscure thirty-something Belgian midfielder in his complaint against the Belgian football federation; his team, Royal Football Club de Liège; and European football's governing body, UEFA. The dispute centred on his proposed move to a French club after his Belgian contract expired, and it alleged that Liège's refusal to let him go by demanding an unreasonably high transfer fee constituted restraint of trade. By siding with the player, Jean-Marc Bosman, the European court's landmark ruling effectively opened the floodgates of free agency. A player could now switch clubs at the end of a contract without his new team having to pay a transfer fee. (Bosman never truly benefited from the decision and retired shortly thereafter. His subsequent plan to sell T-shirts that read, WHO'S THE BOZ? to any player who profited from free agency failed miserably.)

For any club curious or creative enough, all the tools were now in place to exploit one of the Premier League's earliest market inefficiencies: foreign talent.

English football had always been suspicious of foreigners – something about being an island in a post-empire age with a deeply ingrained scepticism of Europe and an unwavering conviction that Britain simply did things better, from its currency to its electrical plugs. In 1978, the European Union had forced the FA to lift its restrictions on foreign players. And by the mid 1990s, fans were beginning to wrap their heads around the handful of Scandinavians that had trickled into English clubs during the previous decade because they were culturally similar in both football style and the appreciation of cold, muddy afternoons. But when Frenchmen, Spaniards, Italians, and Germans started showing up, English football went through a profound culture shock.

Ostentatious displays of skill – a dancing turn, a not-strictly-necessary stepover – were written off as flamboyance that warranted a crunching tackle from one of the local goons in defence. Southern Europeans were mocked for being delicate flowers when they wore gloves and long sleeves in winter. And should you dare to fall over under anything less than grievous bodily harm while holding a foreign passport, you would reliably be branded a 'diver,' a sneaky fraud who tries to dupe referees into calling fouls for non-existent contact.

Nothing confirmed their suspicions more than Cantona's self-destruction in the 1994–5 season, when he earned an eight-month ban for launching a kung fu kick at a fan after being sent off. English supporters now knew for sure that all these foreigners had a screw loose.

But for the Premier League owners watching at home, there was a lesson to take away from Cantona: for all of his Gallic foibles, he had proven that there was gold to be found beyond Britain's shores. And for the first time in its young history, the Premier League could afford it. The clubs just needed to know where to look.

In the pre-internet, pre-DVD, pre-wall-to-wall-football age, English clubs often had no idea what a nineteen-year-old player in France or Spain or Italy might look like. He could be the next Pelé, and an English director's only opportunities to see him would be during coverage of the Champions League, or at a World Cup, or on a grainy video mailed their way by a scout. The foreign game was so obscure that David Dein had to fight to convince his Arsenal manager, Bruce Rioch, to sign the impossibly gifted Dennis Bergkamp from Internazionale. 'But he's struggled at Inter,' Rioch told Dein in 1995. Dein replied by freeing up £7.5 million to acquire him immediately.

Bergkamp, with 87 goals and 94 assists in 315 Premier League appearances, stayed with the Gunners for eleven years and remains one of the most brilliant players, foreign or domestic, the Premier League has ever seen. (Rioch, to no one's surprise, lasted just eleven more months at Arsenal.) And yet Bergkamp wasn't even Arsenal's most significant import of the mid 1990s. That distinction belonged to the manager that Dein hired in 1996: a lanky, polyglot Frenchman in glasses that Dein remembered from a game of charades in 1988.

Dein first met Arsène Wenger when he was coaching AS Monaco in the French league, where he fitted neatly into the tradition of cerebral managers who smoked on the sideline and wanted nothing more than for their teams to play stylish football with the ball on the ground – none of that 'hoof it long' stuff. Wenger had particularly impressed Dein by acting out *A Midsummer Night's Dream* in a game of charades at a London dinner party, which would end up changing the course of Arsenal Football Club. The late 1980s weren't yet right to bring him to England, but Dein took note of him. This was not your average tracksuit manager. For the next six years, Wenger stuck around the French Riviera before moving in 1995 to the football hinterlands of Nagoya, Japan, to run a club called Grampus Eight, which was built by the heirs to the Toyota fortune. 'Wengeru', as he was known in the Far East, stayed for two years until Dein came calling.

When Arsenal unveiled Wenger in September 1996, he was only the second non-British or non-Irish manager of the new Premier League era. He was urbane, exotic, and instantly recognizable to precisely no one. The *Evening Standard* asked in a block headline, ARSENE WHO? The players thought he looked like more like a geography teacher than a football manager. And before asking 'Will he help us win?' or 'How will he have us play?', what the club's long-serving captain, Tony Adams, really wanted to know was 'Does he even speak English properly?'

As it happened, Wenger did, because Wenger speaks no fewer than five languages. Raised with French and German in the Alsatian village of Duttlenheim, the former altar boy and unremarkable central defender, who spent his French military service giving driving lessons, had enrolled in a Cambridge University English course for a summer in the 1970s, somehow knowing it would come in handy down the line. Add that to the Spanish, Italian, and Japanese he picked up on his travels and Wenger could converse in more languages than the entire Arsenal squad put together. Through the addition of one middle-aged man in thick spectacles, the 110-year-old club was about to become the most cosmopolitan spot north of the Thames.

Before he could revolutionize English football, however, Arsène Wenger had to revolutionize lunch.

He did away with a few of the club's less productive English traditions: beer, steak, and chocolate bars. The Tuesday Club, the senior Arsenal players' weekly booze-up, was cancelled. There would be no turning up to training hung over – albeit on time – and sweating out last night's pints. Post-match Mars bars disappeared despite the squad's singing on the team bus to ask for them back. And a greasy steak was no longer considered appropriate pre-match food. Wenger hired a nutritionist to revamp Arsenal's cafeteria. Grilled chicken, unseasoned rice or pasta, and steamed vegetables became the norm. Exciting it was not. But just as Blackburn discovered when Rovers moved into their new training ground the season they won the title, small improvements in professionalism went a long way in the Premier League of the 1990s.

So could a little bit of obscure expertise. As the first Frenchman to manage a club in the English top flight, Wenger had a distinct advantage when it came to sourcing talent back home. A *Bonjour* from Arsène Wenger on the phone to poach a French club's most talented nineteen-year-old went over a lot better than a grumpy *Parlez-vous anglais?* from any of his English counterparts. If they even knew the right person to call, that is. Wenger had nearly three decades' worth of contacts in France's football market, from academy coaches to club presidents. So it made perfect sense when five of his first eight signings at Arsenal came from across the Channel. All-time Premier League greats Robert Pirès and Arsenal's record goal scorer Thierry Henry would make the same journey to north London in the years that followed. France was always Wenger's ace in the hole.

People figured that one out early on. Wenger breathed new life into the ageing group of English stalwarts at the back by providing what might have been their first encounters with a salad and sprinkled the team with dashing, largely unheard-of foreign imports: a Parisian teenager named Nicolas Anelka, signed for half a million pounds; his French midfield pairing of Patrick Vieira and Emmanuel Petit; and Dutch winger Marc Overmars. In May 1998, twenty months after ARSENE WHO?, Wenger became the first non-British or non-Irish manager to win England's top title. For good measure, he tacked on the FA Cup, too.

That summer, two of Wenger's French boys went off to join their national team at the 1998 World Cup in their home country. Les Bleus marauded their way to the final, where they overpowered Brazil, 3–0. The final goal was swept in by Petit and assisted by Vieira. In London the next morning, the front page of the *Mirror* carried a photo of those two players locked in a hug beside a headline that showed just how much their stodgy old London club – and English football – were changing.

It read, ARSENAL WIN THE WORLD CUP.

While a French revolution unfolded in north London, a handful of other clubs also clocked the confluence of English TV money, plentiful European talent, and free agency. A more cosmopolitan future was within reach for any team willing to look beyond its borders and change its very identity, perhaps irrevocably.

Nothing about Chelsea Football Club in 1995 suggested that it would be one of those teams.

A team that hadn't been top-flight champions since 1955 – 'You won the league in black-and-white' was the chant from the away section – or lifted a major trophy of any kind since the 1970s, Chelsea were a deeply local concern with a legacy of shaved-head hooliganism. Their home stadium, Stamford Bridge, might have been tucked into a posh corner of west London just off King's Road – think antique dealers, French cafés, and maisonettes for merchant bankers – but Saturday afternoons brought a more feral, urine-soaked vibe. The fan situation at this otherwise sleepy club had become so grim in the mid 1980s that it briefly considered installing electrified fences to herd supporters like cattle.

Not that the cattle had much to be excited about. Chelsea spent the first five seasons of the 1990s in the bottom half of the table, where no one gave the Blues much thought. Their chairman, yet another self-made wheeler-dealer named Ken Bates, who struck gold in the ready-mix concrete business, had saved the club by buying it for a pound in 1982. He protected their future at Stamford Bridge by creating the Chelsea Pitch Owners association, a non-profit designed to head off any attempts to move the club elsewhere. (The crux of it was this: anyone could own the club and try to uproot it, but the true Chelsea FC could play only on the pitch that belonged to the fans.) Bates later floated the club on the AIM stock exchange, London's less stringently regulated market for smaller companies, and drummed up a little interest from some mysterious investors in Hong Kong, whose identities never emerged. But everything else about the club was British, including nearly all of the playing squad. The most exotic thing in the team was Russian goalkeeper Dmitri Kharine's sense of style – no matter the weather, he played in long baggy tracksuit bottoms instead of shorts.

'Sexy football' changed all of that.

In 1995, out of the blue, the team pulled off a free transfer for Ruud Gullit, the dreadlocked Dutchman with a better football pedigree than all of Chelsea Football Club. The signing of Gullit – made possible by the Bosman ruling – sent shockwaves through

English football. Here was someone who had seen all there was to see and won all there was to win in Europe's gold-standard league, Italy's Serie A, and he was actually choosing to move to the Premier League. Gullit wasn't a defender or a midfielder, fans were told, he was a *libero*, a kind of free-spirited hybrid. He'd been the heartbeat of AC Milan as it redefined modern tactics in the late 1980s. He'd been a European Champion with the Netherlands in 1988. And, unlike most of the footballers he was about to call his teammates, he had something to say for himself. When he was voted 1987's European Footballer of the Year, he dedicated the award to a then-little-known political prisoner from South Africa named Nelson Mandela. To English football, Gullit might as well have beamed in from an extremely advanced alien culture.

On the pitch, Gullit's comically superior standard was obvious. From his position behind the defence, he would bring down long balls on his chest and then volley a pass out to his fullbacks just to hear the crowd gasp. (The more traditional English approach in that situation would have been to hammer the ball into the next parliamentary constituency.) But when he tried to build Chelsea's play from the back in the Dutch style he'd always known, Gullit ran into trouble: he'd pass the ball to his fellow defenders only to find that they didn't want the damn thing. Eventually, manager Glenn Hoddle changed things up. 'Ruud,' he told Gullit, 'it might be better if you do these things in midfield.'

Gullit was given the chance to spread his gospel even further when he was handed the keys to the whole club. In the summer of 1996, when Hoddle left Chelsea to take over the England national team, Bates appointed the Dutchman player-manager.

Calling each of his players 'lovely boy' and preaching what he called 'sexy football', Gullit set about turning Chelsea into one of the most stylish teams in the country. The squad now had a Frenchman, a Jamaican, a Romanian, two Norwegians, and three Italians, all of whom became Chelsea folk heroes: the aristocratic Gianluca Vialli, who came from Juventus on another Bosman free transfer; the diminutive Gianfranco Zola from Parma, who taught himself English by reading John Grisham novels in one hand and an English-to-Italian dictionary in the other; and the quietly efficient

Roberto Di Matteo from Lazio. Stamford Bridge was officially Serie A's embassy in London.

Right around then, Chelsea's players noticed that little things had started to shift. They still trained at a place called Harlington, a facility they borrowed from a local college and had to vacate by 1 p.m. on Wednesdays. But for the first time, they felt genuinely famous. Five years of unprecedented television coverage meant that the general public knew the players' faces – it certainly helped that Chelsea were such fun to watch now. People who weren't traditional football fans began stopping them in public. Defender Graeme Le Saux was strolling along Sloane Street when a woman stopped him to ask him to sign her Filofax. As he walked away, mildly bemused, Le Saux thought to himself: *The game is changing*.

Le Saux knew that for sure when he saw the transformation of Dennis Wise, a tough-as-nails, five-foot-six bruiser who'd been part of Wimbledon's hard-drinking, practical-joking 'Crazy Gang' of the 1980s. The level of teasing was so intense inside that Wimbledon dressing room that younger players routinely broke down in tears. There was enough hazing to make the military look tame. Not one of the Crazy Gang even blinked when a player's car was literally set on fire as part of a prank.

Now at Chelsea, even Wise was fit for polite company. He stunned his teammates by turning up in London's swankiest restaurants, including Chelsea's favourite post-match spot, San Lorenzo, an Italian osteria around the corner from Harrods.

'I always wanted to go experience football in another country,' Le Saux said. 'But in the end, football from another country came to me.'

The United Colors of Chelsea project reached its peak on Boxing Day 1999 ahead of a forgettable game against Southampton. By now, Gullit had been turfed out by Bates – despite being the first non-British manager to win a major trophy in England with the 1997 FA Cup – and Vialli was the new player-manager. But as he named his side, he had no idea what a can of worms he was opening up.

Vialli was only trying to figure out how to plug some gaps in his flu-ravaged team. The solution he landed on with the best, healthiest players available to him that day was to field a Dutch goalkeeper; defenders from Spain, Brazil, France, and Nigeria; midfielders from Italy, Romania, Uruguay, and France; and a pair of forwards from Italy and Norway. None of the players had noticed anything special until they saw the larger-than-usual crowd of photographers that awaited them when they exited the tunnel.

That's when someone told them. They had just become the first starting eleven without a single British player in 111 years of English professional football.

PART III

Invaders on the Shore

'We had all the money in the world.'
Trevor Birch, Chelsea FC

10

CHELSEA'S NEW APPROACH brought the club trophies, glamour, and some long-awaited recognition. They were all things the club wanted but not exactly what the club needed.

That would have been cash. Because, by 2003, Chelsea were flat broke.

Even as money flowed in from the Premier League's £1.2 billion domestic TV rights deal, signed in 2001, Ken Bates seemed to remain the same old boardroom Scrooge he'd always been. Since the dawn of the Premier League era, Chelsea had signed sixty-three new players, making the most of all the freebies he could find in the post-Bosman market. The problem with those Bosman babies, as Bates later discovered, was that they all joined Chelsea expecting long contracts and hefty salaries. Even if they never played. In 2000, for example, one of Vialli's final acts before being sacked was to pick up the Dutch defender Winston Bogarde, whose contract had just expired at Barcelona. Chelsea handed him a four-year, £40,000-a-week deal that would earn him nearly £10 million.

That worked out to slightly more than £750,000 per appearance: in four years, Bogarde played for the club only twelve times. The only thing he weighed on more than Chelsea's bench was Chelsea's books.

Bates didn't appear much savvier with improvements to the rest of the club either. Unless he saw a chance to monetize an upgrade, the upgrade wasn't worth making. Take the training ground at Harlington. Chelsea had come a long way since European champions first pitched up in west London, but the players were still training on a borrowed college field. 'It was the most shocking thing I'd ever seen,' said World Cup-winner Marcel Desailly. 'I'd just arrived

89

from Milanello,' AC Milan's storied training ground. Bates saw no reason to change this arrangement. He briefly considered building a new training facility complete with a Chelsea megastore – essentially a souvenir shop with a practice pitch attached – before realizing that no one was going to drive out as far as Heathrow Airport to buy a shirt. He had also dreamed up a project through the club's holding company, Chelsea Village, that would see a hotel, restaurants, and a members-only, state-of-the-art health club attached to Stamford Bridge. (The players, squatters at Harlington, did not take it well when they learned Bates was building a gym they couldn't use.)

Bonus negotiations were the worst of all. Bates didn't just squeeze every penny, he had a reputation for gleefully tormenting his employees in the process. In 1999, after Chelsea qualified for the Champions League, the squad designated three veterans – the law firm of Le Saux, Zola, and Wise – to talk to Bates about boosting their European incentives. Bates initially acceded to their demands. But when the contracts landed just before the season started, Le Saux noticed something was amiss. Where were the bonuses?

'Have you got it in writing?' Bates asked Le Saux when he called.

'No. But we sat down with you and spoke about it.'

'Well, if you haven't got it in writing, then you can't have it.'

'Ken,' Le Saux said, already thinking about how he'd have to explain to his teammates that they'd been screwed, 'the three of us know that you sat with us and agreed to it.'

'Maybe it's a lesson for you, Graeme,' Bates said, before secretly reinstating the bonuses. 'You should get things in writing.'

Bates was singing a different tune in 2002. The club was in such dire financial straits that he brought in an Ernst & Young restructuring specialist named Trevor Birch to serve as Chelsea's chief executive. His only mission: save the club from bankruptcy.

Birch had plenty of first-hand football experience before his two decades as a numbers man. He'd been a player in Liverpool's system before leaving the game at age twenty-three to study accountancy. But he never quite expected to be in charge of tightening the belt on a Premier League club's outrageous personnel spending. Nor did he think that, come May 2003, he would have to inform the squad that there was much more than three points at stake when they played Liverpool in the final game of the season.

But in the days before that match, the secret was already out. Chelsea's finances were in desperate need of restructuring and Birch had to come clean. The players suspected something was up when rumours of unusually meagre contract extensions spread through the team. So when the papers began touting Chelsea–Liverpool as the '£20 million game', the squad paid attention. The reason for the high stakes was that the winner would finish fourth and clinch the final spot in the 2003–4 Champions League, giving them access to a vital injection of cash. No English match had ever been described in these terms before.

For unprecedented circumstances, Chelsea were going to take unprecedented measures.

The night before the game, the club moved the team into the Royal Lancaster Hotel off Hyde Park instead of letting the players sleep in their own beds at home, a practice that was still years from becoming standard among Premier League clubs. And after dinner, it was Birch, rather than manager Claudio Ranieri, who addressed the team. He told them in no uncertain terms that this would be one of the most significant matches of their lives. For this occasion, he had hired an American military veteran to give a motivational speech about the Vietnam War to this international squad of Europeans, Africans, and twenty-something Brits. This wasn't just any veteran either. He was General Charles Chandler 'Chuck' Krulak, a marine who served with distinction in Vietnam and the Gulf War, received the United States' third-highest military honour, and rose over a thirty-six-year career to become Commandant of the Marine Corps, the force's highest-ranking officer. It's the kind of CV that used to prime Americans for a run at the White House. Instead, Krulak was standing in a London hotel ballroom preparing a football team to invade Liverpool's midfield.

The general spoke of honour and valour and taking hills against the odds. In clipped cowboy tones, he told them a story about manoeuvring his unit to higher ground in a tropical jungle under heavy fire from the Viet Cong. When he finished, the Chelsea players were ready to kick the stuffing out of Liverpool right there in the hotel ballroom. Unfortunately, they had to go to sleep. 'I felt like I had thirty-two espressos,' Le Saux said. 'I wanted to abseil out of my room and carry out a military operation in Hyde Park.'

The next afternoon, moments before kick-off, there was one last motivational touch. The players were sitting in the dressing room fiddling with their laces and tape as Stamford Bridge rumbled around them. Birch dropped in to remind them of how critical this match was to all of their professional prospects.

For one day only, Chelsea got a pre-match team talk from an accountant.

While Birch sweated to secure Chelsea's present, another character far from the Stamford Bridge dressing rooms was secretly pondering the club's long-term future.

Pini Zahavi, a former Israeli football journalist, was one of the people training his sights on European football's new economy, and no one smelled greater opportunity than he did. Technically, he was an agent, but for those who knew him, a true assessment of his occupation proved more complicated.

Harry Redknapp went with something straight out of a gangster flick: 'A man who can get things done.' Zahavi's ex-wife, in a tabloid interview, preferred 'dirty rat'.

Zahavi's deal-making schtick includes much more than telling a club what a wonderful forward his client is and how this player is precisely the piece they are missing. Zahavi started his career at a newspaper called *Hadashot Hasport*, which sent him on a life-changing trip to the 1974 World Cup in West Germany. Israel didn't qualify for the tournament, but that didn't stop Zahavi from scoring major results of his own. Running around matches for a month, he made plenty of friends 2,500 miles from home. By 1979, Zahavi had nurtured those connections (many of which happened to be from the north-west of England) and slid friendship into business. The journalist turned agent orchestrated his first deal when he helped a little-known defender named Avi Cohen move from the Israeli team Maccabi Tel Aviv to Liverpool, then defending champions.

Over the next twenty-five years, Zahavi grew his network, his portfolio of players, and his wallet until he became the most influential agent in English football. He broke the British transfer record. He seemed to have as much say in Manchester United's transfer dealings as Alex Ferguson did.

But his biggest coup came about when he made a simple introduction between the chief executive of a cash-strapped west London club and a shabbily dressed thirty-six-year-old Russian from near the Kazakh border who ran the Sibneft oil company, had a personal fortune of more than £7 billion, and counted Boris Yeltsin and Vladimir Putin among his personal friends.

This is how Chelsea Football Club made the acquaintance of Roman Abramovich, English football's first oligarch, a high school dropout who was worth ten Jack Walkers. And how Zahavi went from dealing in players to dealing in entire clubs.

Abramovich had had English football on his mind ever since attending a Champions League quarter-final at Old Trafford between Manchester United and Real Madrid in the spring of 2003. As he explored his options, Abramovich had first spoken with Tottenham Hotspur's chairman though he was left unimpressed with the club's location in north-east London. While his Mercedes trundled along Tottenham High Road that day, he looked out the window, and said in Russian to his associate, 'This is worse than Omsk' – a reference to the grim Siberian outpost where Sibneft had a refinery.

Abramovich wasn't immediately sold on acquiring Chelsea either. If he had one stipulation before dropping nine figures on a hobby, it was that the club should be playing in the Champions League. If the Blues could do that, then maybe he was interested. The players going at it with Liverpool at Stamford Bridge on that afternoon in May 2003 knew the stakes were huge because Birch had told them so. But they had no idea just how dramatically things would escalate. Behind the scenes, the £20 million game was secretly turning into Chelsea's £7 billion game. Except, of course, for that single minute of the match when Chelsea trailed Liverpool 1–0 and it was briefly the bankruptcy game.

The Blues came back to win 2–1. Which was good enough for Abramovich. In the first week of July, he and his entourage met with Trevor Birch to agree to purchase the club. Birch and the Chelsea camp hadn't been able to do much due diligence on him since Abramovich was effectively invisible in the West. Birch's Google search turned up very little except a mention of the oligarch in *Forbes*. That Abramovich turned up with what Birch called 'blue-chip advisers and blue-chip banks' plus a lawyer from the New York firm Skadden Arps reassured him despite the oligarch's scruffy appearance and jeans. Abramovich liked to have a Russian translator present, too, even though he clearly understood English – a tactic that had been used by Soviet foreign ministers for decades to buy themselves time in delicate meetings. But for this particular negotiation, in a suite overlooking the pitch at Stamford Bridge, there was little need for high-level gamesmanship. They struck a £140 million deal in less than thirty minutes.

'No, it's not about making money,' Abramovich said in a rare interview with the BBC after the takeover. 'I have many much less risky ways of making money than this. I don't want to throw my money away, but it's really about having fun and that means success and trophies.'

As it did every year, early July brought about the least favourite part of Chelsea manager Claudio Ranieri's summer, the time when he had to slip back into his car and leave his native Rome. It was an eighteen-hour drive up through the boot of Italy, over the Alps into France, and all the way to the ferry that would carry him across the English Channel. Once he got to England, pre-season training could begin. Six weeks of drills, sprints, and putting his players through the heavy physical labour that would whip them into shape to run from August 2003 to May 2004. There would be more money in the club accounts now that they knew there was European football in Chelsea's future, but not that much more. They were talking about enough to keep the lights on at Stamford Bridge, not exactly enough to go on a pan-European player spending spree. In other words, Ranieri was looking at another pre-season with the same bunch as the previous summer.

Ranieri was somewhere in France when his mobile phone rang. He recognized Trevor Birch's number in London. He had news.

'Claudio,' Birch said. 'The owner's changed. A Russian has bought the club.'

Ranieri paused. 'It's good?'

'Yeah, it's fantastic!'

Had Ranieri's problems evaporated while he sped along the autoroute? He turned this over in his mind. The season hadn't even started and he could already tell that nothing would go as he'd planned. 'Fantastic,' he told Birch slowly. 'But be careful. Because me and you are the first who go home.'

'Why Claudio?'

'Yes! Arrive new owner, the first thing is change you and change me.'

Abramovich would change more than an accountant and his Italian manager.

The combination of his cash, ruthlessness, and ambition positioned Chelsea to crash the Manchester United and Arsenal party – the two clubs that had won every league title between 1996 and 2004. Abramovich was going to borrow the Uncle Jack recipe, stir in some caviar, and use it every season, not just for one year of Premier League folly.

'I only want you to bring us the best players,' Abramovich told Ranieri in their first meeting.

'I'll try, but who can sell us their best?' Ranieri replied.

Abramovich didn't care. He knew that every club had its price for every player. The difference now was that he was someone who was willing to pay it whatever the number. 'We had all the money in the world,' Birch said. 'There was disbelief everywhere, because it had literally never happened in football.'

In his first summer as Chelsea's owner, Abramovich oversaw some £110 million in spending on fourteen new players. The following year, Abramovich sacked Ranieri, spent another £90 million on nine players, and hired a cocky young manager who had just won the trophy that Abramovich coveted most, the Champions League, with the Portuguese club Porto. His name was José Mourinho.

Abramovich never met Uncle Jack, but he'd understood the same basic lesson. Upending the Premier League's established order took financial brute force. In the spring of 2005, Chelsea won their first league title in sixty years. Even Martin Edwards, by now retired from Manchester United, couldn't believe it. He thought he had seen off the last of the clubs bankrolled by wealthy benefactors – Blackburn's Jack Walker and others such as Newcastle's John Hall had come and gone. It turned out they were only the warm-up acts.

But rather than knocking Arsenal and United off the mountaintop, Chelsea joined them there. Led by the three most famous managers in Premier League history – Alex Ferguson, Arsène Wenger, and Mourinho – the old guard and new money alike began developing new strategies to give the Premier League an infrastructure that would compound its growing advantage, an aggressive approach to pull the quaint and tribal world of football into the twenty-first century.

And the battles between them – with their warring cults of managerial personality – became the backdrop of the 2000s, a decade of unchecked growth for the Premier League in which its teams could do no wrong. From 2004 on, the three superclubs shared every domestic title for eight years. And salaries climbed so fast that players from around the world grew desperate for English contracts. They didn't even need Arsenal or United or Chelsea to be interested; any move to the Premier League would do.

II

With Manchester United erecting a commercial empire up north and Chelsea waving their chequebook across town, Arsenal could sense their universe was shifting. The Gunners, English football aristocrats, still boasted one of the most sought-after squads in Europe and two titles in four years, but they could see the invaders beyond the walls. They were wearing blue kits and proudly singing about their lack of history. David Dein had been around English football long enough to know that this was unprecedented – Roman Abramovich was no Jack Walker. Dein had to do something. So he took the invaders to lunch.

Roman Abramovich had dispatched Chelsea representatives all over the Continent to stock his new team with stars. But after an initial wave of overseas spending, the club's gaze settled closer to home – on Arsenal. The Gunners were playing precisely the kind of stylish football that Abramovich hoped to emulate, with world-class talent all over the pitch. Better yet, Arsenal had proven willing to part with those stars if Arsène Wenger, the only manager in the league with a degree in economics, felt the offer was right. In 1999, he'd sold his deadliest striker, Nicolas Anelka, to Real Madrid for forty-four times what he originally paid to sign him. The following year, he'd let Marc Overmars and Emmanuel Petit, two key members of his first league-winning team, leave for Barcelona.

The deputies Abramovich sent to meet with Dein in a posh restaurant off London's Piccadilly in late 2003 were aware of all of this. They weren't there to poach any Arsenal player in particular but rather to inquire casually about where everyone stood. In the coy game of football transfers, where courtships are more convoluted than a Jane Austen romance, this was the 'I'm not asking if you're not selling' stage that can quickly become the 'Unless, of course, you *are* selling, in which case I may or may not be interested' stage. This situation plays out hundreds of times a season in fancy restaurants, hotel lobbies, and motorway rest stops all over the country. On this particular afternoon, the list of players Chelsea definitely were not asking about – and that Dein definitely wasn't selling – amounted to pretty much the entire Arsenal squad. Under the terms of the lunch, only one player was expressly off the table, according to one of the Chelsea executives: Thierry Henry. Wenger had discovered Henry as a teenager at Monaco and brought him to London in 1999, where he converted the fleet-footed kid from a winger into a centre-forward. Henry had been breaking records and terrorizing Premier League defences ever since. (He would go on to be the league's top scorer in each of the next three seasons.)

Over appetisers in a secluded corner of the dimly lit room, the Chelsea executives started running through the list of names as Dein answered, 'No, you can't have him.' 'No, he's not for sale.' When they reached Francis Jeffers – a jug-eared forward from Liverpool who had joined Arsenal as a goal poacher but failed to turn into the 'fox in the box' they needed – Dein, who said he never sold a player Wenger wanted to keep, saw an opportunity to shift some unwanted stock. The new billionaires on the block weren't interested.

The soup course arrived without the two sides reaching an agreement for any of Arsenal's players. Only one name hadn't been spoken: Wenger's protégé, the man who had basically won the Gunners the title in 2002. Everyone at the table had stuck to their promise not to bring up Thierry Henry. Now his name hung in the air like stale cigar smoke.

Dein interjected. 'If you don't mention his name, then it's not a real offer . . .' one of the Chelsea executives present recalled. And if it wasn't a real offer, Dein would be under no obligation to inform the Arsenal board. To Abramovich's delegation, the message was clearer than a bottle of Russian vodka.

'Thirty million' came Chelsea's opening non-offer.

No. Don't be silly.

'Thirty-five million.'

Come on.

'Forty million,' the Chelsea representatives shot back, quickly barrelling towards the world transfer record of £46 million that Real Madrid had paid to pry France's world and European champion Zinedine Zidane from Juventus in 2001.

'Forty-five million.'

No again. Chelsea tried one more time. 'How about £49.999 million?' Which was just short of a figure that might have caused the tabloids to spontaneously combust.

Dein paused to consider the figure's absurdity. He knew that buying Chelsea had cost Abramovich only £140 million. Had his fortune already warped the transfer market so dramatically that a single player could now be worth 35 per cent of an entire team? Besides, if Abramovich wanted Thierry Henry this badly, there was surely a much simpler way to get him.

'Why didn't you just buy the whole club?' Dein asked.

The answer came down to Abramovich's due diligence before buying into football. In the spring of 2003, he had hired the Swiss bank UBS to examine the Premier League landscape. One of its findings, along with Chelsea's distressed financial situation and Tottenham's vague potential, was that Arsenal were categorically not for sale. When Dein heard this, he smacked the lunch table so hard that soup spilled out of his bowl, one Chelsea executive said. He cursed UBS and he cursed Abramovich.

Because if Abramovich had come knocking on the door at Highbury instead of Stamford Bridge that summer, Dein was convinced that Arsenal's owners would have cashed out. You'd have been crazy not to. Abramovich could have had his London-based plaything, the Arsenal directors – including Dein – would have pocketed a fortune, and the club's galactic transfer budget in the hands of a recruiter as skilled as Wenger might have built a football dynasty. What is certain is that Arsenal, not Chelsea, would have been the first club with a billionaire sugar daddy.

Dein had just experienced first-hand how powerful that could make a club. Chelsea, on the brink of bankruptcy in the spring, could now waltz in and bid for his best player. (Later that year, Abramovich would personally make a failed attempt to pry Henry away in the director's box at Highbury.) But a football El Dorado had slipped away because a few Swiss bankers didn't know what they were talking about.

And now there was soup all over the table, too.

Without a billionaire benefactor, Arsenal would have to count on a different plan to close the gap on their money-spinning rivals. As of 2003, that plan consisted of a pile of three-dimensional renderings and a newly purchased rubbish dump.

It was somewhere on the site of that dump across the train tracks from the Gunners' home that they intended to build the first of the Premier League's ultra-modern stadiums. There would be no more retrofitting of charming old venues. It was time for something purpose built to support Arsenal's global ambition. The new stadium had to be physically imposing enough to match the stature of the club. It needed enough corporate hospitality to turn every match day into a windfall. And, like the palaces going up in the NFL, it needed to look good on television. Arsenal's new stadium wouldn't just be a venue for 60,000 fans attending in person, it would be a backdrop for the 60 million watching around the world.

Since before the First World War, Arsenal had lived at Highbury, an intimate art deco venue that was less a cathedral to football and more one of the game's universities, all white walls and mahogany interiors. Away fans may have mockingly dubbed Highbury the 'Library', but the place genuinely looked like a hangout for post-graduate students. Everything about the stadium was tight – purposely so. It had to fit among the residential terraces and narrow streets of Islington. And as Wenger built one of the league's most powerful teams through the late 1990s and early 2000s, its dimensions worked to the Gunners' advantage. His team of superathletes squeezed opponents clean off the narrow pitch – and often into the front row of the stands.

On match days, fans would stream from the nearby Tube stations past tidy rows of two- and three-storey houses squashed up against one another. They poured out of Arsenal station – the only stop on the entire Underground named for a football team – took a right onto Avenell Road, and meandered past tiny front gardens until the walls of the North Bank and the East Stand appeared out of nowhere.

Thousands more supporters came from Finsbury Park, the station slightly farther away that gave them the added advantage of being able to stroll by the Auld Triangle pub and burger vendors hawking several varieties of mystery meat on soggy buns.

At its peak in the 1930s, Highbury could cram 73,000 people onto the terraces. It stayed pretty much unchanged for five decades after that, visited occasionally by German bombs during the Second World War, and by Muhammad Ali, who fought Henry Cooper there in 1966.

Redevelopment of the Clock End shrank Highbury a little in the late 1980s, but the ban on standing sections following Hillsborough and the Taylor Report cut Highbury's capacity nearly in half. So in 1993, Arsenal tackled the biggest renovation project the ancient stadium had ever known. The club rebuilt its storied North Bank stand.

To finance the project, Dein cooked up a bond scheme that required season-ticket holders to pay a onetime fee of between £1,000 and £1,500 – more or less the equivalent of an extra season ticket – for the lifetime right to renew, which briefly made him the most hated man in north London not wearing a Tottenham shirt. Still, the programme did what it was supposed to do. Arsenal raised enough cash for construction of the new North Bank to begin ahead of the 1992–3 season. But that only raised another issue: what to do with the eyesore of a construction site behind one of the goals? This was the first season of the new, televised Premier League after all. Highbury couldn't be allowed to look like a mess in front of all those cameras.

But Dein had another trick up his sleeve. He and Arsenal director Ken Friar commissioned a £150,000, thirty-five-foot-tall mural to hang along the north end of the field with 8,000 Arsenal fans painted on it. Only after the odd facade was installed did someone notice that every single one of the 8,000 cartoon fans was a white male, prompting Arsenal to call back the artist for some hasty revisions – and some added diversity.

'At least I didn't get booed,' former Arsenal fullback Lee Dixon said of the mural.

Arsenal fans were too busy bemoaning the mural to gripe about their own players, especially those spectators who had given up their regular seats to a giant tarpaulin. Only away fans had anything nice to say about the mural. Having snoozed in the Highbury Library before, they felt the Potemkin supporters actually improved the atmosphere.

When the mural finally came down, it revealed a 10,000-capacity stand that the architecture firm behind it, Populous, called a 'great leap forward in stadium design'. It had two tiers, sweeping views, and no sign of the now-banned standing sections. What impressed David Dein and the Arsenal brass the most, however, was a detail that couldn't be seen from the field: the bathrooms. In the battle that Dein had been waging for decades, he had finally won a breakthrough.

The directors had been 'quite toilet obsessed' from the beginning of the North Bank project, the architect Chris Lee recalled. But for people like Dein, who remembered the days of hooliganism, bathrooms were weirdly significant. They were the first thing fans trashed when tensions flared, and even when they didn't, the loos remained foul-smelling hellholes – an unspoken message telling fans exactly what English football's authorities thought of them. 'If you treat people like animals,' Friar used to say, 'they will behave like animals.'

Arsenal were going to treat fans like more than just human beings. They were going to treat them like customers. And that started in the restrooms, where every finish was upgraded, from the tiling to the mirrors. Dein, who had fought to increase the length of half-time from ten minutes to fifteen, also insisted that they install twice as many urinals as were recommended under current industry standards. 'In a way, that was my calling,' Dein said. 'If they're drinking beer and Coca-Cola and coffees and teas beforehand, they've got to be able to go at half-time.' He could tell that his personal crusade was won about a year after the stadium opened when he was invited to an architecture awards dinner – to collect a toilet-shaped trophy for the best stadium facilities.

No matter how many bathrooms they upgraded or how many extra seats they crammed in, Arsenal knew they were brushing the capacity ceiling for Highbury. Their hands were tied when it came to expanding the East and West stands by the very thing that made them special: they were historically listed buildings. Dropping an extra 10,000 seats on top of them wasn't an option. The club had barely completed the North Bank when they turned back to the architects for another conversation about the club's future. 'We all came to the conclusion that they couldn't get what they wanted out of Highbury,' said Lee.

As it turned out, the North Bank had been the practice run. After ninety years in their understated Islington home, the Gunners were about to build a grandiose new one from scratch.

For a club renowned for its sober, fiscally conservative approach, there was no shortage of wild schemes thrown around. One proposal was to build a tyre-shaped arena (not unlike Bayern Munich's current stadium) directly on top of Finsbury Park Tube station. Sticking with the railway theme, Arsenal also looked at moving into the undeveloped area around King's Cross – which would have been convenient for Wenger's foreign legion arriving from Paris on the Eurostar. The club held talks about borrowing, or even buying, the England national team's home at Wembley Stadium, and even considered proposals to move more than ten miles away, beyond the M25. But no one felt quite right about taking the club outside of Highbury and Islington. Football clubs do not budge.

The bond between an English club and its supporters is both a pillar of the Premier League's appeal and the hardest thing to manufacture, not only because it demands a commitment that outlives most marriages but because it also spans generations. The clubs serve as flags and time capsules of their neighbourhoods. And in places where the club has outlived the industry that built them – Leeds or Stoke or Huddersfield, for example – it's those teams that ensure their towns and cities remain on the football map long after they have faded as economic poles for Britain. If an owner tried to pack up a club and move it elsewhere, he would be met in the streets by a pitchfork-wielding mob. Wimbledon learned that the hard way when they lost much of their fan base after moving all of sixty miles to Milton Keynes and renaming themselves MK Dons.

Arsenal had moved north from south London in 1913, but that was before the club had fully taken root. Nine decades later, the furthest move the club's directors could sell the fans on was almost spitting distance from Highbury.

The idea was to get the move done quickly and, relatively speaking, on a budget. 'We're just a football club,' the late Arsenal director Danny Fiszman, a former diamond dealer who became the driving force behind the stadium, told the architects. 'We don't want to take an inch more land than we have to. We just want to build a stadium and be done with it.' That was before mission creep set in. The basic cost of construction was £170 million until various concessions to the borough council, local businesses, and public relations piled on a series of smaller construction jobs that included a row of apartment buildings. The garbage dump had to be relocated – and they made Arsène Wenger cut the ribbon on a new one. By the time the stadium finally opened, Arsenal Football Club was one of the largest home builders in London for the previous year, according to Populous. The final bill came in at £390 million. And Arsenal were on the hook for all of it.

Combining piles of cash, a bond offering, and more than a half-dozen lenders, the Gunners' payment structure was gargantuan though hardly unorthodox for a project of this size. Except for one particular stipulation imposed on Arsenal's board by the banks: the club would need to retain Arsène Wenger as manager for at least five more years. This was a tricky proposition when superpowers at home and abroad were making regular overtures to him.

Manchester United's Martin Edwards had pitched Wenger at his north London home after Alex Ferguson first discussed retirement in 2001, and Real Madrid were feeling him out, too. But Wenger declined every time. Only as Arsenal's imperial manager could he be a coach, psychologist, and CEO all wrapped into one. He signed the contract extension.

For the first time in the history of English football – and probably in the history of English finance – the manager of a football team was written into the terms of a bank loan.

'The gamble we are taking is that Arsène continues to work the miracles that he's worked for the past seven years or so,' Arsenal chairman Peter Hill-Wood said at the time. 'Will he stay at the club? I sincerely hope so – he might even be chairman!'

Arsenal's directors wondered constantly whether they were doing the right thing. Over five years of internal conversations, one person or another was always asking if the Gunners really needed to go through with this. The price of the project kept increasing. Once they settled on a site, there were businesses and residents to relocate, ancillary buildings to reconstruct. Highbury, meanwhile, would be left behind and developed into luxury apartments. When the board informed Wenger the budget was now closing in on £400 million, even he thought to himself, *This is a kamikaze mission.*

The requirements for avoiding a financial crash and burn were stiff. Arsenal would need to make sure they filled at least 55,000 seats every game and qualified for the Champions League in three out of the first five years while significantly lightening the wage bill. 'That's when I really concentrated on making the project work, because it was important for the future of the club,' Wenger said. 'I knew it would be difficult.'

Once the club broke ground at Ashburton Grove in 2004, it was too late to turn back. The remit from Fiszman to the architects was brief, Lee recalled. '"I want a 60,000-seat stadium that is the most beautiful and the most intimidating"', came the instruction from Fiszman, who died in 2011. 'And that was it. There was nothing more than that simple sentence.'

Say what you will about the aesthetics and how menacing (or not) the stadium turned out to be, but there is no question that the monumental new arena broke with everything that came before it in English football. Arsenal's new home was the first purpose-built club venue of its scale in the modern era. The only other English club to build an entirely new stadium with more than 40,000 seats in the previous forty years was Sunderland, which opened the Stadium of Light in 1997. And even then, Arsenal's was going to be more than 20 per cent larger.

For inspiration, the team from Populous toured the United States, where the stadiums had blown Dein away three decades before. They bounced from gargantuan NFL stadiums to ballparks, including the Baltimore Orioles' Camden Yards, which tried to manufacture an air of history and tradition. There were significant differences. Nearly all of the American parks were located far outside downtown areas, parked next to highways and shopping malls. In England, they'd have to squeeze something into a residential neighbourhood where people would be living quite literally in the shadow of the new ground. On the other hand, they wouldn't have to worry about providing acres of parking – no one in Europe drove to games anyway.

But the Populous team saw plenty to fire their imaginations. The design they landed on out of more than 170 different possibilities was something else entirely because Arsenal had the chance to build a football stadium with a pair of major new considerations in mind: corporate boxes and television.

There would be an unheard-of forty-one camera positions. Lee had learned up close how significant those could be when he worked on the Olympic Stadium for the 2000 Summer Games in his native Australia. Every time he complained about cutting another ten or fifteen seats, some International Olympic Committee official was there to remind him that the cameras were beaming the show to 100 million people. 'So the backdrop, how it looked on screen, was incredibly important,' Lee said.

So was how it looked to the people buying the most expensive tickets. This was a demographic that football clubs had barely chased until the 1990s – people, or companies, prepared to spend five or ten times the price of a regular ticket, all for the use of a private box and a spot of lunch. A few corporate boxes had been around a handful of stadiums since the 1960s, but it wasn't until the 1980s that Irving Scholar became an early pioneer of corporate hospitality at White Hart Lane, Tottenham's home since the nineteenth century, where giant view-obstructing pillars were considered a necessary evil and the sheet-metal roof on the East Stand made it look more like a country railway station. His bold, if controversial, move was to destroy the Shelf, a two-tiered terraced area in the stadium's East Stand, which was home to 20,000 of the cheapest tickets – and most committed supporters. The section was dynamite for atmosphere but terrible for match-day revenues. Scholar's ploy to take Tottenham public and his knack for merchandising had already given Spurs a reputation as English football's 'corporate club'. Now Scholar was doubling down. In place of the Shelf, he installed hospitality boxes that outstripped the income supplied by the old tickets by a factor of ten every weekend.

Martin Edwards soon followed Scholar's lead at Manchester

United. In 1992, he converted the centre of the Stretford End, which had housed the loudest section of standing fans right behind the goal, into executive boxes. 'It was very unpopular, but I had to pay for a £10 million stand,' Edwards said.

The booing was worth it to the balance sheet. The boxes boosted match-day revenues so much that the stands eventually paid for themselves. But they didn't earn Tottenham or United many friends. United's own players complained about the effect of the corporate crowd on the atmosphere. 'They have a few drinks and probably the prawn sandwiches, and they don't realize what's going on out on the pitch,' club captain Roy Keane lamented in 2000. 'I don't think some of the people who come to Old Trafford can spell football, never mind understand it.'

Yet the whole experience of attending games in the Premier League's early executive boxes at old-school English grounds could be a strange one. Guests wearing the obligatory ties and jackets arrived through a separate lobby, went up a lift or a set of private stairs, and walked along an interior carpeted corridor until they hit a plain door with their box number on it. Awaiting them inside was usually a spread of spectacularly bland food accompanied by a couple of bottles of plonk. The whole thing was more like a mediocre Mediterranean cruise than a professional sporting event. The $15,000 Yankee Stadium luxury suites with Scotch, steak, and sushi these were not.

As the most modern stadium in the league, the Emirates sought to bridge that gap. It went from 48 executive boxes at Highbury to 150, which, on top of the various other club seating areas, brought the total of premium tickets to roughly 8,000 per game – 13 per cent of the whole stadium. This was never going to help Arsenal shake their old Highbury Library nickname or the reputation they had built in the 1920s as the Bank of England Club. Nor was the steady increase in ticket prices. (In the season Wenger arrived, the average ticket cost around £12. By the time the Emirates opened a decade later, it had more than tripled to £40.) But the club did notice a change in fan behaviour. At Highbury, the Gunners used to have to replace hundreds of seats every season due to damage caused by away fans – or disgruntled home supporters. In Arsenal's first decade at the Emirates, the club replaced an average of three per season. With cleaner, more expensive surroundings, the improved facility had actually managed to change how supporters conducted themselves. For better or for worse, Arsenal had signalled to the league what the future of English football looked like.

'We had always been used to cranky, slightly idiosyncratic buildings – which we loved – with incredibly tight concourses and bad food,' Lee explained, 'but the Emirates set a new bar.'

Wenger knew from the beginning that the stadium would shape his legacy as much as any side he fielded for Arsenal. He was so intrinsic to the project that the club commissioned a bust of him to put in the directors' lobby, an honour that most managers immortalized in bronze don't receive until they die – or at least not before they retire. His biggest preoccupation when it came to the physical design of the place was the players' areas. Inspired by what he'd learned in Japan about hygiene and how one space should flow into another, he was punctilious in his demands for the areas his team would inhabit pre- and post-match, laying down strict instructions on everything from the location of the treatment areas to the dimensions of the pathway between the tunnel and the showers. As for the dressing rooms, Wenger had seen first-hand all the horrors English football had to offer. In many places, they felt like glorified public toilets minus the graffiti. Wenger wanted space. He insisted on a wide oval shape where the team could actually breathe. The dressing room, he always said, belonged to the players. But that didn't stop him from telling the architects precisely where he intended to stand when addressing those players. Wenger's towering presence was sketched into the blueprints. After all, everything that would happen at Arsenal's new stadium would start, in some way, inside that dressing room.

Every aspect of the Emirates project had been part of a deliberately considered, meticulously thought-out strategy that was intended to cement the club's position among the leaders in European football for decades to come. Arsenal were taking the leap that United had made in the 1990s and customizing it precisely for the demands of twenty-first-century entertainment.

But by the time the Gunners finally cut the ribbon at their new stadium in 2006, the Premier League had spun around them again.

12

No one paid much attention in Manchester in the autumn of 2003 when a reclusive American investor bought a 2.9 per cent stake in United. Rich men from around the world had been acquiring pieces of the club here and there ever since it went public more than a decade earlier.

And at first, Malcolm Glazer seemed no different. A red-bearded native of Upstate New York and the son of Lithuanian Jewish immigrants, he had taken over the family watch repair business at the age of fifteen when his father died. Then he moved into corporate real estate before evolving again into a corporate raider, aggressively seizing control of companies from Formica to Harley-Davidson, and flipping them at handsome profits. The world of sport learned his name in 1995 when Glazer purchased the NFL's Tampa Bay Buccaneers franchise for a then-record $192 million, a baffling choice considering the team hadn't posted a winning season since the early 1980s. Then again, Glazer's intentions when it came to sport would always be a mystery.

So when he began hoovering up shares of Manchester United in the weeks and months after his initial buy-in, it seemed obvious what Glazer was trying to do: take over the club. It just wasn't clear why.

During the following year, Glazer and his sons quietly increased their holding until they closed in on owning 30 per cent of the club, at which point the law requires investors to make the other shareholders an offer for the entire business. United – and the league as a whole – had been so inspired by what it saw across the pond in the NFL that it seemed only fitting for an NFL owner to take the next step and buy into English football. The Glazers forged right ahead. By the summer of 2005, they had agreed to hand over $1.3

billion to take over 98 per cent of the club. Now they had everyone's attention. Malcolm signed off on the deal without even travelling to England, dispatching his sons Joel and Avram instead.

Waiting to welcome them to Old Trafford were several hundred fans chanting, 'Die, Glazers, die!'

When they arrived, the club sealed off both ends of the tunnel under the East Stand and spirited the new owners into their club in vans with tinted windows, surrounded by a police escort. Chief executive David Gill gave them the tour as everyone attempted to ignore the fracas outside. The furious backlash from United supporters had begun the moment they heard the words 'leveraged buyout', an obscure Wall Street instrument that had been fashionable among the pinstriped Gordon Gekko set in the 1980s. United fans might not have understood the technicalities of an LBO at the time, but they understood the gist of it: United were about to be saddled with an eight-figure debt *on purpose*, all for the financial gain of some rich Americans.

To be clear, not all of the risk transferred to the club. One major loan for $265 million came from a group of banks headed by JPMorgan and wound up on United's books. But another, totalling $75 million, came from US hedge funds in the form of 'payment-in-kind' bonds, a financial product that meant the Glazers – not Manchester United PLC – were personally on the hook.

'This guy was an unusual person,' former Tampa mayor Dick Greco told the *Tampa Bay Times* when Malcolm died in 2014. 'He didn't fit what you'd think a sports personality would be. Everybody expects somebody in sports to be loud and boisterous and say funny things. Mr Glazer was not a sports person at all. He didn't know much about football. He just knew business. And to him, it was a business.'

The same was true about English football. The Glazer sons had grown up as fans of the North American Soccer League's Rochester Lancers in the 1970s, but the Lancers were about as far from Manchester United as your 5-a-side team is from the Champions League final. Besides, if this were strictly about business, they had more than enough money to buy into any number of other profitable sectors where they could have racked up profits in peace without death threats or angry Mancunians screaming obscenities outside their offices. 'The opposition to Glazer's takeover is not about some xenophobic or superficial prejudice,' wrote the *Red Issue* fanzine – though some of the fans' chanting sounded suspiciously like xenophobia – 'but has at its core a sense of deep loss of people who hold the essence of a football club so close to their hearts. That this loss should be inflicted – jeopardizing the very future of a club which has been a pillar of Mancunian life for so long – so that a grotesquely rich man can chase a vain punt of plundering ever greater wealth, whilst effectively forcing those from whom he seeks to profit to pay for his buyout, well it's a wonder that there hasn't been more opposition.'

The Glazers had never seen anything like it at home, where NFL owners are more or less interchangeable versions of rich old white men. Besides, beating the Oakland Raiders to win Super Bowl XXXVII in 2003 had bought the Glazers all the credit they needed with fans in Tampa Bay. In Manchester, their tentative efforts to assuage the locals fell on deaf ears. 'Man U has a tremendous history, and we respect that history,' Bryan Glazer told the *Orlando Sentinel* in July 2005. 'We're not going to try and Americanize the game. We're not going to bring in cheerleaders.'

Of course, the Premier League had already tried cheerleaders. It hadn't worked.

But Manchester United's entire outlook and its position as one of Europe's leading clubs appeared to now rest in the hands of its enigmatic new owners. Rumours circulated that the Glazers would cap United's transfer spending at £20 million a season, that they would buy Old Trafford and lease it back to the club, that they would even change the logo. All around the stadium, stickers cropped up proclaiming, LOVE UNITED, HATE GLAZER. The Manchester United Supporters Trust soon ordered scarves in green and gold, the club's original colours from their days as a collection of railway workers in Newton Heath, which they pushed as a symbol of resistance against the Glazers. One disaffected group of United supporters left United altogether and formed a semi-professional outfit they dubbed FC United of Manchester.

Through all of this, the Glazers remained impassive: 'It'll pass.'

Within a year, the new American-owned, highly leveraged

Manchester United even caught the attention of *The New Yorker*, which marvelled at how the flagship of English football was changing. In a ten-page profile of the club under Glazer rule, the magazine picked up on an anonymous letter in *Red Issue* that explained why 'Old Trafford is shite'. In the 1980s, one despondent fan wrote, 'It was the crowd at OT itself. 50K+ badly behaved men, all older than me wanting to rip limbs off opposing fans and who made the walls shake with the noise they created. Bad language, bad behaviour – the best escape possible. I used to watch them open-mouthed as they jumped over the pens of United Road towards the opposition. A week later, I was doing it with them. The place is wank now. Too controlled, all seating, sensible middle-class shite.'

Even Alex Ferguson felt the heat. When a group of fans confronted him about the Glazers after an away game in Hungary, he told them that if they didn't like it they could 'go and support Chelsea'.

Only the Glazers took the revolt in their stride. Seldom spotted at Old Trafford, they did little to extinguish the inferno that raged around the club. In their few public statements, they came off as oddly unbothered, insisting that they hadn't acquired the club to flip it, as they had with so many other businesses in Malcolm's corporate past. They were in English football for the long haul. That didn't seem to reassure anyone.

Especially not Manchester United's biggest sponsors. Six months after the Glazer takeover, the telecom giant Vodafone informed the club that it no longer wanted its name and logo on the front of United's kits. Two years earlier, it had renewed one of the richest shirt sponsorship deals in football, committing £36 million over four years. Now the company was cancelling halfway through by exercising a break clause inserted in the contract in case of a change in ownership. Publicly, Vodafone said the reason for reneging on the deal was that it would rather focus on its sponsorship of the Champions League. But the timing made it clear that the company's real focus was on getting away from the Glazers and their tornado of negative publicity. Even the Manchester United Supporters Trust had urged Vodafone to sever ties with a club it described as a 'tainted brand'.

Gill received the Vodafone news on a business trip to Japan. He dreaded having to tell his bosses that one of their most visible partners was bailing out. But when he finally made the call to Joel Glazer, he was stunned by his chairman's reaction. Glazer was thrilled. He didn't think a telecommunications company had any business being a global shirt sponsor anyway. That sector was more suited to regional deals, he explained. Gill had never heard the strategy presented that way. But soon he would see it in action every day as Manchester United spun its NFL sponsorship know-how and chopped up the market into as many pieces as possible. From a new office in London sandwiched between two hedge funds across the street from the Ritz Hotel, a commercial staff that soon outnumbered the playing squad cut as many regional deals in as many categories as they could think of, knowing that the sum total would add up to far more than a handful of sponsorship megadeals. In the telecoms category, United turned around after Vodafone's exit and signed Saudi Telecom as the Official Integrated Telecommunications Partner of Manchester United for Saudi Arabia – one of ten 'media partners' it now has around the world. Today, for every major sponsor the size of Adidas or DHL, the club also has dozens that most United fans would have never heard of, including Cho-A Pharm, the club's Official Pharmaceutical Partner for Korea and Vietnam, or Chi Limited, the Official Soft Drinks Partner for Nigeria. Within ten years, United's sponsorship revenue exceeded £95 million a year.

The Glazers were always confident that the fans would eventually come to welcome their business savvy despite some powerful evidence to the contrary. 'I think the supporters appreciate it if you're doing everything you can to put a successful team on the pitch,' Joel Glazer said in a 2005 interview with United's in-house TV channel. 'I think people are forgiving if they know you are doing that.'

Perhaps. But in the mid 2000s, one thing was getting up fans' noses every bit as much as the takeover: the team Manchester United put on the pitch was no longer that successful. And for that, they had to thank a London club they hadn't worried about in half a century.

If the settings for United's revolution were the Old Trafford board-room and the floor of the New York Stock Exchange, Chelsea were upending the dynamics of the league right in the Stamford Bridge dugout. By 2006, the Blues weren't just a rich, ambitious club any more.

Three years into the Abramovich administration, they were a rich, ambitious club with back-to-back league titles to their name.

Chelsea's slick-haired secret – the man who figured out how to turn all of Abramovich's cash into silverware – was José Mourinho. The courtship had been long and public and right under Claudio Ranieri's nose, but this was how the club did its business nowadays. Chelsea were shameless. They knew what they wanted and would spend money until they got it. Mourinho fitted the club's new-found exceptionalism perfectly. In his first press conference, the son of a former mid-level goalkeeper and a primary school teacher introduced himself to the British media with the words that would follow him around for the rest of his career, 'I am not one from the bottle. I am a special one.' The Special One's accent, which sounded more like a Russian spy's from a cold war film than an Iberian football manager's, only bolstered his status as English football's new full-time heel.

Mourinho's first taste of the big time had come when former England manager Bobby Robson hired him as a translator at Sporting Lisbon in 1992. The pair got along so well that when Robson moved to Porto the following year he brought his walking, talking English-to-Portuguese dictionary with him. And by the time the double act bounced again to Barcelona in 1996, Mourinho had taken on some assistant-coaching duties. The young man with the jet-black hair and an easy rapport with modern players was starting to make a name for himself.

That's also when the ego first began to shine through. Mourinho had to give up his translation responsibilities at Barcelona when it became obvious that he was taking liberties with Robson's words, liberally sprinkling in his own opinions, insight, and tactical analysis. Still, whatever he said must have impressed someone at the club, because when Robson left Catalonia, Barça kept young José around to work under new manager Louis van Gaal.

With his apprenticeship completed, Mourinho broke into management in 2000 at Benfica. There, his unique blend of confrontation, bluster, and unimpeachable results set him on a course to the instant success and short tenures that would come to define his career. In the space of two years, he left Benfica and took over União de Leiria, then left União and landed at Porto, where he remained for all of two years until Chelsea came calling. At the age of forty, he was already coaching royalty in Portugal. Which was enough to land him a job in the Premier League but meant precisely nothing to a fan base that barely knew who this Portuguese upstart was – even if he had just won the Champions League.

'If I wanted to have an easy job,' Mourinho said after moving to west London, 'I would have stayed at Porto – beautiful blue chair, the UEFA Champions League trophy, God, and after God, me.'

It wasn't long before Chelsea fans held him in similarly high esteem.

In the Premier League, the forty-one-year-old Mourinho found he had to share the spotlight with a couple of other incarnate deities, both more than fifteen years his senior – Arsène Wenger and Alex Ferguson. Those two had shared every title since 1995. Wenger had landed the most recent punch in 2003–4 by guiding the Gunners through the first undefeated league campaign in more than a century of English football. Fergie was already plotting his revenge, tying up a deal that summer for a promising eighteen-year-old named Wayne Rooney. Mourinho wasn't simply looking to add his name to the conversation. He wanted to end the conversation – and knock them both into early retirement.

Mourinho's attack was two-pronged. He went after Wenger and Ferguson on the pitch, beating Manchester United 1–0 in the first game of the season. And he went after them off the pitch as often as he could, the sharp-tongued pipsqueak inserting himself into a playground fight. He accused Fergie of intimidating referees and labelled Wenger a 'voyeur', because 'he speaks, speaks, speaks about Chelsea'. To opposing fans, Mourinho's press conferences took on a pantomime quality. To the press, they were manna from heaven. However you viewed it, this Mourinho brand of psycho-tactical warfare paid off immediately. Ten months after anointing himself the Special One, he lifted the Premier League trophy with a then-record ninety-five points after losing just one game all season. Arsenal were second, twelve points adrift, with United and Ferguson left seething in third.

In the following season of 2005–6, Mourinho did it to them again. 'Cracks are starting to appear' in the House that Fergie Built, Sky Sports announced before Chelsea's trip to Manchester United.

'A new dynasty is threatening to take over.' In an act of sneering contempt for his rivals after lifting the hallowed Premier League trophy for a second season running, Mourinho took off his winner's medal and casually lobbed it into the crowd at Stamford Bridge. He didn't need a piece of metal around his neck to tell the world who the Premier League's big dog was in 2006. 'One day we'll lose,' he said, 'but for now we are the best team in the country.'

Being the best team in the country was exactly what Arsenal had envisaged when they began work on their new stadium. But in 2006, mere months before Emirates Stadium would open, the club found themselves in a precarious position.

In the long term, their new home would set up the Gunners for sustained success, a self-financing edifice that would turbocharge match-day revenue and establish Arsenal as a permanent member of the Premier League's financial elite. But until then, paying back the loans that had financed its construction would require some careful financial management. Under Arsenal's self-imposed austerity drive, the transfer budget for new players was cut, the club's internal wage cap stayed flat, and long-term contracts for veteran players past the age of thirty were unofficially outlawed. Finances became so tight that summer that Arsenal ran out of money to complete a planned landscaping project surrounding the new stadium. Instead, the club's opulent new home would be encircled by a vast grey concrete plaza.

For Wenger, who had already earned a reputation as English football's resident fiscal conservative, the budgetary constraints that built Arsenal's new home were a point of pride. The way he saw it, Emirates Stadium was the gold standard in sound financial planning for a club's future. But what Arsenal hadn't realized when they embarked on the biggest infrastructure upgrade any club had attempted for the best part of a century was that sound financial planning would soon be seen as a charming relic in English football along with hobnail boots, baggy shorts, or that time England actually won a World Cup. The Premier League's era of overseas investment was coming.

Roman Abramovich's arrival in English football had been greeted with a degree of suspicion. The Glazer family had been welcomed with outright hostility. But any notion that the parochial outlook of the Premier League would dissuade other foreign investors from pitching up on Britain's shores would soon be dispelled.

In May of 2006, the league's sale of its latest three-year package of domestic TV rights eclipsed $3 billion for the first time, with Sky splitting the rights with Irish subscription-TV firm Setanta. Overseas rights fees would take the Premier League's total TV revenue to more than $4.5 billion, which was more than enough to pique the interest of global financiers, international investors, and ambitious entrepreneurs looking to leverage the league's growing global footprint.

Later in 2006, Randy Lerner, an American real estate and financial services billionaire, and owner of the NFL's Cleveland Browns, was searching for an arbitrage opportunity when his sights settled on the Premier League. In a meeting in London, Lerner was reliably informed by the league that all but four or five clubs were up for sale to anyone with a few million in the bank and a decent line of credit. It didn't take long for Lerner to make his pick: Aston Villa, the biggest club in Birmingham, with a roll-call of esteemed supporters that included His Royal Highness Prince William, the future Prime Minister David Cameron, and Geezer Butler, the guitarist from Black Sabbath. What drew Lerner to Villa was partly the club's proud history. Founding members of the Football League in 1888, Aston Villa were seven-time league champions, seven-time FA Cup winners, and had lifted the European Cup as recently as 1982. But Lerner admitted that he was also attracted by the club's location. As the owner of an NFL franchise in America's Midwest, the idea of owning a football club in Britain's West Midlands struck him as rather poetic. On 25 August 2006, he duly agreed to pay £63 million to take control of the 132-year-old club.

Aston Villa weren't the only grand old institution of English football to come under overseas control. The following year, an even more iconic name was snapped up when Tom Hicks, a Texas private-equity investor, and Colorado businessman George Gillett Jr completed a joint £219 million takeover of Liverpool. Desperate to avoid the sort of backlash that had greeted the sale of Manchester United, Hicks and Gillett began their tenure as owners by pledging not to 'do a Glazer' by loading the club with debt. Within twelve months, they proceeded to do exactly that, setting the tone for an acrimonious four-year tenure characterized by miserable on-field results, a spectacular boardroom falling-out between the two owners, and a series of jaw-dropping public-relations pratfalls, highlighted by the time Hicks's son, Tom Jr, then a director of the club, fired off a late-night email to an aggrieved Liverpool fan that read simply: 'Blow me, fuckface.'

Still, the investors kept coming. Later in 2007, American real estate magnate Stan Kroenke acquired an initial 9.9 per cent stake in Arsenal. In 2008, Ellis Short, a private-equity billionaire with a history of investing in distressed assets, gained a controlling interest in underperforming Sunderland. All told, within a decade of the Glazers' leveraged buyout of Manchester United, twenty-seven of the forty-four clubs in English football's top two divisions would wind up with foreign owners – with fifteen billionaires among their number – as ancient football clubs from Britain's working-class towns and old industrial heartlands suddenly emerged as objects of desire for high-net-worth individuals across the world.

Even star-crossed West Ham hit the jackpot. The Hammers' plan to launch a Premier League dynasty had gone awry with a crop of home-grown superstars that resulted in relegation, a fire sale, and two years spent flailing about in English football's second tier. But they had finally clawed their way back into the top division when they caught the eye of the world's 799th richest man, an Icelandic billionaire named Björgólfur Guðmundsson.

Guðmundsson's chairmanship of Landsbanki, one of the tiny nation's largest banks, had allowed him to amass a fortune built on cheap foreign debt, the buoyant global housing market, and the inscrutability of the Icelandic banking sector. In November 2006, just as international hedge funds began buying credit default swaps to short Iceland's banks, Guðmundsson parted with £85 million of that fortune to take control of West Ham United. The club's fans, who should've known a thing or two about bubbles bursting, greeted him as a hero, someone who could help West Ham finally fulfil its untapped potential. Within two years, Guðmundsson had been declared bankrupt and his net worth was listed as exactly $0.

Untapped potential was exactly what Mohamed Al-Fayed, the owner of Harrods, had on his mind in 1997 when he paid £6.25 million to acquire another venerable establishment in an affluent west London neighbourhood: Fulham Football Club. Perched on the banks of the River Thames in its 25,000-seat Craven Cottage stadium, a ramshackle old pile that takes its name from a royal hunting lodge that stood on the site of the pitch, Fulham had a lot to recommend it to Al-Fayed. There was the modest wage bill, their disproportionately middle-class fan base, and a reputation as the friendliest club in English football. What they didn't have in 1997 was a place in the Premier League. Or even the second tier. In fact, when Al-Fayed acquired Fulham, the club had just won promotion from the fourth division of English football and were playing home games in front of an average crowd of 6,000. But the Egyptian-born Al-Fayed had been trying to buy his way into English high society for forty years. Running Harrods, known as the grocer to the queen, had certainly helped, though he applied for British citizenship twice and failed. If it took running a football team, too, so be it.

Al-Fayed was not a subtle public figure. He was always picking foul-mouthed fights with some millionaire or another. In the 1970s, he'd bought the Ritz Hotel in Paris. At Harrods, he imposed a dress code so he could turn away tourists in shorts and flip-flops. And in football, he promised to guide Fulham to the Premier League in five years. Improbably, the club reached the promised land a year ahead of schedule in 2001, making him one of the league's first foreign-born owners. But that's not why the rest of the old boys' club considered him eccentric.

They considered him eccentric because the man had no filter. His favourite gag with his players and rival executives in the direc-tors' box was to press one of the little blue sweets that he always carried with him into their hands and tell them it was Viagra. 'Take this before the game,' he said with a wink.

That's when he was in a good mood. In a bad mood, he made people even more uncomfortable. During an ugly run of results in the 2010–11 season, he stormed into a Fulham training session and ordered the squad to assemble in a meeting room. After a rant about their performances, he dragged the manager, the hard-nosed former

Manchester United player Mark Hughes, into the centre of the room and pointed to him.

'Shall I sack this man?' he shouted. 'Shall I?'

The room of grown men fell silent. They stared at their feet.

'Well, what about you?' Al-Fayed pointed at the Fulham captain, Danny Murphy. 'You're the captain. Maybe I should sack you.'

Al-Fayed saw no reason to treat his players any differently than he treated Harrods' shop staff. Hughes and Murphy ultimately survived the most awkward team meeting of their lives, though Hughes would resign that summer. But if ever they needed a reminder that their owner was a man of fleeting and dramatic whims, that was it.

Well, that and the gift Al-Fayed offered the fans that spring. To truly appreciate the magnitude of Al-Fayed's gesture, it's important to remember that when club chairmen offer up token gifts to their supporters they tend to come in the form of commemorative scarves or discounted tickets or free bus travel to away games. Al-Fayed sourced his inspiration elsewhere. He remembered one of his favourite guests at Craven Cottage, the man he had been thrilled to host for a game against Wigan: the pop star Michael Jackson.

When Jackson died in 2009, Al-Fayed was heartbroken. He was also convinced that Fulham fans shared that grief. The King of Pop once visited Craven Cottage after all. Why wouldn't they be moved by his passing?

So in April 2011, Al-Fayed unveiled a seven-and-a-half-foot, full-colour, resin-and-plaster statue of the singer on a six-foot plinth – complete with the pop star's signature sequined glove. Fulham Football Club and Michael Jackson. Anyone would be forgiven for missing the connection. Supporters hardly knew what to make of it.

'If some stupid fans don't understand and appreciate such a gift this guy gave to the world they can go to hell,' Al-Fayed said. 'I don't want them to be fans.'

They liked it better when Al-Fayed gave them the gift of the Premier League. But as long as he continued to spend money on their club, they were prepared to tolerate pretty much anything.

13

ONCE THESE NEW owners from around the world were ensconced in the boardrooms of their clubs, it became clear that despite their divergent backgrounds they were all fixated on the same goal.

Shortly after their takeover of Liverpool, Tom Hicks and George Gillett Jr announced a plan to move the team from Anfield into a new 60,000-seat venue, with work set to begin 'in the next sixty days'. Within a week of acquiring West Ham, Björgólfur Guðmundsson had announced his intention to move the team to the new stadium being built for the 2012 Olympic Games in London. At Fulham, Mohamed Al-Fayed spent £5 million on architects, lawyers, and planning consultants to design a grandiose redevelopment of Craven Cottage, which would increase capacity to 30,000 and help make Fulham the 'Manchester United of the south'.

None of those plans quite came to fruition – Fulham can't even claim to be the Manchester United of their own London borough – but it soon became clear that the opening of the Emirates had sent a wave of stadium envy through the league. Team owners up and down the country surveyed their own grounds, many of which had been untouched since Queen Victoria was on the throne, and decided an upgrade was essential. Manchester United increased the capacity of Old Trafford to almost 75,000 in 2007, with plans for a further 12,000 seats at a later date. Liverpool, Leicester, Stoke City, and Watford all followed suit with redevelopment projects of varying sizes to increase the capacity at their existing stadiums. And in 2017, Chelsea unveiled a planned £1 billion renovation of Stamford Bridge into a 60,000-seat arena – though it was later cancelled.

Other clubs opted to relocate altogether. Tottenham elected to up sticks from their home of 117 years at White Hart Lane and build a new arena not only to maximize their match-day revenue but also to host pop concerts and two NFL games every season. The club also made a point of setting the capacity at 61,000 seats, exactly 1,000 more than north London nemesis Arsenal's stadium, a sign that one-upmanship in English football was no longer confined to the pitch.

But as clubs took on more debt for bricks and mortar, they were left scrambling for cash to build their squads. Their solution was an era of surging commercialization in which everything but the goalposts went up for sale. Team kits, which had long been scrawled with the names of blue-ribbon corporate sponsors, were soon emblazoned with the logos of decidedly less salubrious institutions: offshore gambling companies, obscure energy-drink manufacturers, and payday loan firms. A fire sale of stadium naming rights saw hallowed old grounds rechristened with less resonant titles, including the bet365 Stadium in Stoke or Newcastle's SportsDirect.com@St James' Park Stadium. No one could match United's marketing sophistication, but that wasn't for lack of trying.

One team was spared the effort and expense of moving into a new home stadium, however. In the autumn of 1995, more than a decade after Rick Parry first spearheaded efforts to bring the Olympics to the north-west, Manchester's grand ambition to stage a major international sporting event was finally realized. In November of that year, after a one-horse race with no other official bidders, Manchester was unveiled as the host city of the 2002 Commonwealth Games.

Granted, 'major international sports event' may be stretching it a little. The Commonwealth Games still includes lawn bowls, after all.

Still, for a city sorely in need of investment following a long and painful period of post-industrial decline, the Commonwealth Games was a game changer. Staging the event kick-started a process of urban regeneration in some of the city's poorest neighbourhoods in east Manchester. Which just happened to be the home of a 115-year-old football team that was in need of some rejuvenation of its own.

Founded in 1880, two years after the Newton Heath railway workers formed what would become Manchester United, Manchester City Football Club had spent more than a century operating in the shadow of their local rival. While United piled up trophies and won admirers across the world, City bounced between the top two divisions, earning a reputation as a lovable loser – that is, when anyone thought about the club at all. There were a couple of league titles and a handful of FA Cup trophies along the way, but mostly City were known for their bumbling losses and bewildering slumps, like when they won their first league championship in 1937 and were promptly relegated the following season, the only time English football's reigning champions have ever gone down. Or the time they became the only team to both score one hundred goals and concede one hundred goals in the same season.

By the 1980s, there was nothing lovable about the losing any more. In the space of a decade, City were twice bumped out of the top flight and had burned through seven managers. The club's enduring knack for shooting themselves in the foot with a bazooka proved so persistent that an expression of weary resignation now doubled as an unofficial club motto: 'Typical City'.

If the 1980s made Manchester City a punchline, the 1990s turned the club into a punching bag. While United emerged as the Premier League's pre-eminent power, City were relegated from the top flight again in 1995–6, and followed it with a season that saw five different managers fail in the dugout. From there, the tailspin continued. In 1998, City became the first British team with a European trophy on their CV to be relegated to the third division.

Then something decidedly atypical happened to City, the first in a series of fortunate events that would transform English football's bungling incompetents into a global force.

The only reason it came off was probably because City had so little to do with it.

The organizers of Manchester's Commonwealth Games remembered a scheme they had cooked up for their two failed Olympic bids. It called for a 38,000-seat venue to be built on the site of a former colliery in an area known as Eastlands. All they needed was a tenant to fill the new stadium after the Games. City raised their hand, and for once, United couldn't get in the way – they had long ago committed to expanding Old Trafford. So in the summer of 2003, Manchester City vacated their Maine Road stadium, an eighty-year-old ground in Moss Side with a guttered roof and gaps in two corners described by the former City striker Niall Quinn as a 'crumbling pile' for a sleek, state-of-the-art facility two miles away dubbed the City of Manchester Stadium.

Technically, City didn't own it. The arena, which was paid for by local taxpayers and revenue from the National Lottery, belonged to the City of Manchester Council, which agreed to rent the facility to the club. But the terms of the lease were so outrageously favourable that it amounted to a gift. The rent owed to the council was to be derived primarily from ticket sales. No money was due if the attendance did not exceed the old 32,000 capacity of Maine Road, and City would turn over only half the revenue from all tickets sold above that level. The only significant contribution required from the club was a one-off £20 million payment to cover the cost of adjusting the stadium for football, excising the athletics track, and putting in corporate boxes, food stands, and club shops. In exchange, Manchester City were awarded a £110 million stadium on a 250-year lease.

For a prospective investor in the club, this was the best possible Premier League sign-up gift. Join today and we'll throw in a free stadium.

It was an even better opportunity for any billionaire with some cash to park abroad and a taste for the adulation of large crowds. Thaksin Shinawatra, a Thai telecommunications magnate who had served as his country's prime minister, was the first to jump on it. He had sniffed around Liverpool and Fulham to no avail. But for the low, low price of £82 million, he could finally have his club. It was barely half as much as Roman Abramovich had spent to acquire the nearly bankrupt Chelsea four years earlier. 'Manchester City is a team with good fans and good infrastructure,' Shinawatra explained later, underlining how the stadium influenced his decision to buy the club. 'So it's not too difficult to improve.'

Though the stadium didn't technically belong to Shinawatra, the city of Manchester let him tailor it to his specific needs. Right at the top of the list was fixing the unlucky vibe about the place. He arranged to have a crystal ball buried underneath the centre circle and elephant statues interred at the four corners of the pitch in accordance with Thai tradition. Smaller porcelain elephants found their way onto the windowsills of every office to keep the east Manchester jinx at bay. In that respect, at least, Shinawatra understood the locals.

And the locals, disappointed by owners in the past, seemed to appreciate him. Finding the new owner's name tricky to pronounce, the fans nicknamed him 'Frank' – to Mancunian ears, Shinawatra sounded like Sinatra.

That the former prime minister of Thailand also liked to sing in public was merely coincidence. Shortly after acquiring the club, he threw a party in Manchester's Albert Square for 8,000 supporters, where he laid on a Thai noodle buffet and flew in a pop star from home to perform before launching into his own crooning rendition of City's adopted anthem, 'Blue Moon'.

What wasn't to like about this fifty-nine-year-old charmer?

Well, one thing. It turned out that he was an alleged human-rights abuser.

During his years as prime minister of Thailand, from 2001 to 2006, the former police officer with a degree in criminal justice from Eastern Kentucky University oversaw a war on drugs that led to allegations of more than 2,000 extrajudicial killings by law enforcement officers. The United Nations were more than alarmed. Shinawatra's response: 'The United Nations is not my father.'

By chance, it was while he paid his non-father a visit for the 2006 UN General Assembly that his enemies in Thailand launched a military coup to oust him. Only after that did he send himself on a mission to burnish his image and stash some of his considerable assets abroad. In May 2007, he got himself elected to the presidency of Thailand's Professional Golf Association. And a month later, he moved to acquire Manchester City. Despite the allegations against him, he passed the Premier League's 'fit and proper persons' test for owners with flying colours, much to the surprise of organizations like Human Rights Watch, which don't usually get involved in football but couldn't ignore the attempted whitewashing of an alleged murderer.

'In light of the widespread, serious and systematic human rights abuses perpetrated in Thailand under Mr Thaksin's [sic] leadership,' the organization wrote to the league's chief executive Richard Scudamore, 'we are very concerned that you concluded that he is a "fit and proper person" to purchase Manchester City Football Club.'

The Premier League's answer, in effect, was that the fit and proper persons test is designed to smoke out any financial irregularities, not moral bankruptcy. 'The issues that you raise are of course extremely important,' Scudamore wrote back; 'so much so that they fall to the UK government, the statutory authorities and the European Union to consider and decide upon.'

In other words, unless someone locked him up, Shinawatra was free to enjoy one of the best bargains in Premier League history. His tenure in Manchester didn't last long. But if it taught the league anything, it was that picking up a nearly free stadium was the kind of open goal that is practically impossible for an owner to miss.

14

THE RAIN WAS pooling in Alex Ferguson's shoes. His clothes were soaked through. And on the touchline of the Luzhniki Stadium, the chill in the Moscow air bit into his sixty-six-year-old bones. He had played and managed in worse conditions than this a million times in his career. He was from Scotland after all. But this was May and it was well after midnight now and this infernal game – the 2008 Champions League final between Chelsea and his Manchester United – just wouldn't end.

The ninety minutes of normal time came and went and the score was still 1–1. Then another thirty minutes of unspeakably tense extra time in which either team could have snatched the trophy. Manchester United had a chance cleared off the line. Chelsea whacked the underside of the crossbar. Through it all, the red-faced Ferguson chewed gum like his jaw was powered by steam.

Ferguson had always felt that United should be more successful in Europe. For all of their dominance at home in the Premier League era – ten titles and four FA Cups by then – the club had won the Champions League only once in his tenure. Something about United's swashbuckling attacking style didn't quite translate year after year on the club's foreign adventures. Like so many British tourists, they spoke only one language and then wondered why they couldn't get service abroad.

In the seasons building up to 2008, however, that was finally changing. Not just for Manchester United but also for the likes of Chelsea, Liverpool, and Arsenal. All of a sudden, every Champions League semi-final seemed to feature a Premier League club if not two. It was only logical that the most prestigious match on the European calendar would be an all-English affair eventually.

'Everyone felt this was a terrific piece of theatre, one of the best European Cup finals,' Ferguson wrote later. 'It was satisfying to be part of a show that displayed our league in such a good light.'

Not that this was at the front of Ferguson's mind as he and his assistant coach Carlos Queiroz paced around his exhausted players on the pitch after extra time. Ten yards away, he could see the Chelsea squad lying around, just as dead, the same players that United had pipped to the Premier League title two weeks earlier. Dripping wet and his jaw still working overtime, Ferguson inspected his troops, looking each of them in the eye. He needed to make sure that five men among this bunch still had heads clear enough to make one more contribution this evening. The Champions League final would be settled by penalty shoot-out.

Ferguson knew he could trust his guys – they had held their nerve to knock out Barcelona with a single goal in the semi-final. But thirty years of experience also told him that big-match tension could do funny things to footballers in shoot-outs. He had the scars to prove it. No Ferguson team had ever won a shoot-out in major competition. He lost three as manager of Aberdeen and three more as manager of United. If ever Ferguson needed to break the streak, it was now. His watch ticked past 1 a.m.

Ferguson set his line-up of five shooters. Right in the middle of it was the Champions League's top scorer that season, Cristiano Ronaldo, who had outgunned that diminutive kid from Argentina named Lionel Messi and earlier bagged United's only goal that night.

But first came Carlos Tevez, the Argentine rottweiler Ferguson had poached from West Ham the previous summer. As Tevez strutted up to the penalty spot at the United supporters' end of the stadium, Ferguson retreated to the dugout and took a seat. Queiroz stayed on his feet – 'I don't have a heart as strong as Sir Alex's,' he said. There was nothing else for them to do. The final was out of their hands.

But no matter who won, United or Chelsea, something else was happening in the Luzhniki that night, 1,500 miles from home. The larger point had already been made. The line between the best teams in Europe and the best teams in England had blurred completely.

There was no longer any question: in 2008, the Premier League was the greatest football show on earth.

This was the high-water mark.

The surprising thing about that all-English final was that it surprised exactly no one. Between Ferguson's trip to the Champions League final in Barcelona in 1999 and that rainy night in Moscow nine years later – an eternity in football – the Premier League had become an irresistible force.

Every season produced another era-defining team. The Arsenal Invincibles of 2003–4, who won the championship without a single defeat. José Mourinho's first Chelsea team in 2004–5, which posted a record ninety-three points and conceded just fifteen goals on their way to the title. And then the revival of Alex Ferguson's Manchester United as they won three titles in a row from 2006, inspired by that preening winger signed from Portugal, Cristiano Ronaldo.

All the fantasies that English clubs had dreamed up in the 1990s were finally coming together. The colossal commercial and stadium revenues meant England's top clubs paid better than nearly everyone else in Europe. And foreign players were no longer a curiosity in a line-up. 'Who could believe that Brazilians could play in England?' said the superagent Pini Zahavi, one of the chief importers of that foreign talent. 'Who could believe that other South Americans would come? But that happened. This is a fact. The dream was always Spain or Italy, not England. But it changed.'

In the eyes of Europe, and the rest of the world, this is when the Premier League became the *Premier League*.

Manchester United's Champions League campaign of 1998–99 was brilliant, but it stood more as a triumph of English football's spirit of blood, toil, tears, and sweat than of any technical and tactical superiority. United were never a favourite as they picked off Juventus and Bayern Munich. And besides, United stood alone among English clubs; no other Premier League team were yet capable of hanging with the Continent's elite deep into the spring the way Ferguson's team did.

The league rankings formulated by UEFA were a reflection of that. Based on how teams from each country performed on the

European stage, England didn't crack UEFA's top three until 2003 and still trailed far behind Spain's La Liga and Italy's Serie A.

English clubs knew what they had to do.

The statement victories came slowly at first, an upset here and there. Then came the steady drumbeat that no one could ignore. Arsenal marauded into the San Siro in Milan and stunned Europe by stomping Inter 5–1. The next season, José Mourinho's new-look Chelsea dumped Barcelona and Bayern Munich out of the Champions League. In 2005–6, Arsenal booted Juventus again and then bossed Real Madrid in their own backyard on their way to the final. The following year, Manchester United vaporized Roma 7–1 at Old Trafford.

The gem in the collection, however, belonged to Liverpool. From the first minute of that crazy night in Istanbul in 2005, everything went wrong. The Reds' Champions League final against AC Milan had barely started when the Italians landed a sucker punch off a set piece. After Milan struck twice more in the six minutes before half-time to make it 3–0, the shell shock among the Liverpool players was palpable. They looked to their Spanish manager, Rafa Benítez, for inspiration. He grabbed his lucky Montblanc pen in the dugout and started scribbling.

The defensive set-up had to change – Benítez went to a back three instead of four and squeezed the midfielders together. He sent one of his starters back to the showers. With the noise building outside and confusion swirling in the dressing room, Benítez briefly lost track of things and almost sent twelve players out for the second half. But the error was caught in time. The coaching staff's final instructions as they filed back into the tunnel was to do something for the travelling support before the night was over and score at least one goal.

Liverpool scored three. In the space of six minutes, Steven Gerrard, half-time substitute Vladimír Šmicer, and Xabi Alonso pummelled Milan to make it 3–3. The final went on for another thirty minutes of normal time after the equalizer, and thirty more minutes in extra time, without either side finding a winner. Now it was time for Liverpool's Polish goalkeeper to take over. Ignoring the cues from the bench about which way to dive, Jerzy Dudek did a Bruce

Grobbelaar-style rubber-legged dance on the line and saved three of Milan's five efforts in the shoot-out. England's most successful team in Europe were bringing the Champions League trophy home again.

'I don't really know how we did it,' Dudek said.

Liverpool may have won the title in a shoot-out, but nothing about the Premier League's success in Europe was a fluke any more. Between 2005 and 2009, English clubs occupied twelve of the twenty Champions League semi-final slots, and the Premier League was represented in every final. And if they didn't win it every year, whichever team did knew it would have to survive a knock-down, drag-out fight against an English club somewhere along the road.

'If you want to win the Champions League you have to play with the best in Europe,' then-Barcelona manager Pep Guardiola said in 2009. 'So we'll take the challenge. It would be nice to taste success against one of the English sides.'

By flooding the knockout rounds, English teams also scooped up the Champions League's prize money by the tens of millions of euros. Their success raised the alarm in corridors of power all over Europe, including the Zurich headquarters of the game's world governing body, where FIFA president Sepp Blatter was worried about – of all things – powerful entities stuffing their pockets.

'Shall we let the rich become richer and say nothing?' he asked in 2008, years before he was accused of unethically enriching himself during his decades at FIFA. 'This season, there were four English teams in the last eight, three in the semi-finals and two in the final. The Champions League has been very successful financially but it has also favoured national inequality.'

To remedy the situation, Blatter proposed that FIFA set limits on how many foreign players a team could field. His idea was to cap the number at five, forcing each side to include six domestic players and restore some semblance of nationality to a country's clubs. The proposal was never adopted – partly because it was ludicrous and partly because it probably violated European Union labour law. But in its own twisted way, it showed that even Blatter understood what underpinned the strength of the English squads. More than a decade after their money-spinning gamble on forming the Premier League, the clubs could afford to import the technical ability of the most expensive players in the world, which they combined with the speed and power inherent to English football. By 2005, three of the top four players in Ballon d'Or voting plied their trades in England: Chelsea's Frank Lampard, Liverpool's Gerrard, and Arsenal's Thierry Henry. Premier League teams were now bigger, faster, and often more skilful than their European opponents. As the level rose at home, those teams entered Europe more battle hardened than ever, living proof that iron sharpens iron.

The Premier League now ran so deep that the fight just to get into the Champions League became one of the focal points of every season. England had been awarded a fourth automatic berth in 2002 and, to ambitious clubs, grabbing a top-four finish became the absolute minimum requirement. In one section of north London, qualification was treated almost like winning a trophy. Which was fine with Arsenal fans until manager Arsène Wenger started using it to replace actually winning trophies.

'For me, there are five trophies every season: Premier League, Champions League, the third is to qualify for the Champions League,' Wenger told Arsenal's shareholders years later. 'The fourth is the FA Cup and then the League Cup.'

The race for the top four places now gave more spice to the final weeks of a season even in years when the title was already settled. Media coverage had more permutations to play with to ramp up the tension, never failing to remind fans of what was at stake with a Champions League berth: a far-fetched shot at European glory, sure, but more important, a guaranteed eight-figure payout to your club. That was practically enough for a new striker right there.

The teams most consistently on the brink of qualification during that period were Everton and Tottenham Hotspur, a pair of clubs with ancient stadiums, old-school owners, and a fraction of the transfer budget of the top four. Yet the allure of Champions League football, combined with the new level of talent they were able to attract, was enough to keep them in touch with the third- and fourth-place clubs, often pushing them until the dying moments of a league campaign.

Unless, of course, they ate something funny.

This is the point in the history of the Premier League when the tale takes a brief detour to the buffet of the Marriott West India Quay Hotel in east London, the scene of an incident known thereafter as Lasagne-gate.

Heading into the last day of the 2005–6 season, Tottenham were finally close enough to a first Champions League qualification that they could taste it. Sitting in magical fourth place, one point ahead of Arsenal, they needed only to match the Gunners' result to book their spot in Europe – and keep out their hated rival as a bonus. Spurs were due to play West Ham at Upton Park. Arsenal had Wigan at home. Neither opponent was expected to trouble them, especially since neither mid-table club had anything left to play for in the league.

Tottenham prepared for their game as they normally would and holed up in the Marriott ahead of what was supposed to be one of the prouder days in the club's history. It turned into one of the most effluent.

Lights flicked on and off along the players' hallway all night as they scrambled into their toilets. The lasagne they'd had for dinner – it wasn't sitting well. By morning, the casualty list was at least seven players long, one-third of the entire squad. Spurs chairman Daniel Levy phoned the Premier League in a panic, hoping to postpone the game. The Premier League wasn't having it. The rules made no provisions for food poisoning. Any failure on Tottenham's part to play in the game, Richard Scudamore told Levy, would see Spurs punished by the league.

Manager Martin Jol's biggest problem now was finding eleven players who could give him ninety minutes without evacuating their insides. Half the team did just that in the hotel that morning and then again in the dressing-room facilities. When the staff noticed that Jol had skipped his usual pre-match smoke, they knew they were in trouble.

Tottenham made a mess of things and lost the game 2–1. Arsenal ate Wigan for lunch and won 4–2. For Spurs, the Champions League dream was gone.

It was no consolation to the Tottenham players when they heard a week later that the lasagne had been absolved. Tests by the Health Protection Agency had found that the meal was perfectly safe. The actual culprit was a form of contagious gastroenteritis that had spread through the team like a rumour.

It would take Tottenham another three years to wash out the taste and finally earn a seat at the Champions League table. The teams that were qualifying year after year, meanwhile, were learning far more important lessons than how to avoid contagious digestive ailments. Lessons on how to tweak their tactics to play in Europe.

Teams on the Continent might not have had the physical power of Premier League sides, but their players tended to understand the subtleties of the game on a higher level. They built up their play more patiently. They made more clever use of space. They had none of England's hell-for-leather attacking drive. 'When you play Saturday in England against Bolton or against Watford and Tuesday you play Barcelona, you cannot play with the same style,' Manchester United's Queiroz said. 'What is the language when you play Champions League? This is one language. When you play UK football, this is another language.'

It had taken until the 2000s for the top Premier League clubs to teach their home-grown players how to speak that language – and to import enough native speakers for them to start dominating Europe. But by 2008, they had proven so adept at it that the Premier League was officially recognized as Europe's top championship, leapfrogging Spain in UEFA's rankings.

Nothing embodied that growth better than the teams that lined up in the Champions League final in Moscow that year. Between Manchester United and Chelsea, the starting elevens on display exhibited the best of what modern English football had to offer: British cores surrounded by virtuosic foreign talent. Nineteen of the twenty-two starters that night had represented their countries at the most recent World Cup. Bizarrely, five of those nineteen had graduated from West Ham's academy. But it didn't matter where anyone started out any more. The world's elite players would eventually be funnelled into the Premier League's biggest and richest teams.

The only person whose presence on European football's brightest stage raised some eyebrows was the man in the Chelsea dugout, a fifty-three-year-old journeyman manager from Israel named Avram Grant. Nothing about Grant's career up until that point suggested he would ever be in charge of a club as ambitious as Chelsea. The first thirty years of his coaching career had all taken place in the Israeli league, where he won a handful of titles and earned the right to manage the Israeli national team for four years. He got his first taste of the Premier League in 2006 when he took a job as technical director of Portsmouth – a role that few other English clubs had ever found useful or necessary – but he stayed for only a year. In the summer of 2007, he was poached by Chelsea for a plum gig as their technical director, overseeing the club's business in the transfer market. It was intense, but all the conditions were in place for him to succeed: fresh off back-to-back league titles, he had the biggest transfer budget in the country and none of the public pressure. That was all on Mourinho.

What Abramovich hadn't counted on was the Special One's sudden exit from Stamford Bridge a month into the following season. Mourinho had fallen out with Abramovich, who was disappointed after a couple of weeks without a victory. In one telling, Mourinho dared Abramovich to fire him. So Abramovich did. The club, however, was at pains to clarify that there was more to it than that – but wouldn't say precisely what it was.

'José did not resign and he was not sacked,' read the bizarre statement. 'What is clear, though, is we had all reached a point where the relationship between the club and José had broken down. This was despite genuine attempts over several months by all parties to resolve certain differences.'

What was also clear was that Chelsea hadn't given the least bit of thought to his successor. Which is how the defending champions of England found themselves hiring Grant in a pinch and throwing him into battle against the likes of Alex Ferguson and Arsène Wenger. Those men had thirty years of Premier League experience and eleven titles between them. Grant didn't even possess the standard UEFA coaching licences. But he did have one qualification for the Chelsea job that wouldn't have shown up on any CV: he was close personal friends with Abramovich.

'He was pretty much unknown in this country, and to get a position like that from being at Portsmouth is unusual,' Ferguson said of Grant in May 2008. 'But I had a feeling when he went to Chelsea as director of football there might be something more to it. And there was. Now he's in a Champions League final. Jesus Christ!'

It was fitting that Chelsea's first European final of the Abramovich era should take place in Moscow, the city where he had made his billions. This was the stage he had envisioned for himself ever since he sat in the stands at Old Trafford in 2003 to watch Manchester United play Real Madrid – the night he decided to buy an English football team. That United were now the team in his way hardly mattered. Despite conceding the first goal, Chelsea were on top for most of the second half, and Abramovich imagined himself celebrating the fifth anniversary of his pricey hobby with the trophy he craved most.

Lampard nearly made it happen for Chelsea in extra time, but his shot slammed against the crossbar instead. Then Blues captain John Terry had another chance to end it in the penalty shoot-out. Except he slipped in his run-up to the shot and hit the post. With that, the evening swung definitively back in United's favour.

Ferguson watched it all in near silence, never moving from his seat in the dugout, not even when Ronaldo missed his penalty in the middle of the shoot-out. He trusted that his staff had equipped their goalkeeper, Edwin van der Sar, with a secret weapon that might make the difference: a towel with a piece of paper taped inside that he could consult whenever he wiped down his gloves. Prepared by United's analysis department, it listed the tendencies of every Chelsea player who might take a penalty kick.

Through the first six rounds, the towel hadn't helped. Van der Sar had yet to make a save – on the one Chelsea miss, which cancelled out Ronaldo's, he went the wrong way. When it came to Nicolas Anelka, however, everything clicked into place with Van der Sar's bluff of pointing to his left and the double bluff of diving to his right. The goalkeeper met Anelka's shot squarely and kept it out.

Ferguson could barely stand up. In the centre circle, Cristiano Ronaldo broke down in tears face down in the turf where he'd been ever since missing his own attempt moments earlier. The two best teams in the Premier League had proved themselves to be the two best teams in Europe. It had taken 120 minutes of football and fourteen penalty kicks to separate them. And now, by the narrowest margin – the width of a towel – Manchester United were champions of Europe for the third time.

All around the UK, this made for unmissable television. More than a quarter of the country's 62 million residents tuned in, with a peak of 14.6 million watching on ITV and another 2 million on Sky. Around the world, UEFA estimated the total audience for the game at more than 140 million, far exceeding that year's Super Bowl.

But among those many millions around the world that night, it's surprisingly easy to pinpoint who was the most significant viewer as far as the course of Premier League history is concerned.

His name was Sheikh Mansour bin Zayed Al Nahyan, the thirty-four-year-old brother of the ruler of Abu Dhabi. And as he watched United and Chelsea duke it out, he liked what he saw.

15

WHEN THE TIME comes in an ambitious young person's life to purchase a professional team, the process is usually smoothed over by having several billion dollars in your pocket. It's even simpler when you can easily prove that you're good for all that cash by, for instance, being a royal in the country that controls 8 per cent of the world's oil reserves. At that point, you pick a team that's for sale and keep adding zeros to your offer until everyone says yes. This was how Sheikh Mansour expected to do business when he decided to buy into English football in the summer of 2008.

The only hitch was that the clubs on top of the pile, the ones that matched Abu Dhabi's level of ambition, were all taken. Manchester United and Chelsea, the teams he had watched slug it out in Moscow, had each been adopted by billionaire sugar daddies in the past five years. He thought about Liverpool and Newcastle, too. And while Arsenal, with their new stadium and London location, would have made an ideal candidate, the sense in Abu Dhabi was that the Gunners weren't available to them. Besides, American investor Stan Kroenke was already in the process of ramping up his stake in the club to add it to his growing portfolio of sports teams.

Sheikh Mansour would have to look elsewhere.

As a thirty-something with more money than he could spend in several lifetimes, Sheikh Mansour didn't fit the usual profile of a Premier League owner – certainly not that of the local businessmen who bought clubs in the 1980s and 1990s, but also not that of the billionaire investors who arrived later. For one, he was born into unimaginable wealth as a result of being literal royalty.

The fifth of Sheikh Zayed's nineteen sons, Sheikh Mansour landed on a lucky branch of the complex Al Nahyan family tree. Because of who his mother was, the man who would be crown prince of the emirate happened to be one of Sheikh Mansour's full brothers, which put him in prime position for one of the influential political gigs that are sprinkled around the family.

It was not immediately obvious, though, that he'd be capable of handling one of those gigs. While many of those families dispatch their scions to Harvard, Princeton, and other prestigious institutions on the east coast of the United States, Sheikh Mansour enrolled in 1989 to study English at Santa Barbara City College, a two-year party school by the beach, whose most famous former student is not a Nobel Prize winner but the pop star Katy Perry. US intelligence cables detailing Sheikh Mansour's background point out that his 'academic record was poor'.

Still, he must have done something right besides perfecting his American-inflected English. In 1997, he was appointed to head the presidential office, an influential advisory group to his father, Sheikh Zayed. That job later turned into minister of presidential affairs, which he tacked on to his other responsibilities, which included the chairmanship of the First Gulf Bank and the Al-Jazira Club's football team, plus seats on the boards of the Abu Dhabi Investment Council and the International Petroleum Investment Company, who decide how to spend the nation's tide of profits. The degree in international relations he received back in the UAE might have served him well when he married the daughter of the ruler of neighbouring Dubai – or the time he helped negotiate a $10 billion government bailout for Dubai in the midst of the global financial crisis.

As luck would have it, Sheikh Mansour's interest in English football perked up at precisely the right moment. Some 3,500 miles from the Emirati desert, a struggling club in the rainiest city in England was freaking out about what was going to happen to their owner.

Thaksin Shinawatra had run into a spot of rather serious financial trouble.

It's not that Shinawatra didn't have any money. There were $1.4 billion of assets in his name sitting back in Thailand. It's just that it was awkward for him to get to them at this precise moment because, well, a Thai court had frozen his bank accounts. Shinawatra was being accused of abusing his power and had been sentenced *in absentia* to two years' imprisonment for his role in a crooked land deal. The British press was also renewing its interest in the spate of extrajudicial killings by Thai police, which he allegedly consented to during his time as prime minister – a somewhat graver crime than losing 8–1 at home to Middlesbrough.

Shinawatra couldn't go back to Thailand for fear of being arrested. And he couldn't spend time in Manchester because he didn't much like the place. Instead, his self-imposed exile took him to London and Dubai. And in late May 2008, he put the club's operations in the hands of a new CEO that he'd headhunted from Nike, a globe-trotting Englishman with a set jaw and silver hair named Garry Cook. For the previous few years, Cook had overseen the international side of Nike's Michael Jordan line. As far as football experience was concerned, he had been around for a pair of milestone deals for the Premier League, too: in 1992, he worked at Mitre Sports International when it signed an agreement to supply the league's official ball, and eleven years later, he was involved with Nike's blockbuster deal to produce Manchester United's kits. There was little the world of sports business could throw at Cook that his career hadn't already prepared him for. At least until he landed in east Manchester with the erratic former prime minister of Thailand for a boss.

Cook got off to a rocky start. In one early interview, he was asked about the various criminal allegations chasing Shinawatra from the other side of the world. Cook considered the question and put his foot squarely in his mouth. 'He's embroiled in a political process and I've chosen to stay out of it,' he told the *Guardian*. 'Is he a nice guy? Yes. Is he a great guy to play golf with? Yes. Does he have plenty of money to run a football club? Yes. I really care only about those three things. Whether he is guilty of something over in Thailand, I can't worry. I have to be conscious of it. But my role is to run a football club.'

Running that football club proved equally delicate to navigate. In addition to whatever Shinawatra might have been guilty of over in Thailand, he was certainly culpable of letting his football club run itself into the ground in the north-west of England. Everything Cook learned about City in those first few weeks gave him cause for alarm. 'Financially, it was a black hole,' Cook said. On at least two occasions that season, City had to borrow £2 million from its former chairman John Wardle. The club was also lining up two more bridging loans for £25 million apiece – one from a bank and one from a Greek shipping magnate who happened to be friends with Shinawatra – that were leveraged against future TV revenue and ticket sales. Much of the money that Shinawatra had put into the club to fund transfers had also turned out to be loans rather than straight-up investments by the owner. With the interest on some of these debts exceeding 11 per cent, Manchester City might as well have been paying for players with their Amex.

In the year ending 31 May 2008, a time of record payouts from the Premier League to its clubs, Manchester City recorded a loss of £29.7 million.

'When you got into the business and had a look under the hood, you could see we were actually heading for a bit of a road crash,' Cook stated. 'We were strongly influenced by agents. We were spending a lot of money on agents' fees. We were leveraging any equity we had in the business to bring cash forward.'

Everywhere Cook looked, another disaster was brewing. Six weeks after being hired, he had only one piece of advice for Shinawatra: 'Get out of here as quickly as you can because this thing is going to collapse.'

On 28 June, Shinawatra gave Cook permission to start speaking to buyers.

Not that buyers were exactly queuing up for this car crash of a club. The mess Cook was selling for somewhere between £150 and £200 million had fewer salvageable parts than most. Anyone who bought City would immediately be on the hook for some of the most disproportionate salaries in the league. There wasn't much of a real estate angle to play either since the stadium was leased from the city. 'And, of course,' Cook said, 'everybody thought we lived in the shadow of Manchester United.'

No sane buyer would have taken the plunge. City needed a

billionaire or a consortium or a *deus ex machina* who could absorb huge financial losses and perhaps had an agenda that went beyond football because Manchester's second team didn't exactly strike fear in the rest of the football world. Cook marketed the club for more than a month with no success. Shinawatra, meanwhile, had bigger fish to fry. He was hanging out at the Beijing Olympics, hoping to find a way to re-enter Thailand.

It was around this time that Cook, through acquaintances of acquaintances, was introduced in London to a pair of potential investors, Amanda Staveley and Ali Jassim. Staveley, who counted Prince Andrew as an ex-boyfriend, was well known in financial circles as a regular intermediary for money from the Gulf. Jassim was an adviser to Sheikh Mansour. And they were preparing to help him spend an awful lot of money. At the same time as they were enquiring about Manchester City, Staveley and Jassim were preparing to help Sheikh Mansour acquire a multibillion-pound stake in the seriously distressed Barclays bank at the height of the global financial crisis. (He would end up spending £3.5 billion on it that autumn.)

Cook had no idea what other expensive irons Staveley and Jassim had in the fire when he first met with them. But if an Emirati royal was dispatching a pair of lieutenants to investigate Manchester City, Cook figured he might find his seriously distressed club a saviour after all.

In a meeting room at the City of Manchester Stadium on 24 August, ahead of City's opening home fixture against West Ham, Cook delivered a forty-five-minute presentation that laid out why someone didn't necessarily have to be crazy to buy this club. The £150 million price tag was incidental, he told Staveley and Jassim. Whoever was stumping up the cash wasn't just buying membership into the most watched league in the world. They were buying a slice of global legitimacy, a PR campaign that played fifty games a year to an audience of millions. You couldn't put a price on that. For today's image-conscious billionaire, a Premier League football team was a must-have accessory.

'Nobody had ever heard of Roman Abramovich until he bought Chelsea Football Club,' Cook told the pair. 'If you're developing your nation and you're looking to be on a global stage, we are your proxy brand for the nation.'

That nation, at the time, was nine years younger than Manchester City's manager.

But even though the United Arab Emirates were founded only in 1971, the region's relationship with the United Kingdom ran much deeper. In the seventeenth century, the locals survived mainly on fishing, pearl diving, and a little bit of piracy. Well, more than a little bit. Attacks on British ships were so frequent that sailors dubbed that stretch of the Persian Gulf the 'Pirate Coast'. The British Empire, however, couldn't give up on shipping waters that close to India. So it applied its age-old peacemaking strategy: 'If you can't beat 'em, trade with 'em.' In 1853, Britain and the local tribes signed the Treaty of Maritime Peace in Perpetuity – the locals hoped that the British might enforce some peace between the region's tribes during the all-important pearling season. That agreement grew into an exclusive trade arrangement, and the Pirate Coast soon became known as the Trucial States when they were folded under the umbrella of British India. No one had any clue yet that fishing and pearl diving would eventually become afterthoughts.

It took until the 1930s for anyone to start scouring the desert for the resource that would turn the region upside down and until the 1960s for Abu Dhabi to start pumping it out of the ground. But once they did, the sheikhs that had carved out patches of sand quickly understood what they were sitting on. Now there was just the small question of how to handle the British.

Unlike many subjects of the Crown who were agitating for independence after the Second World War, the sheikhs quite enjoyed having the British around. They kept the local borders intact and propped up their royal houses. It gave the sheikhs authority. The problem was on the other side: the British had no inclination to stay. With anti-colonial uprisings elsewhere in the Gulf, Prime Minister Harold Wilson decided that the expense and hassle of hanging on to the Trucial States were no longer worth it. In 1968, he ordered all UK troops out of the region, much to the chagrin of the sheikhs, who tried offering to foot the £12 million annual bill for the British forces themselves. But Britain was not interested in renting out its army. 'Who asked them to leave?' asked the ruler of Dubai, according to *The Prize*, Daniel Yergin's global history of oil. 'Britain is weak now where she was once so strong,' added the emir of Bahrain. 'You know we and everybody in the Gulf would have welcomed her staying.'

The rulers in the desert were left with the biggest 'Now what?' in the region's history. Desperate to fill the power vacuum, they spent the next three years locked in tense negotiations over what to do with their borders with the Saudis next door and, more important, how to manage the riches that now came spurting out of the ground. The solution they came up with when the final administrative ties to Britain expired in 1971 was for six of the sheikhdoms to band together as the United Arab Emirates. A seventh, Ras al-Khaimah, joined the following year, but Qatar and Bahrain, which had also enjoyed Trucial protection, weren't interested.

There was no question that Abu Dhabi and Dubai were the senior partners in this new arrangement. Abu Dhabi, despite having no paved roads and only a handful of permanent buildings, represented 84 per cent of the country's landmass and controlled more than 90 per cent of its oil and gas. It also understood that in order to launch itself towards the twenty-first century, all of that oil money would have to pay for more than sports cars, chandeliers, and shopping trips to London for the royal family. Black gold was going to build their entire society.

In the space of forty years, it turned Abu Dhabi into a shimmering oasis of glass and steel.

But because of its youth, because of its wealth, and because of its outsize influence for a nation of only around 500,000 citizens, Abu Dhabi became intensely aware of the image it projected to the rest of the world. It didn't want to be seen as an irresponsible nouveau riche petrostate with more money than sense. But Abu Dhabi also knew that wanting to be taken seriously on the global stage came with a high degree of reputational risk. The Western powers Abu Dhabi was doing business with weren't going to ignore the elephant camped in the room: the emirate's disgraceful human-rights record.

The list of sins that Amnesty International routinely laid at Abu Dhabi's door included the nation's strict restrictions on freedom of the press, its limitations on women's rights, its ban on homosexuality, its habit of 'disappearing' political dissidents, its use of torture and show trials, and its continuing reliance on the exploitative kafala contracts for the migrant workers who make up around 90 per cent of Abu Dhabi's workforce.

The government, while denying any wrongdoing, knows these are liabilities. Which is why Abu Dhabi undertook a charm offensive around 2006 to soften its image. The vision was to paint a picture of a globally relevant, dynamic, welcoming nation built on the traditional values of the Gulf. Laid out in a couple of documents with sexy names – *Policy Agenda 2007–08* and *The Abu Dhabi Economic Vision 2030* – Abu Dhabi's soft-power offensive relied on, among other things, three crucial tools.

The first was the Abu Dhabi Tourism Authority, created to 'contribute to the international reputation of the Emirate'. Armed with an initial advertising budget of £10 to £20 million a year plus shiny new offices in London and Frankfurt, its sole purpose was to paint Abu Dhabi as a viable tourist destination with every modern amenity you could think of – and definitely not as an obscure air-conditioned oasis.

Then there was Abu Dhabi's very own international airline, Etihad Airways, quite literally a vehicle for exporting the Abu Dhabi name to the world and bringing business home. No one cared that it operated at a loss for years after its founding in 2003. That wasn't the point. After finishing its first full year of operations with six aircraft, it built that fleet to forty-two by 2008, at which time it announced an order for a hundred more aircraft from Airbus and Boeing at an estimated cost of $20 billion – more than double the market value of every Premier League club combined.

Finally, Abu Dhabi sought to make its presence felt in international sport. And they weren't talking about events like the bowling championship Sheikh Mansour once presided over. In the two years before taking an interest in Manchester City, Abu Dhabi launched an international golf tournament, successfully bid to host the FIFA Club World Cup in 2009 and 2010, secured the rights to a Formula One

Grand Prix, and broke new ground with a Ferrari-themed amusement park called Ferrari World that boasted such attractions as the Formula Rossa rollercoaster and a kids' ride called Khalil's Car Wash. The trend continued after the summer of 2008 as Sheikh Mansour grew his personal influence in the world of sport everywhere he could. In 2009, he became chairman of the Emirates Racing Authority, which presides over the annual $10 million Dubai World Cup, the richest horse race in the world.

How much Sheikh Mansour actually cared about football and the fate of a Premier League club was unclear. People with knowledge of his thinking believe that he was more enamoured with the idea of a globally visible property for Abu Dhabi than he was with the intricacies of whether City played a 4-4-2 or a 4-2-3-1.

Whatever his reasons were, after hearing back from the delegation he sent to Manchester City vs West Ham, Sheikh Mansour gave the purchase the green light. This would not be an acquisition by Abu Dhabi's sovereign wealth fund – this came out of Mansour's pocket.

Over the next few days, there was minimal back-and-forth. At no point did anyone working for the Abu Dhabi United Group, the purchasing vehicle for the club, dig deep into City's books. In fact, there was almost no due diligence at this stage – that could wait till later. Six days after the presentation at the City of Manchester Stadium, on the evening of 30 August, Shinawatra's right-hand man, Pairoj Piempongsant, summoned Garry Cook to London to tell him where he'd been. A secret deal had been struck in Abu Dhabi to sell the club and the mountain of debt hanging over them would soon disappear.

There was only one highly unusual condition attached to the sale: Manchester City needed to sign a superstar player immediately. Otherwise, he told Cook, Abu Dhabi would consider backing out. It didn't matter who the superstar was. He just had to be big enough to match Abu Dhabi's ambition. And Cook and Piempongsant needed to get on it right now.

The transfer window was closing in twenty-four hours.

On the morning of 31 August, Garry Cook and Pairoj Piempongsant sat in Shinawatra's offices on Old Park Lane desperate to spend a wad of cash. They just needed to find another club that would take it. As Cook paced around, Piempongsant, a former senior government adviser in Thailand, lay on a sofa with his shoes off while the two men tried to figure out which international footballer to buy with Abu Dhabi's money.

They drew up a shopping list of starry names they thought might please their new masters in the Gulf. They were all strikers, of course. Blowing £30 or £40 million on a defender wasn't going to bowl anybody over. Cook and Piempongsant spent all morning on the phone to agents and executives while the office back in Manchester faxed off a string of ludicrous offers to clubs all over Europe. Few outside the room had any idea what kind of stress the two City men were under.

In the confusion, Cook got a call from Manchester asking him if he was sure they wanted to go ahead with a bid for Barcelona's Lionel Messi. Cook was perplexed – this was the first he'd heard of it. But Piempongsant had apparently given it the go-ahead. Without a second thought, Cook also signed off. 'Sure, just do it. If it works, great.'

Then he turned to Piempongsant. 'This is getting ridiculous.'

'Yes,' Piempongsant replied from the couch. 'Very messy.'

'*What did you say?*'

Cook realized what had happened. Between the shouting into phones and Piempongsant's accent and the panic in Manchester, someone had misunderstood the orders. Manchester City had just bid more than €50 million for one of the best players in the world completely by accident.

Barcelona wasted no time in dismissing it.

But the chaos was only beginning. Rumours of the Abu Dhabi takeover had started to spread through the media in the late morning. By noon, it was confirmed. The club had signed a memorandum of understanding to sell the club to the Abu Dhabi United Group, who were acting on behalf of a member of the emirate's royal family. The takeover's front man was Sulaiman al-Fahim, a thirty-one-year-old real estate developer, chess champion, and the host of an *Apprentice*-style reality show on Emirati TV. His catchphrase: 'Impress me!'

No one seemed to be better at impressing Sulaiman al-Fahim than Sulaiman al-Fahim. Embracing the role of a gregarious new Premier League owner – even though he didn't own the team and it wasn't clear he'd ever heard of half the clubs in the league – al-Fahim declared immediately that 'our goal is to make this football club one of the best not just in England but also in the world. To reach that goal there is no limit.'

Great, Cook thought. Now everyone knew that City would pay through the nose. Al-Fahim also let it be known that City were in for Valencia's David Villa and Stuttgart's Mario Gomez. What the rest of Europe still didn't realize was that City had to get a deal done today, the most chaotic day on the football calendar. Deadline Day had become like scrambling around the supermarket on Christmas Eve – except all of the turkeys had agents.

Across town, in the Osterley studios of Sky Sports News, this was perfect. For a few years now, producers had wondered if they could jazz up their coverage of this final day's trading. 'Let's make an event of it,' executive editor Andy Cairns had told his staff. He wanted to go from having an overhead shot of two telephones on a desk to dispatching camera crews around the country. In his mind, he envisioned the full election-night treatment: live updates from reporters standing outside stadiums and training grounds, snippets of breaking news left and right, lots of interruptions. 'There's a touch of tongue-in-cheek about it,' Cairns said.

But before 2008, the Premier League had never quite produced enough Deadline Day intrigue to support it. On 31 August, that changed for good.

As afternoon turned to evening inside the office on Old Park Lane, City's gaze was settling on two players after carpet-bombing Europe with offers. The first was the tall Bulgarian striker from Tottenham, Dimitar Berbatov, with more than enough talent to mask his habit of sneaking the occasional cigarette. The second was a tricky Brazilian winger from Real Madrid named Robinho. The issue with both of them was that other clubs were already ahead of City in the hunt.

Manchester United had spent most of the summer attempting to wrangle Berbatov away from Spurs, and he was already on a flight to the north-west. City's plan was to throw in a late bid – a British record of £34 million – and station someone at the airport to meet-slash-kidnap the player in a last-minute coup. Everyone involved knew only too well that in the world of football transfers nothing meant anything until the player was in your building holding up a shirt for the cameras. Without that, no deal was immune from being hijacked.

As for Robinho, Chelsea had been in talks with Real Madrid for weeks. Chelsea's chief executive, Peter Kenyon, flew back from Madrid on Saturday, 29 August, convinced that he had done enough to secure the player's signature and could expect Robinho in London soon. Snippets of information about the deal soon flooded the BBC's Deadline Day live blog, updates of dubious origins from around the country with no way to verify them. 'My cousin works in the booking centre for British Airways – she just processed a seat from Madrid on a 4 p.m. flight for one Robson de Souza aka Robinho,' wrote one. 'I work in the shirt sales at Stamford Bridge. I was told this morning to prepare Robinho shirts with number eight,' another texted in.

The first piece of bad news came from Manchester. United had matched City's bid for Berbatov. Not only that, their local rivals had mobilized a welcoming committee of their own to meet the player at the airport: Sir Alex Ferguson himself. It takes a brave man to stare down Ferguson in an airport and tell him you were about to sign for City. Berbatov, Cook quickly surmised, was not that man.

Piempongsant and Cook were down to their last throw of the dice: negotiating with Robinho and a coterie of representatives who hadn't been able to deliver a straight answer all day. They threw Real a bid for £32.5 million, promised Robinho the moon, and hoped something stuck. If everyone could get on the same page, City told them, there would be a private jet in Madrid waiting to whisk Robinho and company to London at a moment's notice.

Still nothing. Cook could see the Abu Dhabi deal falling apart before his eyes if this twenty-four-year-old Brazilian kid didn't board that plane in Spain. Then the phone rang for the millionth time. The deal was done.

As far as football moves go, they didn't come much more nouveau riche than this. A Brazilian winger is a bit like a Maserati. Not many people know how to use one properly but damn if they don't look good. By 11 p.m., the cat was fully out of the bag. Real Madrid president Ramón Calderón was on Spanish radio stating, 'We have agreed to sell the player for human reasons, for footballing reasons – and for an important quantity of money.'

The moment Robinho's £32.5-million feet touched down on English soil, he was whisked to central London to finalize the transfer and, most important, take the obligatory pictures. Until he held up Manchester City's sky-blue shirt in the Old Park Lane office sometime around 11.30 p.m., it wasn't clear to Cook and Piempongsant that Robinho knew which club he had signed for.

But that hardly mattered now. City had its marquee player.

The coast was clear for Abu Dhabi to turn the Premier League upside down.

Robinho was just the beginning. At least if you believed Sulaiman al-Fahim.

Manchester City's newest executive had made the mistake of giving out his phone number to any football reporter who asked. When they rang, he never failed to deliver incendiary copy. He promised early on that City would bring in a minimum of eighteen new players. And not just any old veterans who happened to be knocking around on the transfer market. He wanted all those famous names City had flirted with on Deadline Day and more: Spanish forwards Fernando Torres and David Villa, Dutch striker Ruud van Nistelrooy, Wayne Rooney, and the ageing Brazilian Ronaldo, whose balky knees and precipitous weight gain were mere trivialities as far as al-Fahim was concerned.

'Ronaldo has said he wants to play for the biggest club in the world, so we will see in January if he is serious,' al-Fahim said. 'Real Madrid were estimating his value at $160 million but for a player like that, to actually get him, will cost a lot more, I would think $240 million. But why not?'

Al-Fahim wanted to treat the grand clubs of Europe and his rivals in the Premier League as if they were a Dubai supermall, popping into one luxury store after another and walking out with the most expensive item they had. For Garry Cook, it made things 'somewhat awkward' at the season's first Premier League owners' meeting a few days later.

Al-Fahim and his bluster didn't last long. On the orders of the royal family, the club quietly replaced him with the individual who would soon become the key figure in the entire Manchester City organization, Khaldoon al-Mubarak. An Emirati native with narrow glasses and a neatly kept beard, he was a classic example of the savvy entrepreneurs Abu Dhabi stations on the front lines of its international mission to win friends and influence people. Like Mansour, al-Mubarak was educated in the United States. But unlike his boss, al-Mubarak didn't spend his college years soaking in the California sun. Al-Mubarak went to Tufts University in Boston, where he studied economics and finance, and then rose to the rank of chief executive of the Mubadala Investment Company, a strategic investment fund with a portfolio worth tens of billions of dollars. For a man used to ploughing money into projects like the construction of the largest aluminum smelter in the world or a 230-mile gas pipeline from Qatar to Abu Dhabi, a $200-million football team normally would have constituted a minor play. Right before joining City, for instance, al-Mubarak signed off on Mubadala spending nearly seven times that for a 7.5 per cent stake in the Carlyle Group, the international private-equity firm that has counted US presidents and British prime ministers as advisers. But al-Mubarak understood that Manchester City gave Abu Dhabi a level of global exposure that few other properties could ever hope to match. Fifty thousand people have never bought season tickets to a metal smelter.

Working alongside al-Mubarak on City's board were a pair of high-fliers who had never been near a football club, but like Sheikh Mansour's hand-picked chairman, they knew how to play in the big leagues of international business. In New York, they hired Marty Edelman, an eye-wateringly expensive lawyer whose most recent relevant experience was helping the American property tycoon Stephen Ross acquire 50 per cent of the Miami Dolphins for $550 million. And in Abu Dhabi, they leaned on a man who knew everything there was to know about managing risk and reputation, an English expatriate PR guru named Simon Pearce.

Pearce came from an international firm called Burson-Marsteller, the most notorious name in the spin and crisis-management business. Since its founding in 1953, the firm has acted to improve the public perception of the Argentine military junta in the 1970s, the Romanian dictator Nicolae Ceauşescu, the royal family of Saudi Arabia in the wake of the September 11 terrorist attacks, Big Tobacco, the company behind the Three Mile Island nuclear plant that partially melted down in Pennsylvania, and the Union Carbide Corporation, whose 1984 gas leak in Bhopal, India, exposed half a million locals to toxic chemicals and killed around 3,000 people. No client had too many skeletons in its closet for Burson-Marsteller.

Pearce had been putting all that expertise to work for Abu Dhabi in his capacity as a member of the Executive Affairs Authority, the influential group of fifteen to twenty unelected officials who advise the government on all manner of strategic issues. They assess risk, study the landscape, and figure out how best to position Abu Dhabi in the world. Pearce had been one of the authors of the nation's vision documents. But neither Pearce nor Abu Dhabi had ever had a promotional apparatus like Manchester City at their disposal. The tourism authority and the airline were all well and good, but neither of them reached as many people as often and as reliably as a property in the world's most popular league in the world's most popular sport.

The decision to buy into the Premier League had not, in fact, been the whim of one man, according to people familiar with the process. Decisions by Abu Dhabi's rulers are always discussed from a strategic perspective by the trusted inner circle and dissected for potential reputational upside and risks. But when it came to buying something as public as a football team, it was helpful to have a figurehead to point to.

Immediately after the final formalities of the takeover went through in late September – the Abu Dhabi United Group had aced the fit and proper persons test – Sheikh Mansour issued a humble, if slightly jarring, open letter to his 'fellow Manchester City fans'.

'I am a football fan, and I hope that you will soon see that I am now also a Manchester City fan,' he wrote. 'We are ambitious for the club, but not unreasonably so. We understand it takes time to build a team capable of sustaining a presence in the top four of the Premier League and winning European honours . . . We know a little of the history at City also and whilst we want to bring in the best players in the world, we also want to see the academy continue to develop talent and give Mark Hughes the chance to bring home-grown players into the team. We are building a structure for the future, not just a team of all-stars.

'In cold business terms, Premiership football is one of the best entertainment products in the world and we see this as a sound business investment.'

It would take two years for Sheikh Mansour to sample that enter-tainment product in person. In August 2010, he flew in to take in his club's match against Liverpool. The club needed pictures of him inside the City of Manchester Stadium. He waved to the fans from his seat in the directors' box between Khaldoon al-Mubarak and Garry Cook, appeared to enjoy himself, and never went to another game again. The club's official position is that he doesn't care for the hassle. Critics argue that he doesn't care at all.

That may be true for Sheikh Mansour, but the same can't be said about the people involved with actually running the club.

In its mission to radiate good vibes from day one, City made good on its promises to invest in the eastern part of Manchester, teaming up with the city council to build a two-hundred-acre sport and leisure complex in Eastlands and becoming one of the area's major employers. But that belied the fact that the ambition – the very purpose of the club – wasn't exactly about what happened between the white lines on a Saturday afternoon. The institution founded in 1880 by a church to keep rowdy men away from booze and violence at weekends was about to become a slick international business.

'We're not a football club, we're actually a sports entertainment media company,' Cook said internally as the new owners swept into City. 'So we must create content. We must provide events, we must create shows, we must create drama. And we must be part of the news, front page and back page, in every way. Am I competing with the other football club down the road, Manchester United, or am I competing with Walt Disney, with Amazon?'

Cook's experience with the world's leading sportswear manufacturer and history's greatest basketball player informed every decision he made for the second-most-famous football team in Manchester. In the States, Cook had been struck by seeing cash machines inside stadiums, tiny monuments to convenient consumption. In England, 'You'd be lucky at a football stadium if you had a functioning toilet,' he said. 'I looked at American sports and thought, *This is entertainment. I am entertained.*'

At a club where some staff in the box office used to celebrate going out of the FA Cup because it meant having to do less work, the global entertainment pitch would take some time to resonate. City's new owners were up against a much more serious cultural barrier than they had anticipated. What they had on their hands was a club traumatized by its history. But more than anything, they had a club traumatized by sharing a city with Manchester United.

Because of that, City had learned to revel in everything that was explicitly not United. In other words, their own mediocrity. Cook could see it first-hand in every department of the club. But nothing brought the particular neuroses of City fandom home quite like his trip to the stadium shop during his first season in charge. In the course of his normal diligence, he asked the staff member behind the counter what the best-selling item had been that season, expecting it to be the home kit, or perhaps a scarf.

'We've had a good year this year with the DVD.'

'Which DVD do you mean?'

The salesman pointed at a rack. 'United home and away.' City, despite finishing ninth the season before the Emirati takeover, had beaten their arch-rivals twice in the same league campaign for the first time in thirty-eight years. Fans couldn't get enough of it. This was a success they had never imagined was possible.

What they had yet to wrap their heads around was that City's expectations were now set much higher. Beating United needed to become incidental to the kind of dominance that al-Fahim, uncouth as he was, had expressed out loud. The likes of Cook and al-Mubarak wanted the same thing, only they knew to keep their ambition in-house.

'If you feel nervous about where we're going, you should,' Cook told staff. 'Because nobody's ever been where we're going. Nobody's ever done what we've done.' His instructions from Abu Dhabi in his quarterly meetings with ownership were clear: create a culture of excellence at every level. 'Best in class' was the phrase that kept coming back, as if they were describing a luxury saloon. Even the groundsmen got a 'strategic meeting' pep talk.

'What are you going to do to get in the top four?' Cook asked them.

The club looked all over for inspiration. Not many sporting projects get to start effectively with a blank slate. City hired Brian Marwood, a former player who had worked with Cook at Nike, to be the club's director of football operations. He studied baseball, basketball, music, and the overachieving Olympic programme at the Australian Institute of Sport, borrowing whatever he could find about fostering elite performance. In some cases, that meant updating sagging facilities. In others, it was about giving players the logistical support to function as human beings when they went home from training. Signing so many players from abroad created a need for translators, childcare, and real estate help. So Marwood hired four full-time staff exclusively to look after the needs of players and their families. Until the takeover, that department had never existed.

'We needed to remove the excuses,' Marwood said. 'We wanted to create a best-in-class environment, but then we needed to know what best in class looked like.'

For all his globetrotting, Marwood knew he didn't really need to look that far. During his daily shuttling between City's three locations – the offices at the City of Manchester Stadium, the academy at Platt Lane, and the training ground at Carrington – he often took a deliberate detour past Old Trafford. It wasn't for the scenery. It was a reminder of what greatness looked like.

In the space of one international break, Marwood oversaw a radical overhaul of the training ground. The gym, which previously looked like your local discount fitness club, was decked out with all new state-of-the-art equipment. Outside, City made as many cosmetic changes as it could execute quickly; if anyone knew that appearances counted for something, it was the club's new owners.

'We put some nice lawn down and some nice trees,' Marwood said. 'It kind of felt like you were coming into a country club.' Inside, they overhauled every aspect of sports nutrition, player health, and club operations. For the first time in their history, Manchester City had a real human resources department. All the changes that United, Arsenal, and later Chelsea had made in the 1990s – the trappings of life as a rich club in the money-spinning Premier League – were finally coming to east Manchester.

But amid all that progress, City soon ran into a question that it had never even considered: was greatness something the fans really wanted?

For City fans who remembered the club's ugly slump into the third tier – which is to say, any fan with a memory longer than a fruit fly's since the relegation happened only six years earlier – the takeover triggered mixed emotions. On the one hand, the club's new owner was unimaginably rich and not personally a human-rights abuser as far as they knew then. On the other, were they mortgaging their credibility for ever? With a sugar daddy as an owner, a big stadium, and a fancy international airline as a sponsor (instead of a fax-machine company), were Manchester City now any different from the sell-outs across town?

City had always prided themselves on being more authentically Manchester than United. Matches at Old Trafford were so full of tourists that opposing fans sang, 'We'll race you back to London'. Meanwhile, City's fan base included the likes of Oasis, Manchester's most famous export this side of British cotton. The club was cool. They were bad at football, true. But they swaggered. If United were all money and prawn sandwiches, City were a dark nightclub and a packet of cigarettes. Their authenticity lay in their fatalism. 'City till I die' was their mantra, closely followed by 'Typical City'.

Equal parts jealous and appalled, fans of rival clubs who saw hapless City catapult literally overnight into the ranks of world football royalty wasted no time in ripping the team apart for abandoning its roots. 'You're not City, you're not City, you're not City any more' went the song from opposing fans. A few City supporters agreed. Some even posted back their season tickets.

The slick Emiratis weren't worried about City's history of ineptitude. For them, the future was now.

In the new owners' first five transfer windows, from the last day of summer 2008 through to the summer of 2011, Manchester City spent in excess of £300 million on twenty-three new players. If you include the players who returned from loans and those City promoted from their youth academy, the total influx came to more than forty. 'You definitely got to meet a lot of people,' defender Vincent Kompany said. In trying to create a new DNA for the club, City borrowed wholesale from anyone they admired – it was no coincidence that five of those first twenty-three players signed had been on Arsenal's books at one time or another. 'It was quite scary. For me, we put the roof on before we built the walls,' Marwood said.

Cook went even further: 'Nobody really knew whether we were doing the right thing or the wrong thing.'

What looked to the outside like fishing with dynamite was the product of a carefully studied approach inside City. For every acquisition, Marwood produced a thirty- to forty-page colour-coded dossier that included the classic analysis technique borrowed from corporate America known as SWOT – a visual representation of any business proposition's strengths, weaknesses, opportunities, and threats. City saw no reason why this couldn't help them choose, say, a new left-back.

In January 2009, the magnitude of what City were attempting knocked Cook over the head while he was watching BBC News with his American ex-wife. They had perked up when she caught sight of Cook's name on the news ticker because he'd accused AC Milan of messing up a transfer for the Brazilian midfielder Kaká. But that wasn't the surprising part. What blew them away was that this item somehow preceded the day's other important news on the ticker: Barack Obama being sworn in as president of the United States.

'Welcome to England,' he told her.

Not everyone City managed to reel in was a hit. They spent £22 million on a Brazilian forward named Jô, who made a grand total of twenty-one appearances for the club and scored just one goal. Togolese striker Emmanuel Adebayor, despite his fifteen goals in thirty-four games, proved to be more trouble than his £26 million price tag suggested. Robinho wound up making only forty-one appearances for the club – though his appearance record in Manchester's nightclubs was unmatched. But the club slowly got better at this game. It added experience, if not flash, with players such as Gareth Barry and Patrick Vieira, who raised the standard internally through their professionalism and work ethic. Young talent was blended in too; defender Vincent Kompany, for instance.

And in the summer of 2009, City went for fireworks.

Through a convoluted web of agents and brokers with rumoured ties to Sheikh Mansour, City's brass in Manchester were presented with the fait accompli signing of an Argentine striker they knew all too well: Carlos Tevez, the man who'd been banging in goals on the other side of Manchester for the past two seasons. No internal dossier had called for his signing. No one was even sure it was possible to get him. But once he landed on City's books at a reported cost of £47 million, the club were determined to make the most of it. That's when the billboard went up on Manchester's busiest shopping street. A sky-blue image of Tevez celebrating a goal over giant white letters spelling out, WELCOME TO MANCHESTER.

For the first time in the club's modern history, Manchester City were sufficiently emboldened to fire across United's bow. They had something to gloat about even if gloating ran contrary to every fibre of a City fan's being. Was this how United fans felt all the time? It would take some getting used to.

On the red side of Manchester, Alex Ferguson wasn't impressed. 'They think taking Carlos Tevez away from Manchester United is a triumph. It is poor stuff,' Ferguson scoffed. As far as he was concerned, the score was still 11–0 on Premier League titles. 'It's City, isn't it? They're a small club with a small mentality.'

Then he turned the screw again.

'All they can talk about is Manchester United. They can't get away from it.'

PART IV

Premier League Inc.

'The intensity, the chaos, it either smokes some truth out of you, or you turn into one of them.'
Randy Lerner, Aston Villa

16

ALEX FERGUSON COULD live with losing Carlos Tevez to Manchester City. Because in the summer of 2009, there was another transfer that was making him crankier than usual. It had been gnawing away at him for more than a year. And now he finally had to face up to the fact that the best player on the planet was fed up with life at Old Trafford.

Cristiano Ronaldo was leaving Manchester United, the club that had turned him from an awkward teenager into a global football god, the team he'd carried to three consecutive Premier League titles and two Champions League finals. And there was nothing Fergie could do about it.

Getting Ronaldo to United in the first place had been one of the major transfer coups of the decade, a plot more than a year in the making. Ferguson had heard whispers about a teenager from the island of Madeira, part of the Portuguese archipelago off the coast of Morocco. The kid was fast, mad about training, and routinely put older defenders on their backsides. Everyone who'd seen him at Sporting Lisbon raved about him as if they'd seen a fifteen-year-old Mozart.

'He wasn't afraid of anything in the game,' his youth coach Leonel Pontes said. 'When he was in the game, he was like, "This is my place. This is where I belong."'

In order to convince Ronaldo that where he actually belonged was the north-west, Ferguson had the perfect partner in crime: Carlos Queiroz, a former Sporting manager who knew Portuguese football inside and out. Queiroz had joined United as Ferguson's assistant manager in 2002 and immediately felt as if he'd spent his whole life with this grumpy old Scotsman though their backgrounds could hardly be more different. The connection, he said, 'was magic'. Ferguson, the son of a shipbuilder, came from working-class Glasgow and grew up in football as a successful striker. Queiroz, eleven years his junior, was born in Portuguese Mozambique and had a brief pedestrian career as a goalkeeper. But the two men were indistinguishable on the training pitch, bad cop and bad cop. They soon got into the habit of eating breakfast together every day at Carrington at the crack of dawn.

One of their first conversations when Queiroz arrived in England was, naturally, about the talent brewing in Portugal. In the vastness of the football landscape, every coach of a certain age is expected to be a walking encyclopedia of players in their own region. Queiroz gave Ferguson the names of two kids at Sporting: Ricardo Quaresma and Cristiano Ronaldo. Asked by United's recruitment department which one he preferred, Queiroz was clear. 'There is no doubt,' he said. 'Both.'

United were skittish about raiding Sporting's youth system to gamble on a pair of Portuguese teenagers. Forced to pick just one, the club settled on the younger player, the one with braces on his teeth and dyed-blond streaks in his hair who went by the name Ronaldo.

Ferguson wasn't the only one who knew the boy's name. By 2002, word of Ronaldo's exploits and determination had made its way around the sharpest scouts in Europe. Here was a kid with the talent to terrorize defenders and who had such a thirst to be the best that he used to race cars away from traffic lights in Lisbon. Someone was going to snap him up soon. Ronaldo sensed it, too. In preparation for the first major transfer of his career – wherever it might take him – Ronaldo had hired a former nightclub promoter and video-store owner named Jorge Mendes to act as his agent.

Mendes began touting the teenager around right away. He mentioned Ronaldo to Inter in Italy. In November of 2002, he took young Cristiano to visit Arsenal's training ground at London Colney, where he met with Arsène Wenger. Mendes nearly did deals with Valencia, Liverpool, and Juventus. He also made sure to put Ronaldo on the radar of Real Madrid.

So how did United steal a march on everyone else? Well, they had a rather elaborate plan for that.

In 2002, thanks to Queiroz's links, United struck up a 'strategic relationship' with Sporting. The tie-up would allow the two clubs to share coaching advice and various best practices. Nothing sinister. Nothing explicitly about poaching the best player ever to come through Sporting's youth ranks. Sporting and United were just pre-eminent clubs in their respective leagues with storied histories hoping to exchange ideas – at least that's how Queiroz sold it. Ronaldo's name was never mentioned. As a result of that partnership, Sporting asked United for a favour. Late in the summer of 2003, the Portuguese club planned to open a new stadium in Lisbon; would United join them there to christen the ground with a friendly? For United, the fixture wasn't exactly convenient. The club knew it would be heading back from an exhausting pre-season tour of the United States. Portugal was hardly en route from Philadelphia to Manchester. But in the interest of keeping Sporting sweet, United agreed. So there they were that August, sunburnt and jet-lagged, touching down in Lisbon.

One man who didn't board that flight was Queiroz. He had quit United after only one year to take over the vacant post as manager of Real Madrid. His first instruction to Real's president was to pay whatever it took to poach Ronaldo.

Ferguson suspected that this conversation might be happening in Spain. By that point, United had made a little progress with Sporting, hoping to complete a deal for Ronaldo and then leave him in Portugal to mature for at least another season. But two factors changed Ferguson's mind. One was the knowledge that sharks like Queiroz were circling. The other was Cristiano Ronaldo's first-half performance against United in the Lisbon game.

Ronaldo absolutely murdered them.

The poor soul across from Ronaldo that night was United's twenty-two-year-old Irish right back John O'Shea. He never saw Ronaldo coming. By the end of the first half, O'Shea was so traumatized by the trickery from the spotty teenager that he had resorted to fouling Ronaldo whenever he got close enough. After forty-five minutes of this torture, Manchester United retreated to the dressing room, where Ferguson was accosted by two of his senior players, Rio Ferdinand and Roy Keane. Sign this kid, they told him. Sign him now.

'I've got it sorted,' Ferguson answered, fudging the truth slightly. He didn't have it sorted quite yet, but he would soon. Ferguson dispatched the kit man to haul United's chief executive Peter Kenyon down from the directors' box to get busy locking up Ronaldo's transfer to United even before the game was over. 'John O'Shea's ended up with a migraine!' Fergie screamed at Kenyon. 'Get him signed.'

Ronaldo barely had time for a shower afterwards before Kenyon and Ferguson bundled the kid and his agent into an office inside the stadium. The rest of the United squad were waiting on the bus. But Ferguson wasn't leaving Lisbon without Ronaldo's signature. The old plan of stashing him in Lisbon for another year had gone out the window, Kenyon told them. Ferguson promised the seventeen-year-old a minimum of six starts in the Premier League next season. There would be no more wait for the big time.

If he agreed, Ronaldo could be in Manchester in under twenty-four hours.

United hired a private jet to fly Ronaldo and his mother back to England before anyone else – especially Queiroz – could squeeze in on the deal. The situation evolved so quickly that Ronaldo didn't even pack a change of clothes. He assumed he'd be presented to the media and flown back home to sort out the details. Ferguson had other ideas. He expected him to report for training the next morning.

The next twelve months would redefine Ronaldo's career.

Immersed in the culture of Carrington, the showboating teenager began to add more substance to his game. He bulked up. He improved his passing. Wearing the No. 7 vacated by David Beckham, he made forty appearances that first season, far outstripping the meagre six he'd been promised. Hearing Ferguson talk about the work ethic of his father and northern England resonated with the teenager from Madeira for some reason, just as it had over the years with the Premier League veterans that made up the United squad. 'When you have Roy Keane in a team,' said Queiroz, who returned to the club in 2004 after one unhappy season at Real, 'there is no room for jokes, no space for entertainment. Every single training session was commitment.'

Ferguson so trusted Queiroz that the Portuguese coach became Ronaldo's primary care-giver at training, the one who worked closest with him on all the technical aspects of the game. Ferguson wrote later that Queiroz 'was the closest you could be to being the Manchester United manager without actually holding the title'. (He even took over some of Ferguson's post-match interview duties during Ferguson's years-long feud with the BBC, remaining true enough to his boss's style to draw a Football Association reprimand for insulting referees.) What the two men loved best about Ronaldo was his utter devotion to the cause. For all of his flash on the pitch, for all the time he spent admiring himself in the mirror, for all of his silly haircuts, Ronaldo practically lived at the training ground.

Over their 7 a.m. breakfasts, Ferguson and Queiroz could observe that Ronaldo was the first player to arrive at Carrington every day, followed shortly by Wayne Rooney, who was eight months younger. Training didn't formally start for at least another hour, but the teenagers couldn't wait to get in and start kicking about. They played football tennis and other games they invented. They had what Queiroz called, 'their little kingdom of activities'.

The coaches could tell Ronaldo had the hallmark of other great players: they're never in a rush to go home. 'They take long showers, they go to the gym,' Queiroz said. 'For me, when I see this, I start to think I have something special in front of me. There is nothing at home that is more important than the game for them.' Ronaldo started sticking around Carrington so late that Queiroz would have to chase him off one of the outer pitches after training. Ronaldo wanted to stay out to work on his dribbling skills and free kicks – an echo of Eric Cantona, another previous owner of the No. 7 jersey. The United staff just wanted to go home.

'I saw many great professionals, but some of them are more great than others,' Queiroz said, reaching for an analogy. 'You have the colour blue – but you can have dark blue and light blue.'

Over the next four years, United shaped Ronaldo into the greatest player in the world. And in turn, Ronaldo returned the club to its position of dominance. In 2006–7, they broke their longest title drought of the Premier League era and lifted their first championship trophy in four years. Ronaldo scored twenty-three goals in fifty-three appearances. The following season, he positively exploded. Playing as a winger, he notched forty-two goals in forty-nine games, lifting United to the Premier League title and the 2008 Champions League final in Moscow. But by the time they reached Moscow, the trouble had already started. Ferguson and Queiroz had always known this day would come. 'How long are we going to be able to keep Cristiano?' was a regular question between them, though they recognized getting five years out of him already counted as a success.

Ronaldo had dropped hints here and there. His agent, Jorge Mendes, meanwhile, did what agents do. He dropped more than hints, and he made sure the right people in world football heard them. The press caught wind of these transfer whispers, but everything remained a rumour, carefully hedged and opaquely sourced. Until the morning of the Champions League final. On that day, *MARCA*, the Spanish sports daily with a reputation as Real Madrid's unofficial mouthpiece, loudly proclaimed on its front page that Ronaldo was heading to Spain. Stories about a possible move to Real then graced the cover of *MARCA* for eight of the next ten days. No prizes for guessing the source.

The reason Spanish clubs can't help themselves when it comes to major declarations about which players they intend to sign comes from a fundamental difference in the way they are structured. Real Madrid, Barcelona, and the other clubs have presidents who must run for the office by laying out their visions for the future. And more often than not, that vision is built around the simplest campaign promise in sport: splurging a load of cash on a superstar. The method is crass and underhanded for turning players' heads when they are still under contract with rivals, but that's how Real Madrid assembled its team of *galácticos* in the early 2000s. Now, in 2008, Real president Ramón Calderón needed a *galáctico* of his own. It could only be Cristiano.

The onslaught of stories promising a world-record transfer fee of €80 million went on for months despite several unconvincing public reassurances from Ronaldo that he wanted to stay at Manchester

United. Everyone involved knew it wasn't true. The Glazers' position on Real was 'to hell with them' – they wouldn't sell – which did plenty to raise the owners' standing in Ferguson's eyes. Calderón told anyone who would listen that Ronaldo was being kept in Manchester and being forced to work against his will.

The Ronaldo soap opera was the talk of the football world. At the top of the game's power structure, Sepp Blatter threw his weight behind Calderón. The FIFA president argued that Ronaldo was being treated 'like a modern-day slave'.

Ronaldo, who was earning a salary of roughly £8 million a year at the time, agreed.

The situation was clearly untenable. Anytime anyone opened their mouth, it made for sensational headlines. They needed to sit down together, Ronaldo and Ferguson, and sort this out in private once and for all. Queiroz, who left United after the Champions League final to take over the Portuguese national team, made it happen.

Feeling a responsibility towards Ronaldo's 'motivation, his commitment, and his happiness', he arranged a meeting in July far from the prying eyes in Manchester and Madrid. The venue would be Queiroz's family home outside Lisbon. Ferguson and club chief executive David Gill, who had replaced Kenyon in 2003, flew in from the United camp. Jorge Mendes represented the player. As for Ronaldo, he tried to pull out at the last minute, making up an excuse about an appointment for some physical treatment, hoping to avoid looking Ferguson in the eye. That's when Queiroz insisted, exercising what he called his 'fatherly coaching authority'.

With Ronaldo's immediate orbit finally in place, Queiroz sent the most decorated manager in English football and the best player on the planet into his living room. 'When you finish this meeting,' Queiroz told them, 'you need to have a solution for both sides.'

With that, he stepped out and left them in peace. He retreated to wait with Gill and Mendes, interrupting Ferguson only to offer him some water. An hour passed. Inside the room, Ferguson did most of the talking. 'You can't go this year, not after the way Calderón has approached the issue,' he told Ronaldo. 'I know you want to go to Real Madrid. But I'd rather shoot you than sell you to that guy now. If you perform, don't mess us about, and someone comes and offers us a world-record fee, then we will let you go.'

Ferguson explained that he simply couldn't be seen caving in to Calderón's bully tactics. 'If I do that, all my honour's gone, everything's gone for me, and I don't care if you have to sit in the stands,' he said. 'I know it won't come to that, but I just have to tell you I will not let you leave this year.'

Ronaldo understood. Ferguson had been like a father to him, especially in the three years since Ronaldo's biological father had drunk himself into an early grave. He hated to disappoint him. So Ronaldo agreed to give United one more season. Real would still be there in 2009.

The secret deal between them didn't stop the rumours, aspersions, and will-he-won't-he back-and-forth drama from bleeding into the season. Calderón, riled by Ferguson's powerplay, used the front page of *MARCA* to denounce the Scotsman, calling him a 'little General Franco' while also speculating that he was turning senile. Ferguson, his wits very much about him, made it his job to drive up Ronaldo's asking price. 'You don't think we'd get into a contract with that mob, do you?' he said that December. 'I wouldn't sell them a virus.'

The end result remained the same. Ferguson could delay the move, but he couldn't prevent it. Others, including Barcelona, tried to profit from the stand-off and made noises about offers of their own. But Ronaldo's mind was made up.

When United finally relented in the summer of 2009, Real coughed up £80 million, making Ronaldo the most expensive player in the history of the game. It was obscene even by football standards. Real had just broken the world transfer record to sign the Brazilian Kaká for £56 million, and now in the same month, they were shattering it again. All over the football world, experts feared that things were spinning out of control. Not Blatter, though. He came right to Real Madrid's defence – they'd just given him honorary membership to the club after all.

'Ten years ago there was a painting from Picasso's Blue Period, which was sold by Sotheby's in London at that time for over £100 million,' Blatter said. 'And what happened to this painting by Picasso? They hid it somewhere so no one could take it away. Nobody can see it. But a football player, you can see him once or twice a week, he is there, he is a star.'

On the day Ronaldo was unveiled in Madrid, 80,000 fans turned out to the Bernabéu Stadium to gawp at him like he was Michelangelo's *David*. He jogged out of the tunnel onto a podium on the pitch, where he joined Real's newly elected president, Florentino Pérez, and a pair of geriatric club legends. Ronaldo wore the famous all-white kit for the first time with all eyes and several dozen cameras on him.

The man who had made it happen, Jorge Mendes, stayed discreetly out of the way, ignored by practically everyone. But the right people knew he was in the centre of the action. For more than a year, Mendes had kept two of the richest clubs in the world dangling by a string. If anyone needed a reminder that the power was shifting from the clubs to the stars and their agents, this was it.

But more than just illustrating the impact of one man in a dark suit, Ronaldo's move from Manchester to Madrid also hinted at a larger tectonic shift of power within European football, one that went largely unnoticed at the time but became more obvious over the years that followed. It marked a transfer of star power from England to Spain.

Not since Ronaldo left for La Liga have the Premier League been able to claim that the best player in the world was employed by one of their clubs. Due in part to natural cycles of talent development and movement but also because of the relative parity of the Premier League, the monopolies and duopolies in Germany and Spain had a small competitive advantage when it came to attracting the absolute elite talent. Over there, the likes of Cristiano Ronaldo and Lionel Messi were all but guaranteed to lift a trophy or two each season instead of having to duke it out in dog-eat-dog English football.

The question now became: did the Premier League even need a Ronaldo? If the players were good enough and the product sparkled enough without impacting the teams' abilities to pull in the most money, so what if the most prized players in the game increasingly plied their trade elsewhere? Their venture was still making money hand over fist. It would take more than the departure of Cristiano Ronaldo to derail English football's runaway success.

17

THE RONALDO SAGA unfolded at the highest end of the transfer market, but the tension between players, agents, and clubs – between loyalty and seeking fatter pay cheques – exists at every club at every level of the professional game, and in the modern era of the Premier League, it came to define the relationships between clubs as much as anything that happened on the pitch. Someone is always trying to leave. Someone always needs to be signed. Transfers are the knee-jerk solution to everything.

As Arsène Wenger loved to remind everyone, 'In England, as soon as you have a problem, people want you to buy.'

The way players move between football clubs is entirely transactional. 'We want your guy and we're going to throw money at you until you're willing to tear up his contract.' Contracts are basically meaningless. Players who sniff a move to a bigger team can strong-arm their owners via their agents to make it happen as long as it takes place during a transfer window. This is the sports world's ultimate free market.

That's not to say there isn't an agreed-upon way of doing business. Here are the basic steps of any Premier League transfer, the framework that everyone in football is constantly trying to bend to their will. (Spoiler alert: the agents always win.)

- Step 1: Your club identifies a player it might want. That used to happen by consulting reports filed from obscure matches around Europe by a network of grizzled scouts administering the eye test. Today, the process more often begins with a spartan office and a team of data hounds with laptops and deep libraries of footage combing through dense spreadsheets of players. When their algorithms spit out a name, that's the cue to dispatch a scout to his next game or six and start investigating his character – make sure he isn't an uncoachable nutter. A high-end Premier League scouting department will sift through more than two hundred scouting reports a month. 'Before we go and watch a player that we really like, there will be an awful lot of background work,' says Steve Walsh, a twenty-year veteran of Premier League player recruitment. 'It's about lessening the risk . . . Anybody who tells you they get everything 100 per cent right when they sign a player is a liar.'

- Step 2: Go see the player. Go see him a lot. When interest escalates enough, send the manager or the chief scout to watch the player in the flesh – but expect TV cameras to spot the manager in the stands immediately, so remind him to take a baseball cap.

- Step 3: Make an offer. As in any negotiation, it should fall somewhere in the region of 50 per cent of the price the club is actually prepared to pay. The usual back and forth ensues as both clubs spend most of their time publicly denying any contact exists. This can take anywhere between a matter of hours, when the seller is motivated, to an entire season.

- Step 4: Agree to personal terms with the player. Once that's taken care of, it means the transfer is effectively done. Only three formalities remain: a medical examination by the buying club to make sure they aren't being sold a lemon, the physical signing of the contract on the dotted line, and a photo shoot with the grinning player holding up a shirt.

At least that's how it works when all goes smoothly. But certain wrinkles can affect everything about transfers, from price to the ambient levels of hostility – wrinkles such as release clauses; how much time is left on a player's existing deal; and, of course, the small matter of agents' fees. Manchester United's David Gill attempted in the 2000s to introduce a league-wide rule forcing players to pay their own agents' fees rather than expecting the clubs to shell out. But enough clubs influenced by enough agents pushed back, and the Premier League found itself in a situation where agents' commissions grew to represent 13 per cent of all transfer spending in England according to UEFA, a figure that amounts to tens of millions of pounds each season.

Here, too, the 1995 Bosman ruling shifted the power back to the players. The existence of free agency created a strange new inflection point in the life of a contract: the eighteen-months-to-go mark. While it is never explicit, that's when clubs begin to realize that they need to begin drawing up a new deal to keep the player tied down – to the extent that this is even possible – or face the possibility of losing him for nothing when the contract expires.

This madness used to go on year-round. There was no restriction on when two clubs could make a deal – players were permanently for sale. From the early 1990s, the Premier League tried to restrict this, with former Tottenham manager Terry Venables leading the charge.

'Terry's idea is that managers ought to be coaches, spending time with their players and not looking around for new signings or fending off agents or having to deal with unsettled players,' Premier League chief executive Rick Parry said at the time.

But a proposal to introduce specific windows when player sales would be allowed was narrowly defeated in a vote of the league's owners. The dissent came from a handful of small clubs who appreciated having the option of offloading a player mid season in case they needed to raise cash quickly. Except that this wasn't the end of it.

After the Bosman ruling sent the transfer market into overdrive, the Premier League again supported proposals to rein in the destabilizing effect of a permanent shopping period. 'It would keep some control over the agents just hawking players around constantly,' Peter Leaver, Parry's successor as league chief executive, said in 1998. 'And I think clubs would also have to start planning ahead properly.'

UEFA agreed and introduced a plan to restrict player movement to two specific windows – one in the summer and one in January. By now, however, in classic English fashion when any idea comes from the Continent, the Premier League clubs had flip-flopped. Not that they had any say in the matter. In 2002, UEFA introduced the two standardized transfer windows across Europe, thinking that this would be the end of it. Now that clubs and players knew where they stood for longer periods, they could stop worrying about transfers for most of the year and focus on the task at hand.

They were wrong.

'Modern football has been defined by players searching for more and more freedom. And that coincides with more and more individualism,' Wenger said. 'Today, we're at a point where even the January window creates earthquakes inside clubs. As soon as a guy's personal interests don't line up with the team's, he gets very bored.'

And who is right there fanning the flames but the salivating tabloid press.

Transfer gossip had been their stock in trade for decades, a product older than the Premier League itself. Look back far enough, and you realize that transfer gossip and the Premier League share a common ancestor. By the time that ancestor became entangled in the Premier League, he sat atop an international media empire. In 1969, however, he was just an ambitious newspaper owner from Australia.

Rupert Murdoch had just acquired the failing *Sun*. And he was facing something of a logistical problem, the first of many in his life caused by football. The scarcity of presses around the country meant the *Sun*'s first edition had to go to print before the end of any late matches. For a man hoping to target Britain's football-loving masses, this was a disaster.

So the *Sun* subbed in a kind of football filler – high in calories, low on nutrition – that would placate its readers baying for headlines. It started printing gossip. Never in the history of anything has gossip been unpopular.

The following decades brought more innovation in football's Gossip-Industrial Complex. In the same way the adult film industry lived at the forefront of video technology – proving decisive in the battle between VHS and Betamax – the Complex embraced whatever new medium was available to it. In the pre-internet 1990s, it was the BBC's on-screen teletext system, Ceefax, rounding up the tabloids' latest rumours. Premium-rate phone services also enticed fans to pay exorbitant amounts to hear which 'World Cup star' might sign for their club. Then the Complex moved online and onto Twitter, where rumours go to catch fire. Today, the transfer gossip column on the BBC website is one of its most read pages on a daily basis. Journalists build huge social media followings based on the occasional accuracy of their transfer rumours alone. The creation of transfer windows did little to curb transfer speculation as a year-round pastime. In the newspaper shorthand of transfer rumours, virtually anything can become a sign of a player's impending move.

Player X answers a reporter's question about whether he might like to play in England with a bland, 'It's the best league in the world – anyone would want to play there for the right club.' That quote is then spun to within an inch of its life and turns into midfielder issues 'COME-AND-GET-ME' PLEA TO PREM CLUBS.

But there is another fundamental issue that influences how transfers – and the Premier League at large – is covered by the British press: a near total lack of access. The Premier League press pack are restricted to brief glimpses of the people they are expected to write about every day. In a typical week, the manager will give one pre-game press conference per match and then address the media again after the game. A couple of players might also deign to speak to a handful of reporters for a moment on their way out of the stadium. And that's pretty much it. Broadcasters get a little more, including guaranteed exclusive interviews before a game they're carrying live – then again, they are paying millions for those rights.

This leads to a careful game played by journalists from rival daily newspapers after every match or press conference. The pack of reporters will huddle together in a move borrowed from political hacks, where they will decide what the juiciest bits were. 'What's the line?' is the question they're all trying to answer. Perhaps they'll lead with the game's red card, or maybe the manager hinted that his club was in the market for a striker. The only certainty is that their stories the next day will all take the same basic angle – because they've agreed on it beforehand.

The press also has a clever trick for creating the illusion of greater access: the embargo. Any given press conference or interview can be chopped up into two or three sections. Take a typical manager's news conference ahead of a Sunday game. Held on the Friday of that week, the first ten minutes are open to newspapers and broadcasters alike – all for immediate use. Then the cameras go off, and there is a second portion exclusively for daily newspapers and websites where the quotes must be held until 10.30 p.m. that night – so the reporters aren't thrust in a race to see who gets them out first. And finally, a third portion is reserved for the Sunday papers. All of that material is, of course, embargoed until late Saturday night. Similarly, anything offered up by the one or two players who might say something after a game – in the so-called mixed-zone interview – is also subject to an embargo determined not by the club but by the senior members of the pack.

Play by the rules and the pack will always forward quotes and transcripts by email so you don't get caught short. Break them and you risk being blackballed, ending up on the end of irate tweets from fellow professionals accusing you of 'letting down the industry' and informing you that you should 'hang your head in shame.' (True story.) Unless, of course, you have an exclusive. At that point, all bets are off. Say an agent or club executive drops a reporter a text with a snippet that may or may not be true about a player's future plans. The timing of those text messages often coincides with uncanny proximity to that player's next contract negotiation. Fast-forward to an opaquely sourced report about one club 'weighing a move' or 'going in for' or 'planning an audacious January swoop' for a rival club's star. In the daily game of back-page one-upmanship, the only thing that counts is a bold-faced or sometimes a gold-lettered head-line and a price tag with plenty of zeros. The crazy part is that these antics fire the Premier League's ambient conversation and layer even more intrigue onto every game. In other words, the Gossip-Industrial-Complex not only draws more attention and eyeballs to the Premier League, it also helps supercharge the markets underlying it.

Crazier still: sometimes these transfers even happen.

Against this backdrop, it is no surprise that the already cut-throat business of Premier League transfers saw the process of buying and selling players become more furious than ever in the late 2000s and early 2010s. When Premier League clubs splashed out £485 million in the summer of 2011, a 33 per cent surge on the previous year, it looked like an anomaly. In fact, it was merely the start of a collective hysteria that caused the combined expenditure of Premier League clubs to jump in each of the next five seasons, culminating in the free-for-all of 2016, when spending by the league's twenty clubs broke the £1 billion mark for the first time.

Don't think for a minute, however, that this world-class cash flow eradicated cheap tricks from the transfer market. If anything, clubs, agents, and even players became even more creative and outrageous in their efforts to force through deals or gazump their rivals. Genteel verbal contracts and handshakes between gentlemen went out the window. Operating in the transfer market had always been like swimming in a piranha tank. Now it was as if someone had introduced a school of ill-tempered manta rays for good measure.

The Premier League got its first glimpse of this a few years earlier, when Roman Abramovich's Chelsea finally succeeded in their mission to poach one of Arsenal's top players. In the end, it wasn't Thierry Henry who made the move from north London to west London but the defender Ashley Cole. The Blues' interest in him made perfect sense: the twenty-five-year-old was one of the world's top left-backs, an England mainstay, and firmly in his prime. The surprise was how they went about signing him. On 27 January 2005, the various parties assembled in the lobby of the Royal Park Hotel, around the corner from the Lancaster Gate where the Premier League had been formed more than a decade earlier. Cole brought his agent, Jonathan Barnett, while José Mourinho and Peter Kenyon made up the Chelsea delegation. The ubiquitous superagent Pini Zahavi was also present, as he would be for seemingly every major transfer that unfolded during that decade.

Over drinks and bar snacks, the group sketched out the vague parameters of Cole's contract with Chelsea, his off-the-pitch requirements, and how he would fit into Mourinho's team. All of which was standard fare for a transfer negotiation except for one minor detail: Cole was midway through a five-year contract with Arsenal, which had received no approach from Chelsea for their player, making the entire meeting a clear breach of Premier League rules. When the tabloids caught wind of the secret transfer talks, it marked the first time most football fans ever heard the term 'tapping up' – the illicit practice of turning a rival player's head and paving the way for a future transfer. It would not be the last.

When the Premier League opened an investigation into the matter, Cole's agent swiftly attempted to defuse the situation, categorically denying that any meeting with Chelsea had taken place. But he hadn't counted on a sharp-eyed hotel waiter, who signed a legal affidavit confirming he had served drinks to Kenyon, Mourinho, and Cole on the afternoon in question.

That summer, Chelsea, Cole, and Mourinho were all found guilty of a breach of Premier League rules. The Blues received a £300,000 fine and were hit with a suspended three-point deduction while Cole and Mourinho were fined £100,000 and £200,000 respectively, though those sums were later reduced. It merely served to delay Cole's switch to Chelsea, however. The defender finally signed for the Blues twelve months later after a protracted transfer saga and a falling-out with Arsenal's ownership, whom he accused of 'taking the piss' with a £55,000-a-week contract offer. In a spectacularly out-of-touch autobiography published shortly after his move to Chelsea, he wrote, 'When I heard Jonathan repeat the figure of £55k, I nearly swerved off the road.' Those ill-considered comments turned Cole into a figure of national ridicule, earning him the nickname 'Cashley' from Arsenal supporters, who waved fake twenty-pound notes at him when the two teams met later that season.

Tapping up was nowhere near a new phenomenon in English football – the former Nottingham Forest manager Brian Clough once boasted that 'we tapped more players than the Severn Trent water board' – but the brazen way Chelsea went about luring Cole in the middle of a busy hotel lobby dismayed fans and rival managers alike. 'Why not do it in the middle of the M25?' Wenger wailed, upon learning of the very public approach for his player. 'Then at least everybody knows.'

The Blues were so unmoved by the indignation stirred up by the Ashley Cole saga that by 2009 they were at the centre of another tapping-up controversy when they were accused of inducing a sixteen-year-old midfielder named Gaël Kakuta to break his contract with RC Lens of France. (Chelsea were later cleared of wrongdoing and reached a settlement with Lens.)

The moral panic over tapping up would soon feel like a more innocent time. Morally questionable practices became so common across the board that they were soon dismissed as the simple cost of doing business. And if there was one lesson from the ruthless modern transfer market, it was that no deal was safe until the ink on the player's signature was dry, photocopied, and filed in triplicate with the league.

That lesson proved an expensive one for West Ham in 2010 when the club appeared to have wrapped up a deal to sign the veteran Icelandic striker Eiður Guðjohnsen from Barcelona. When Guðjohnsen arrived at the airport, West Ham had him driven to a local hospital to undergo a routine medical examination before dropping him at a hotel in Canary Wharf, where he could have a shower and change before proceeding to the stadium to complete the formalities of signing a contract, posing for photos, and telling the world that the chance to represent the Hammers was a dream come true. When club officials pulled up at the hotel to whisk Guðjohnsen to the stadium, however, their plan hit a snag. 'He just disappeared from the hotel,' recalled David Sullivan, the West Ham co-owner. Guðjohnsen resurfaced a few hours later – holding up a Tottenham shirt and telling the world that the chance to represent Spurs was a dream come true. West Ham could hardly believe it. Somewhere between passing the medical and physically signing on the dotted line, Guðjohnsen had been contacted by Spurs manager Harry Redknapp and had his head turned. As far as Sullivan was concerned, this wasn't getting jilted at the altar; it was being divorced halfway through the wedding reception. The Hammers were even left to foot a £5,000 bill for Guðjohnsen's flight, hotel, and hospital visit.

'We thought we had a deal, the player even had a medical,' Sullivan fumed. 'I feel very let down by Tottenham. But I believe in karma and what goes around comes around.'

For once, Sullivan's judgment on transfers proved impeccable. Because karma came around three years later. This time, Tottenham officials were abuzz at having outmuscled Liverpool to sign Willian, the Brazilian winger who had been put up for sale by the Russian club Anzhi Makhachkala after its owner, the billionaire oil tycoon Suleiman Kerimov, grew weary of personally bankrolling the team. Having agreed to a price with Anzhi, Tottenham flew in Willian for a highly publicized medical. He arrived at the Spurs training ground to a flash of photographs and duly went through a battery of tests while Tottenham officials readied the necessary paperwork in an adjoining room. Everything was going smoothly until they tried to usher Willian into that room. The player wouldn't budge.

'I'm sorry, but I go to Chelsea,' he told them.

It turned out that all the hoopla surrounding Willian's medical had alerted Chelsea to the possibility of a deal with Anzhi and Kerimov happened to be tight with Roman Abramovich – a considerable advantage in the modern Premier League. One timely phone call between two Russian oligarchs allowed Chelsea to steal the player from right under the nose of their London rival, a fact that made José Mourinho – by this time back at Stamford Bridge for a second spell – positively giddy. 'That's the danger of medicals before contracts,' he said in a press conference later that day before graciously offering Tottenham some free advice. 'The best thing you can do is do the medical in secret.'

Yet for most of the Premier League, the new transfer economy was no laughing matter. The permanently elevated levels of stealth and panic forced clubs to cut corners as they raced to push deals over the line. Risky signings of injured players, temperamentally suspect players, and downright terrible players became commonplace. By 2012, when Steve Kean, the Blackburn Rovers manager, announced the Deadline Day signings of three guys he had never actually seen play before, hysterical shopping was a staple of the marketplace.

The explosion of agents on the scene only added to the confusion. As the likes of Jorge Mendes and Pini Zahavi grew more powerful and more prosperous, the number of would-be Jerry Maguires looking to cash in on the lucrative business of buying and selling players mushroomed. By 2014, there were an estimated 150,000 registered football agents operating in Europe alone – a number so absurd that simply keeping tabs on them had become an undertaking roughly akin to classifying all the species in a rain forest. Which is why FIFA decided that same year to do away with the concept of licensed agents altogether. The result is that Premier League clubs looking to make a purchase are often confronted by as many as four or five agents and intermediaries, all claiming to represent the same player. 'You don't know who to deal with,' said the owner of one Premier League club. 'And they all expect to be paid – "I've got exclusive rights for England", "I've got official rights for his club", and on and on. You're talking huge sums of money and the threats you get – I've had physical threats, threats of violence against my family. It's scary.'

In all the chaos, even some of English football's most reputable establishments struggled to keep up with the cost of doing business. Everton, one of the Football League's founder members, had emerged as a serial overachiever under David Moyes. But with an ancient stadium, Goodison Park, which had hosted a World Cup semi-final in 1966, and an owner, Bill Kenwright, whose modest personal wealth came from producing West End theatre, the club found itself unable to keep pace with its deeper-pocketed rivals. 'When David started, I told him: "I've got no money,"' Kenwright announced to an Everton supporters' group in a 2011 meeting to explain why proceeds from the £3 million sale of the South African midfielder Steven Pienaar hadn't been spent on acquiring new players. 'You have to battle with the bank, daily for me. They're desperate.' Aston Villa and Newcastle United wound up similarly hamstrung by a lack of disposable funds. Others got caught up in the hysteria and spent anyway, including Portsmouth, which ran up nine-figure debts and ran out of money to pay its players' salaries midway through the 2009–10 season.

Not even Arsenal, one of the most careful shoppers in the country, were immune to a transfer-market disaster.

Weighed down by the crushing debt burden of building the Emirates Stadium and Arsène Wenger's own financial conservatism, the Gunners decided that they couldn't lose in the hypercharged transfer market if they didn't play. The precipitous post-2006 decline in the quality of Arsenal's signings wasn't because Wenger suddenly lost his eye for talent but rather because Wenger wasn't willing to drive the club to ruin or sacrifice his principles to acquire it. It's why Arsenal claim to have nearly signed almost every superstar in world football. Cristiano Ronaldo, Lionel Messi, Zlatan Ibrahimović . . . They were all on Wenger's radar as teenagers before winding up elsewhere . . . In this brave new world, the way he moved in the market was painfully slow. So when he finally identified a player for a price he could stomach, it was often too late to turn back. Even if, as in the 2014 case of Kim Källström, a loan signing from Spartak Moscow, it was determined that the player was already damaged goods – Källström arrived with a broken back.

Worse for Arsenal than being unable to add world-class players was having to offload the ones they already had. Players Wenger had discovered, from Ashley Cole to midfielder Cesc Fàbregas, all bolted for the exit when the Gunners couldn't keep up with the salaries their rivals were offering elsewhere. It was no coincidence when the club's target subtly shifted from winning league titles to simply finishing in the top four. 'Agents knew we had to sell, that we didn't have the same financial power as the others,' Wenger said. 'On top of that, we called on young players. It was a way for us to survive. We had some good teams, but we lacked maturity, because we were younger than Chelsea and Man United.'

Across north London, one club found this volatile transfer economy rather to their liking. No one navigated the world of doublespeak and dirty tricks more expertly than Tottenham Hotspur. And for that, they were indebted to a bald, bespectacled Cambridge graduate named Daniel Levy.

Shy and studious, Levy was an unlikely candidate to emerge as the most feared negotiator in football. But then Tottenham were unlikely candidates to emerge as feared operators in any field until Levy joined the club in 2001. During the early years of the Premier League, Spurs were seen as a soft touch. The club's reputation for stylish football, forged in the 1950s and 1960s, had developed into a fixation for highly skilled players, who invariably commanded high wages but almost as invariably lacked the stomach for the physical demands of a Premier League season. Nothing seemed to sum up the prevailing opinion of the club like the speech that Alex Ferguson once delivered before a match against Spurs, as revealed by Roy Keane. It consisted of just three words: 'Lads, it's Tottenham.' Spurs were lightweights.

But that slowly began to change when they were acquired by Joe

Lewis, a billionaire currency speculator who knew a thing or two about making a profit from declining English institutions. Before buying Spurs, he was best known as one of the people, alongside George Soros, who bet in 1992 on the pound crashing out of the European Union's Exchange Rate Mechanism, which cost the British Treasury an estimated £3.4 billion.

Born in Bow, east London, just a half-dozen miles from White Hart Lane, Lewis had long since relocated to the tax-free sanctuary of the Bahamas by the time he acquired Spurs. Which meant he would need someone on the ground in London to run the club for him. That someone was Levy.

Levy, whose father founded the discount menswear retailer Mister Byrite, had graduated from Cambridge with an economics degree and managed or owned ten retail businesses of his own before he arrived in 1995 at the English National Investment Company, or ENIC, an offshore investment firm financed by Lewis and initially involved in textiles. Levy showed early promise. One of his first moves was to invest £6 million in a British internet start-up. Three years later, ENIC sold its 4 per cent stake in the company, Autonomy, for £150 million. Levy soon identified another investment opportunity he believed could offer similar returns. 'We chose football because it is the most popular sport on earth – and the biggest money-spinner,' Levy recalled later. 'We weren't just looking for a business growing at 10 per cent per annum. We were looking for something exciting.'

In 1997, ENIC waded into the sport, plunking down £40 million for a 25 per cent stake in Glasgow Rangers, where Levy sat on the board. They followed that early foray by acquiring stakes in the Italian club Vicenza, FC Basel in Switzerland, Slavia Prague in the Czech Republic, and the Greek side AEK Athens. An attempted takeover of Spurs in 1998 was rebuffed, but in December 2000, Alan Sugar agreed to sell ENIC a 29.9 per cent controlling interest in Tottenham for £22 million, a figure that delighted Levy. At eighty pence a share, ENIC was paying twenty pence less than it had offered – and Sugar had rejected – eighteen months earlier.

Levy was appointed chairman and immediately took control of the club's transfer activity, where large sums of money were being wasted on underachieving players. 'The club has spent more money than Arsenal over the past few years, and where has it got us?' he inquired at the time. 'It's easy just to keep buying players. But if they don't work out, you end up writing off tens of millions of pounds.'

The answer, Levy had decided, was to assign the business of buying and selling players to someone with a little more financial sense than the guy in a tracksuit sitting in the dugout. Which is just as well, because during his first eight years as chairman, Levy burned through five different managers. 'The English-style manager comes in and wants to get rid of half the players and bring in his own,' Levy told the *Sunday Times*. 'So the club writes off millions, selling at a loss and buying all over again.' So Levy adopted a two-tier management structure, hiring a head coach to train the team and a sporting director to oversee the club's transfers, a model that was common elsewhere in Europe but widely derided in English football. Former PSV Eindhoven executive Frank Arnesen occupied the role initially, followed by French scout Damien Comolli, and later the Italian Franco Baldini.

But it wasn't long before Daniel Levy determined that the best person to oversee the club's transfer business was Daniel Levy. 'I think people get too hung up on job titles,' he said. 'In terms of how we run this club, whether a person is called director of football, sporting director, chief scout, head of recruitment, their job is ultimately to assist the manager in finding quality players. It doesn't really matter what the title is.'

His intuition proved correct – and not for the last time. Levy swiftly earned a reputation as a fierce negotiator pathologically incapable of giving an inch or accepting a deal if it meant he didn't come out on top. When Manchester United finally concluded a £30.75 million deal for Dimitar Berbatov on 31 August 2008 – more than twelve months after the Bulgarian striker first informed Spurs of his desire to move to Old Trafford – Alex Ferguson described negotiating with Levy as 'more painful than my hip replacement'. But driving a hard bargain was more than just Levy's schtick. With each painstaking transaction, he was slowly turning Tottenham into a permanent member of the Premier League's elite, beating his rivals in the transfer market one transfer at a time before beating them on the pitch.

As a football outsider, Levy knew little about the conventions that governed the business of transfers. But he didn't let that worry him. He simply ignored them. When Chelsea identified Spurs play-maker Luka Modrić as their main summer transfer target in July 2011, the Blues submitted a £22 million bid as a way of opening negotiations with Tottenham. Levy refused to enter into negotiations at all. One week later, Modrić announced that he wanted to join Chelsea and revealed he had a 'gentleman's agreement' with Levy that would allow him to leave for a bigger club. Levy denied the existence of such an agreement. On 31 August, the final day of the transfer window, Levy's brinkmanship appeared to have paid off. Chelsea submitted a new £40 million offer for Modrić, paving the way for the want-away midfielder finally to depart for Stamford Bridge for nearly twice the initial offer. Or not. The new bid was rejected, and Modrić was forced to remain at Spurs against his will for a further twelve months. The following summer, he was sold to Madrid for around £30 million.

'He is a calculated guy and he is prepared to wait and wait,' Comolli said. 'That is why he always wins.'

It wasn't only transfer conventions that Levy ignored. According to the Lyon president Jean-Michel Aulas, with whom Tottenham struck a deal to buy the French goalkeeper Hugo Lloris in 2012, Levy frequently disregarded contractual clauses and provisions that he had already agreed to. 'He talks a lot and goes back on what we have agreed in writing,' Aulas complained. 'The negotiation with the Tottenham directors has been the hardest I have ever had to undergo in twenty-five years.' Levy also refused to deal with clubs he perceived to be Tottenham's closest competition. He once inter-vened at the last minute to prevent Emmanuel Adebayor from joining West Ham on loan, ignoring his own advisers, because he deemed it unwise to help a rival for a top-four spot. West Ham finished that season in twelfth.

Yet Levy has proved to be much more than just a stubborn deal-maker. While other chairmen appeared mystified by fluctuations in the transfer market, Levy prospered. The Tottenham chairman was among the first to identify an inefficiency in the new marketplace: young home-grown players – especially those holding British passports – were overvalued relative to other players. Long before most teams clocked this development, Levy made it his business to target youngsters with major resale value, stocking the Spurs bench with up-and-coming English talent and continually renegotiating contracts so that no player ever reached the final eighteen months of his deal. The upshot is that when it comes to selling players, Levy is like a luxury boutique on the Champs-Élysées – nothing is ever on sale. Even those players who don't make the grade at Spurs end up commanding huge fees on the open market. 'Some of the best acquisitions have been players that many may not have heard of or haven't been acquired for large sums of money,' Levy explained. In the summer of 2017, for instance, Spurs ditched five reserve players who had scraped together just 117 Premier League appearances between them. The total sum Levy earned for that dead weight came to a remarkable £46 million.

On the rare occasions that Levy agrees to part with one of his most valued players, as he did with Gareth Bale, his unblinking approach is cold enough to shake down anyone. Even Real Madrid. In the summer of 2013, Madrid had made Bale their primary target just as they had done with Cristiano Ronaldo four years earlier. Levy could see the writing on the wall – no one chooses life on the Tottenham High Road over the Bernabéu. But if Bale was heading for the White Hart Lane exit, it would have to be on Tottenham's terms. And Levy had already put Spurs in the strongest possible position. During Bale's six years at Tottenham, one club insider estimated his contract had been redrafted as many as seven times, ensuring Spurs would receive full value for their most exciting player. When Real submitted an opening offer of £55 million for Bale, Levy decided it was too low. But instead of summarily rejecting the offer, he played the game, twice flying out to Spain on a private jet to discuss terms with Real president Florentino Pérez. Throughout those talks, Madrid officials were adamant that the value of the Bale deal could not surpass the €96 million they had paid to acquire Cristiano Ronaldo from United. Ronaldo was their star man, they explained, and it would be unseemly to spend more for anyone else.

That was a crucial tactical mistake. Real had unwittingly shown Levy how high they were prepared to go.

After dragging on all summer in phone calls and text messages between Real, Levy, and Bale's agent, Jonathan Barnett (the erstwhile architect of the Ashley Cole-to-Chelsea deal), the two clubs struck an agreement in the final forty-eight hours of the window. Tottenham would sell Bale for €91 million. At least, that was the official fee. It later transpired that when Madrid sought to pay that amount in instalments Levy balked. He wanted the cash up front. So with the biggest transfer of the year threatening to unravel before their eyes, Madrid agreed to cough up a world-record €100.8 million fee for Bale provided no one acknowledged the revised figure in public. Levy had done it again.

Not everyone was so shrewd. In their haste to keep up with the Joneses, chief executives around the league sourced cash for transfers wherever they could. Banks weren't exactly inclined to lend to football teams when they knew how irresponsibly they were run – *You plan to take this £10 million loan and blow it on a teenager from where?* Besides, from the time the credit crunch hit Britain around 2008, the banks didn't have that kind of money to fork over. The one thing football clubs had going for them was a guarantee that the money tap from the Premier League would stay open for the foreseeable future. And for a few institutions less respectable than your average City of London bank, that was good enough.

With the full blessing of the league, clubs began borrowing money for transfers from privately held funds against future payouts from the Premier League. The team would have the money wired from a company such as VIBRAC, based in the British Virgin Islands, in exchange for a promissory note stating that in the next round of payouts the Premier League would divert the club's share directly back to VIBRAC. Due to banking secrecy laws in the BVI, no one knew who the money behind VIBRAC belonged to. All they knew was that they had cash on hand and could subsidize their football spending habits.

While it might have felt like English football loan-sharking, everything about it was perfectly legal.

Even more extreme was a financing solution that landed on

Premier League shores from South America in the mid 2000s called Third-Party Ownership. The system was simple. A club has a player on its books but needs to raise some cash quickly – except it doesn't want to sell him. So instead of losing him entirely, it pawns off a stake in his 'economic rights' to any third party prepared to stump up the cash. This can be an individual, an investment fund, or occasionally a letterbox company based in Luxembourg. In exchange for their investment, the third party is entitled to an equivalent share of the transfer fee received by the club when it sells the player on. In other words, the 30 per cent stake it bought in a player for €1 million would later triple in value when that player was sold for €10 million. As of 2015, third-party owners were earning about $360 million a year according to FIFA – some 10 per cent of all spending on transfers.

For many clubs, particularly in Spain, Portugal, and South America, TPO was a vital crutch. Atlético Madrid, despite mountains of debt, reached the 2014 Champions League final with a whole squad of players secured on so-called alternative financing.

But the system has two major flaws.

One is that it perverts incentives. From the moment another club makes an offer for the player, investors have a concrete figure for their potential return. And with dozens of potentially value-damaging factors lurking around the corner – from injuries to sudden dips in form – the investors would prefer to cash in sooner rather than later, so they lean on the club to sell. This is what troubled FIFA and UEFA because those authorities don't want anyone but clubs and players to have a say over how talent moves. One prominent investor in third-party funds rejected the premise that he had any influence over when anyone was sold – though his defence was perhaps even more frightening.

'I never even met 95 per cent of the players I owned!' he protested.

The other problem with TPO was that the whole marketplace for 'economic rights' was completely unregulated, leaving it exposed to fraud, tax evasion, and money laundering. The precise ownership and financial backing of the funds disappeared down warrens of shell corporations dotted around the usual list of tax havens and tax-friendly hideouts – Luxembourg, Ireland, the Caribbean. Some funds were so desperate to remain untraceable that they set themselves up as bearer-share companies, meaning the owner is whoever happens to be physically holding the paper certificate.

At Premier League headquarters, the words 'Third-Party Ownership' were first mentioned around the year 2000 when chief executive Richard Scudamore learned about it from someone who knew far more about English football's transfer market than the chief executive of the Premier League. Pini Zahavi explained the whole system to him. Zahavi, of course, knew intimately how it worked. The Israeli agent was one of its most loyal users.

TPO, in fact, helped Zahavi and Jorge Mendes become so influential over the next decade – directly and indirectly through various investment vehicles – that according to one president of a major European club, who asked to remain anonymous, every transfer on the Continent somehow involved 'Pini and Jorge, Pini and Jorge' if you looked hard enough. And that was certainly true of the deal that would eventually bring about the end of TPO in the Premier League: the transfers of Carlos Tevez and Javier Mascherano.

The pair of Argentine stars had been plying their trade at Corinthians in Brazil. Mascherano was a tough-tackling defensive midfielder; Tevez had just scored twenty-five goals in thirty-eight games. West Ham wasn't an obvious destination for a couple of players of that calibre – their future stints at Manchester United, Man City, Liverpool, and Barcelona would make that much clear. But there was a compelling business reason for them to land in east London. Their agent and the owners of their economic rights were involved in a takeover bid for West Ham by an Israeli businessman and hotelier named Eli Papouchado.

The players had to arrive before the takeover actually went through because the deals had to be done within the transfer window. So a deal was hastily arranged, Tevez and Mascherano landed at West Ham, and the paperwork was sent off to the league office. Well, not all the paperwork. Because buried in their contracts was a clause that West Ham didn't reveal to the league, a clause that gave undue control to the company that held the players' transfer rights and that counted among its investors none other than Pini Zahavi. 'It is quite simple. If the players are a big success, I make money,' Zahavi said at the time, by way of clarifying his role. 'Not just if they leave West Ham in the future but if they do well at West Ham.'

When the takeover bid fell apart and West Ham were sold to Icelandic investors instead, Tevez and Mascherano were stuck there. Things became more complicated in March 2007 when the Premier League uncovered the third-party arrangement and charged West Ham with illegally registering the two Argentine players, eventually nailing the club with a fine of £5.5 million.

That would have been the end of it had Tevez not been such a damned good player.

He scored seven goals in West Ham's last ten games of the season to save the club from relegation. Sheffield United, the club that went down instead, were incensed. The Hammers had been rescued by a player they were never supposed to have. Sheffield United sued immediately. It took two years for the matter to be resolved, and the two clubs reached an out-of-court settlement in excess of £10 million. The case also led the Premier League to ban Third-Party Ownership years before FIFA would move to do the same.

But most important of all for West Ham, despite their clumsy efforts to keep up with the rest of the league on the cheap, the club were allowed to stay in the Premier League. No amount of transfer-market embarrassment could take that away.

18

MANCHESTER CITY, STILL rolling in Abu Dhabi's initial investment, had no such need for backdoor player-financing schemes. In the first four years as an Emirati plaything, the club spent upwards of £500 million in the transfer market. 'I'm sitting in front of players and I haven't got a cabinet full of trophies,' former sporting director Brian Marwood said of the club's splurge. 'I've literally got some finance and a vision. And I'm saying, "Guys, come and create history with us."'

In order to create that history – any history at all – it wasn't enough for City to vacuum up all the talent it could get its hands on to become stronger. The plan was also to deliberately weaken its opponents. So early on, City identified which clubs were most likely to challenge it for one of the Champions League spots and went about poaching their best players. From Arsenal, City lifted four key players in the space of three years, prompting jokes that the Gunners were just a City feeder club. From Everton, they took a club player of the year in defender Joleon Lescott and midfielder Jack Rodwell. And from Aston Villa, City ripped away the two most reliable professionals in the squad: Gareth Barry and James Milner. 'We crippled Villa,' former chief executive Garry Cook remembered.

The shopping spree began to pay dividends in subtle ways inside the dressing room as the culture slowly evolved. Senior professionals, guys who had won trophies elsewhere, set the tone – even those who didn't see much playing time, former Arsenal captain Patrick Vieira and his balky knees, for example. The first pay-off in silverware came in 2011 when Abu Dhabi's Manchester City lifted the FA Cup, the club's first major trophy in thirty-five years.

The real climax, however, came a year later: the tightest finish in the Premier League era.

Almost untouchable in the first half of the 2011–12 season, City hit late January three points clear of Manchester United. For the first time in decades, they could now be considered title contenders. The club's Cityness soon caught up to them, though. From that perch atop the standings, they tumbled over the next three months to eight points behind United after a loss to Arsenal in early April. That, the City players thought, was that. Eight points back with six games to play meant it was over. United don't throw those leads away.

City's dressing room was tense and manager Roberto Mancini was flying off the handle even more often than usual. He didn't like the squad he had and made no secret of it. That's when City's chairman, the enigmatic Khaldoon al-Mubarak, stepped in for a rare address to the team. Never raising his voice, he calmed things down after Arsenal. He reminded them that City weren't dead yet. There was still time.

The players didn't really believe him until United spun into a mini-collapse of their own. By the end of April, the gap between the sides had eroded completely. The two Manchester clubs arrived at the final day of the season level on points again. City had only a slight edge by virtue of goal difference.

United would have to travel to eleventh-place Sunderland, a side with absolutely nothing left to play for that season in the morass of mid table. City's match-up against Queens Park Rangers wasn't quite as favourable. Though QPR sat seventeenth there was still a danger of going down if they lost and other results broke against them. No one likes to face a team playing for its life, even one with the worst away record in the league.

What happened over the course of that Sunday afternoon, 13 May 2012, would rattle and elate and torment and traumatize every football fan in Manchester, red and blue, over and over again in the space of two frenetic hours. Even in their wildest dreams, the Premier League could have never scripted anything remotely close. It would have been a little too much.

The agony and insanity of that afternoon went like this:

3 p.m. In east Manchester and Sunderland and around the rest of the Premier League, the final day of the season begins with ten simultaneous kick-offs.

3.01 p.m. Wayne Rooney scores practically from the whistle for Manchester United at Sunderland, putting one hand on the trophy. News immediately filters back to the Etihad, where the ensuing feeling of existential dread was all too familiar.

3.39 p.m. At the Etihad, Pablo Zabaleta scores for City to make it 1–0. As it stands, City will win the title on goal difference.

4.03 p.m. Typical City. Moments after the second half kicks off, City concede an equalizing goal and metaphorically push the trophy back into United's hands. (In fact, the Premier League wheeled out two copies of the trophy that day – one in Manchester and one in Sunderland.)

4.21 p.m. City go down 2–1 to QPR. It has to be over now.

4.37 p.m. As Man City head into stoppage time, Edin Džeko, thrown into the game by Mancini after the second QPR goal, gives the home fans a glimmer of hope and equalizes. 2–2.

4.39 p.m. The final whistle blows at Sunderland and United win 1–0. Sky Sports' coverage goes to a split screen.

On the right side, United fans are smiling. They know it's 2–2 in Manchester. They think they're moments away from a twentieth title. Sky cut to a supporter holding a mobile phone to his ear.

On the left side of the screen, City have the ball in the middle of the pitch. 'It's finished at Sunderland,' says commentator Martin Tyler, the tension mounting in his voice. 'Manchester United have done all they can. That Rooney goal was enough for the three points.' City work the ball to the edge of the QPR box. Mario Balotelli controls it, and while all six foot two of his chiselled frame tumbles backwards, he squeezes out a pass to his right towards Sergio Agüero – ninety-three minutes, twenty seconds on the clock. 'Manchester City are still alive here . . . Balotelli . . . Agüerooooooo!'

The Argentine connects with his right foot. The ball hits the back of the net. And City go up 3–2. Agüero rips off his shirt as 47,000 people inside the Etihad lose their minds.

'I swear you'll never see anything like this ever again!' Tyler howls.

'So watch it! Drink it in . . . They've just heard the news at the Stadium of Light. Two goals in added time for Manchester City to snatch the title away from Manchester United.'

Those words, 'snatch the title away from Manchester United'. Four years earlier, the suggestion of City's pulling that off would have been too insane to contemplate. Now the noisy neighbours owned the most extraordinary finish to a season in the Premier League era – a genuinely remarkable football moment – to hold up and vindicate the whole lavishly funded project.

In the Gulf, Sheikh Mansour celebrated with his brother, the ruler of Abu Dhabi, and a white-frosted cake was wheeled out on a cart. It had two versions of the Man City logo and, right in the middle, a one-foot piece of silverware made out of pastry. Which looked nothing like the Premier League trophy.

Through gritted teeth, Ferguson had to congratulate United's local rivals.

'It's a very, very difficult league to win,' he said at the Stadium of Light. 'We know that because, as we've experienced today, we've lost on goal difference.' About thirty seconds of magnanimity were all he could muster before offering a reminder of how he really saw the world.

'They can go on as much as they like,' Ferguson added. 'That's what you would expect, but the history of our club stands us aside . . . It will take them a century to get to our level of history.'

There was no way Ferguson could let City rob him again next season. He immediately began plotting revenge. Without over-thinking it, he decided the solution was more firepower. And in the summer of 2012, the most dangerous weapon in England was that season's top scorer, Arsenal's Dutch striker, Robin van Persie. Thirty goals in thirty-eight league appearances? That would do Ferguson very nicely.

From the moment Manchester United opened talks with Arsenal, the Gunners were at a disadvantage. Van Persie had only one year left on his contract and was refusing to sign a new one. Arsenal could technically enforce it, keeping the disgruntled forward at the club for another year, but then he could leave for nothing the following summer, costing the Gunners a potential fee north of £20 million. It didn't help that Wenger was still sweating Arsenal's finances – he simply couldn't carry the massive salaries that world-beaters like Van Persie commanded in their prime. But perhaps most damning of all, Van Persie had confessed to Wenger that he wanted to leave. At that point, there is little a manager can do except try to get a good price. Ferguson knew it, too. He was prepared to turn the screws on Arsenal in precisely the same way Real Madrid had turned the screws on him over Ronaldo.

Negotiations didn't go as quickly as Ferguson had hoped. Manchester City and Juventus were sniffing around Van Persie, too, and Wenger's preference was to sell the striker abroad rather than to a direct rival in England. In meeting after meeting with Arsenal, in call after call, United chief executive David Gill banged his head against what he felt was an excessive asking price from the Gunners' executives. Finally, when he'd had enough, he told Ferguson that this transfer would have to be done old-school, manager to manager.

On 15 August, Ferguson picked up the phone and dialled Wenger's personal mobile. He found Wenger in a car on France's A13 autoroute speeding between Paris and Brittany. Wenger was on his way to Le Havre for a friendly between France and Uruguay, which he was due to cover as a pundit for TF1.

'*Arsène, it's Alex . . .*'

This is not how deals were done any more. Wenger couldn't remember the last time he'd negotiated directly with another manager about a major transfer. But for all of his scrapes and skirmishes with Ferguson over the years, he respected the man for calling. The two old generals were going to sort this out – but not before Ferguson tried to lowball Wenger first.

The call didn't last long. Over the noise of the car and the A13 rushing by, Wenger nudged Ferguson's offer north until he reached £24 million – £22.5 now and another £1.5 if United and Van Persie won a Premier League title in the next four years.

Fine, then. It was settled.

Wenger 'could run a poker school in Govan', Ferguson would say later. 'He got a great price but we are also happy the matter is concluded.' There was no point in keeping it a secret now. Wenger arrived in Le Havre and confirmed the deal right on French TV during the game.

'It's always sad, but there's the economic reality and the will of the player,' he lamented. 'When you can't extend a player in the last year of his contract, you have no choice but to let him go.'

19

It had become an occupational hazard for Premier League fans that when they bought a shirt with a player's name on the back the £70 garment they just splashed out for now had a shorter shelf life than the latest iPhone.

Not only did the kit designs change every year in a perpetual, ever-so-slight rebranding of the same basic colour scheme and format; the supercharged transfer market meant the playing squads were in a state of permanent flux, too. The star player whose name was emblazoned on the back would soon be replaced in the team by a big-money signing from Spain or Germany or Italy before getting shipped off in the other direction.

What concerned Premier League supporters far more than the players leaving England were the owners and executives flooding in from the opposite direction. From Roman Abramovich to the Abu Dhabi royal family, foreign owners all seemed to want the same thing – modern stadiums, all-encompassing corporate sponsorship, and slightly pricier tickets. And by 2012, buyers had barged in from every corner of the globe. Italian businessmen took control of Watford. An Indian poultry tycoon picked off Blackburn Rovers. Leicester City had been acquired by a Thai duty-free retail magnate. Out of nowhere, English football had become the world's leading playground for billionaires, the 1 per cent of the global 1 per cent, who found that the Premier League was now a more exclusive spot than Monte Carlo or the private dining room at El Bulli.

Only Chinese investors seemed unusually shy about stepping behind the Premier League's velvet rope. Not that they were lacking for invitations. China was linked with a bid for Liverpool in 2010 and a government vehicle later bought a stake in Manchester City.

But the influx from Beijing and Shanghai didn't materialize with the force many expected it to. Businessman Gao Jisheng took an 80 per cent stake in Southampton in 2017, a year after another entrepreneur, Guochuan Lai, took over West Bromwich Albion. Lai's approach was typical of many Chinese investors in football: he hired a local firm to advise him, asked which was the best available Premier League club on the market, and was referred to the second-largest team in Birmingham, for which he stumped up around £200 million. Simple.

By 2018, the prospects for further Premier League club acquisitions from China had dimmed, however, due to the government's efforts to curb capital flight. Chinese investors were more likely to spend their money trying to win promotion with Championship teams, advertising on Premier League kits, or bringing overpaid players to their own domestic league.

Which left plenty of room over the past decade for Americans to move in.

Nowhere on earth went gaga for English football clubs quite like the United States. Between 2005 and 2012, seven clubs fell to Yanks. And the new owners weren't crossing the Atlantic to mess around. Manchester United were the first prize to go, snapped up in the Glazers' leveraged buyout. In Birmingham, Aston Villa went in 2006 to the billionaire chairman of credit-card giant MBNA, Randy Lerner, while a pair of Texans took the plunge at Liverpool in 2007. The Premier League's leadership had no problem at all with these developments. In fact, chief executive Richard Scudamore actively encouraged American investors to dive in because he trusted their standards of doing business, knew where their money was coming from, and generally felt confident they wouldn't cut and run after one bad season. For these characters, pre-vetted by Wall Street, the fit and proper persons test was a formality.

Interest in taking over English football's oldest institutions grew so fervent that more than one billionaire made a play on the same club. That was the case at Arsenal in 2007. The Gunners were one of the most attractive properties in the league – with an experienced manager, a shiny new stadium and, at that point, only a thin film of dust on the trophy cabinet – when they found themselves in the middle of a cold war between two people they'd never heard of: on one side, Stan Kroenke, a reserved Midwesterner who made his money in real estate but made a fortune by marrying a Walmart heiress; on the other, an Uzbek metals magnate named Alisher Usmanov with a personal passion for fencing. Both men mopped up as many shares as they could find. Kroenke sped to a 67 per cent stake in the club as Usmanov built up 30.4 per cent, including the shares formerly controlled by David Dein. The two men disagreed on pretty much everything, from Arsenal's financial prudence – which drove Usmanov crazy – to how to handle the future of Arsène Wenger.

Kroenke was perfectly content to keep the club ticking over on its self-sustaining model, just as he did with the four pro-sports franchises he owned in the United States – the NBA's Denver Nuggets, the NHL's Colorado Avalanche, the NFL's St Louis Rams, and MLS's Colorado Rapids. Accusations that Kroenke prioritizes investment in the buildings those teams play in over actual competitive success are hard to brush off when you consider that through fifty-four combined seasons of Kroenke ownership those teams have exactly two championship titles between them. The Avalanche won a Stanley Cup and the Rapids lifted the MLS Cup. Arsenal have not come close to a Premier League title on Kroenke's watch.

'It doesn't help to turn a blind eye to the reality of the situation and keep thinking of ourselves as being in the same league as Real Madrid, Chelsea, Manchester City and Barcelona,' Usmanov wrote in a scathing open letter to Arsenal's board in 2012. 'To have a fighting chance of success, which means winning trophies, we need to match them in every aspect, including, if not first and foremost, financial.'

Usmanov sided early on with the vocal faction of fans who wanted Wenger out. Yet Kroenke appeared so committed to Wenger that the Frenchman often seemed as immovable as the stadium he helped to build.

From the time it began in 2007, the Usmanov–Kroenke battle simmered for the next ten years with no sign of abating. It could have ended when Kroenke made a widely reported $730 million bid for Usmanov's stake in the club in 2017. But while Usmanov was generally open to a sale, he specified that he would consider only buyers not named Stan Kroenke. That was until he ran out of patience with Stan Kroenke in the summer of 2018 and abruptly changed his mind. He cashed out his stake in a deal that valued Arsenal at £1.8 billion.

Silent Stan, meanwhile, was perfectly content to stick to the model set by the Glazers and keep schtum.

In that respect, the next American to follow the Glazers into purchasing one of English football's national institutions set himself apart. Because silence in the sports world was not a problem that afflicted John W. Henry. Not when he bought the Boston Red Sox. And certainly not when his gaze settled in 2009 on Liverpool Football Club.

Henry, a wispy, grey-haired trader, knew a thing or two about cashing in on storied teams with massive fan bases, celebrated stadiums, and a long title drought. As the owner of the Red Sox, he had delivered the team its first World Series title in eighty-six years. What he knew next to nothing about was English football. That was until he received a text message from Joe Januszewski, an employee in the Red Sox corporate sales department, that contained a simple request: 'Save my club!'

That was the gist of it, anyway. In a follow-up email, Januszewski outlined the parlous state that Liverpool – the most successful team in England in the twentieth century but without a league title since 1990 – had fallen into under its current owners, Tom Hicks and George Gillett Jr. Their takeover of the club, another leveraged buyout, had saddled Liverpool with eye-watering debts of £351 million, including a £237 million loan from Royal Bank of Scotland that was due in a matter of weeks. Unable to meet those obligations, Liverpool faced a genuine risk of bankruptcy. With the deadline for repayment looming, the club's loans had been moved to RBS's toxic-assets division, and the Anfield boardroom had descended into open warfare. The co-owners were no longer on speaking terms; the club were being run by a three-man board that were currently negotiating to sell the team to one of four interested parties despite furious opposition from Hicks, who had unsuccessfully attempted to have them all sacked. By speakerphone.

For Liverpool supporters, this unseemly squabble represented a threat to their beloved club's future. For a sharp-eyed investor, however, it represented a tantalizing opportunity. 'If one group shows RBS proof of funds (something that has yet to happen among any of the bidding groups) to clear off the outstanding debt, Hicks/Gillett may not have any choice in the matter but to accept,' Januszewski explained in his email to Henry. 'The bank will legally be able to force that deal.'

Henry was intrigued. Baseball may have been his passion, but his US sports interests weren't limited to the Red Sox. Fenway Sports Group, the company he had founded with veteran Hollywood producer Tom Werner in 2002, also owned a 50 per cent stake in the NASCAR auto-racing team Roush Fenway Racing, as well as 80 per cent of a regional sports channel. But here was an opportunity to turn it into a global operation. 'In my opinion it would be the deal of the century,' Januszewski wrote in his email. 'Liverpool FC are a top-five sports brand worldwide and are just begging to be properly marketed and leveraged globally among the soccer-mad masses.'

Liverpool had missed the Premier League's first marketing explosion back when Martin Edwards was turning Man United into Merchandise United. But Januszewski was right. The club embodied all of the gritty authenticity and ancient tradition that new Premier League fans around the world were going crazy for. Those supporters dreamed of standing on the Kop, so named more than a hundred years before by a local sports journalist who thought that the wide single tier bore a striking resemblance to the Spion Kop, a South African hill that had proven strategically significant in the Second Boer War. (No team in the world would even think of manufacturing history that obscure today.)

And once those fans made it to Anfield, on the south side of Stanley Park, they all wanted to do the same thing: sing along to a Rodgers and Hammerstein show tune. 'You'll Never Walk Alone' had become the most famous anthem in world football, a spine-tingling chorus belted out before every game. Other clubs became so envious of it that they simply stole it for themselves and built it into their own pre-match routines from Borussia Dortmund to FC Tokyo.

For any Premier League investor in the market for something iconic, this was the club.

On 15 October 2010, exactly sixty-six days after Januszewski's email dropped into his in-box, Henry was introduced as Liverpool's new owner.

'We're here to win,' Henry declared on the steps of the Royal Courts of Justice shortly after completing his takeover of the club. 'We are committed first and foremost to winning. We have a history of winning, and today we want Liverpool supporters to know that this approach is what we intend to bring to this great club.'

It didn't take long for Henry to realize that the winning might have to wait a while. The $487 million that FSG had spent to acquire the club, he realized, had bought a lot of headaches. Hicks and Gillett had left Liverpool with a mediocre squad of ageing players, a deeply unpopular manager, Roy Hodgson, and absolutely no idea what to do about the team's fabled Anfield Stadium, which needed to be redeveloped to bring it up to modern money-making standards or else abandoned in favour of building a new venue altogether.

Still, Henry wasn't unduly fazed. The Red Sox had been faced with similar problems when he arrived there, and as he learned more about his new team and the broader landscape of English football, he began to feel certain that the same tricks he used in Boston would work 4,000 miles away in another cold northern city with rabidly loyal supporters and their own ninety-year-old stadium. 'It became clear to me there were a number of similarities between the Reds and the Red Sox, as well as Liverpool and Boston and their respective fan bases,' Henry said. What English football needed, he decided, was some good old-fashioned American innovation.

The first challenge was to improve Liverpool on the pitch. It was no secret how the owners had done this in Boston. In fact, they were shooting a Hollywood movie about it.

Technically, *Moneyball*, the film starring Brad Pitt and based on a Michael Lewis book, was about the Oakland A's and their stats-obsessed general manager Billy Beane, not the Red Sox. But no team in Major League Baseball had stuck to its central thesis – a data-driven approach to identifying value that others have missed – more scrupulously or successfully than the Red Sox. One of

Henry's first moves after buying the team was to try to hire Beane, though he couldn't be persuaded to leave northern California for the north-east, and the job ended up going to Theo Epstein, who picked up a bunch of players for relative peanuts and helped the Red Sox win the World Series the next year.

Henry knew the formula that built Boston into a baseball champion couldn't be imported wholesale into English football. But he suspected that the embrace of data analytics to drive team-building strategy could yield similar results. So when it came to hiring an executive to oversee player recruitment at Liverpool, Henry knew just the man to talk to.

Billy Beane.

'Billy had been closely studying the Premier League,' Henry said. '[He] called me shortly after the acquisition to recommend Damien Comolli as someone who had a similar viewpoint to his way of approaching baseball.'

Which is how Comolli ended up as director of football at Liverpool not long after the FSG takeover.

With Comolli in charge of recruiting players, Liverpool now needed someone to coach them. The club had made a dismal start to the season, and Hodgson had worn out his welcome with the supporters. Eager to get the fans back onside, Henry replaced him with a bona fide legend: Kenny Dalglish, back at the club for a second spell as manager some twenty years after walking away in the wake of Hillsborough.

The playing side now set, Henry could turn his attention to the club's commercial operations, which he felt were sorely in need of some US sports know-how. Despite a huge global following, Liverpool lagged far behind Manchester United, Arsenal, and even Chelsea in worldwide sponsorship and commercial revenues. If Fenway's marketing machine could put a Red Sox hat on the head of every kid in New England, how many Liverpool shirts could they sell in Merry Olde England – and the rest of the world beyond? The best part of all this, Henry realized, was they would get to keep all that money for themselves. Unlike baseball, where revenues are shared between all thirty teams, Liverpool would directly profit from FSG's expertise. 'We were constrained in MLB to working solely within New England with regard to merchandising and sponsorship,' Henry explained. 'We thought we could significantly boost revenues and work towards getting to a level playing field with Manchester United.' More than all that, Henry felt confident about turning Liverpool around because he trusted his own decision-making process. The other Premier League owners were mostly impatient and undisciplined. But Henry would operate with the same deliberate, analytical approach he had always relied on. After all, it had made him into a billionaire commodity trader with two World Series rings, and football was a simple game.

For once, it turned out Henry had made a small miscalculation. What he would soon discover – to his not inconsiderable cost – is there are few benefits to be gained from a rational approach if you aren't operating in a rational environment. And whatever else has been said about English football over the years, no one has ever accused it of that. Before long, Henry realized his error. The Premier League was a madhouse.

Within days of acquiring Liverpool, he was accused of orchestrating an 'epic swindle' by former owner Tom Hicks, who filed a claim for £1 billion in damages in a Dallas court. In a wide-ranging and thoroughly unhinged interview on Sky News, Hicks insisted that internet terrorists had waged a campaign to oust him as Liverpool owner and that the club's board were engaged in an organized conspiracy to sell the team behind his back. Then he dropped a truly shocking accusation, questioning the integrity of Sir Martin Broughton, Liverpool's independent chairman. 'He's a Chelsea fan – he's not even a Liverpool fan,' Hicks wailed. 'He wanted to be seen as the guy who got rid of the Americans.' Broughton immediately countersued.

Hicks' claims were summarily dismissed, but it wasn't long before Henry found himself battling a controversy that was harder to shake off. In a clash against Manchester United in 2011, Liverpool's Luis Suárez racially abused United defender Patrice Evra, calling the Frenchman *negrito* seven times and then pinching his skin, as if to emphasize the point. Everyone agreed it was utterly despicable behaviour. Or almost everyone. Instead of condemning Suárez's actions, Liverpool's players and coaches offered a robust defence of the Uruguayan striker. 'We support the wee man,' Dalglish said, after the incident came to light. 'The football club and everyone at the football club is totally and utterly fully behind Luis Suárez.' In case anyone failed to get the message, Dalglish had his players warm up on the pitch before their next match wearing T-shirts in support of their disgraced teammate.

Back in Boston, Henry watched events unfold with a mixture of disbelief and dismay. His star player – one of Comolli's early successes in the transfer market – had racially abused a fellow professional. And the club legend he had appointed to run the team, a man as synonymous with Liverpool as the Liver Bird, seemed to be actively endorsing it. Henry had seen some deeply strange things in his time at the Red Sox. But nothing in his time in baseball had prepared him to deal with this sort of unholy mess.

Which kind of showed. Because the sorry saga was somehow allowed to drag on for another four months through an FA investigation, a subsequent charge, a seven-day hearing, Suárez's receipt of an eight-match ban and a £40,000 fine, and, finally, the release of a 115-page FA report into the matter. None of which, amazingly enough, persuaded Dalglish, Suárez, or an increasingly loud minority of Liverpool fans to abandon their contention that Luis Suárez was somehow the wronged party in the whole affair.

Through all of this, Henry simply allowed the episode to play out. It might have rumbled on to this day were it not for the events of 11 February 2012, when someone finally forced Henry to put an end to the saga. It was on that day that Liverpool faced Manchester United for the first time since the incident occurred. And it was on that day that Suárez decided now was the perfect time to throw kerosene on the smoldering dispute by refusing to shake hands with Evra before kick-off. It was the *New York Times* that made Henry sit up and listen. 'If the Fenway Sports Group is to be the responsible team owner in soccer that it has proved to be in baseball,' read their page-one story on the latest Suárez–Evra eyesore, 'it needs to get hold of Liverpool, its club in England's Premier League, and repair its global image fast.' The *New York Times*, it should be noted, held a 7 per cent stake in Fenway Sports Group. Within twenty-four hours of publication, Dalglish, Suárez, and Liverpool managing director Ian Ayre had issued apologies for the club's handling of the matter. The episode was over.

But it was not forgotten. Dalglish was sacked at the end of the season, just twelve months into a three-year contract. It's fair to assume that his conduct during the Suárez affair played a major role in Henry's decision to fire Dalglish. But it's also true that results on the pitch were hardly spectacular, a fact at least partly attributable to Henry's unhappy discovery that football's transfer market was even trickier to navigate than a drawn-out racism controversy.

Henry's championship Red Sox teams were built on identifying market inefficiencies. What Billy Beane and Theo Epstein uncovered is that certain attributes in baseball were undervalued, specifically the ability to get runners on base. They exploited this by signing a bunch of players who excelled at doing exactly that with relatively cheap contracts, and their clubs won a ton of games. But two years into Henry's ownership, Liverpool's efforts to unearth similar inefficiencies in the Premier League were beginning to look like an expensive mistake.

In the two years following FSG's takeover, Liverpool had embarked on a £100 million spending spree that amounted to a pricey bet on their data-driven approach. Suárez was signed for £24 million; midfielders Stewart Downing and Jordan Henderson joined for £20 million and £16 million, respectively; £7.5 million was spent on Scotland's Charlie Adam; and a record £37 million went on striker Andy Carroll, making him the most expensive English player ever.

The sums involved certainly raised eyebrows. Rival clubs were staggered that Liverpool shelled out so much for Carroll, who had then featured in just eighteen Premier League games in his career. But the strategy behind the moves seemed clear, if a little simplistic. One year after finishing sixth in the league partly because of a record of scoring just fifty-nine goals in thirty-eight games, Liverpool had recruited some of the most prolific creators of chances in English football. The club's internal data revealed that Downing, Adam, and Henderson were all ranked in the top eight in chances created the season before yet were cheaper to acquire than many players who finished far below them in those same rankings. If the Red Sox had won games by getting runners on base, Liverpool were going to try to win games by creating shots on target.

It all sounded good in theory. Tom Werner even invoked Theo

Epstein's name when praising Liverpool's transfer dealings that summer. 'There is no question that Damien Comolli is cut from the same cloth as Theo,' Werner said.

But within a few months it became clear that Liverpool's fancy algorithms needed some work. The club's mission to create more scoring chances ended with Liverpool's tying the record for the lowest number of league goals in their history. At the end of the season, Comolli was sacked and followed Dalglish out the door. 'He did not really turn out to be someone who believed in the *Moneyball-*type of approach,' Henry recalled.

What Henry was starting to understand was that the laws that govern US sport – or the worlds of business, finance, or basic maths, for that matter – frequently don't apply to English football. And even those that do weren't applied frequently enough for Henry's liking. Take player contracts. When Liverpool acquired Luis Suárez, he signed a five-year deal, and Liverpool were expected to pay him for the duration of that contract regardless of injury, loss of form, or a sudden proclivity for biting opponents. But if Suárez decided he wanted to move on before that five-year contract expired, he was basically free to do so. Liverpool would receive a fee, of course. But in the world of football, contract law went out the window when a player – or his agent – decided it was time to go. No club could hold a player who wished to leave for long. They would eventually go. They always did.

Henry didn't think much of this arrangement. So he decided to do something about it. As it happened, Suárez did decide it was time to move on in the summer of 2013. His preferred destination: Arsenal, who were in the market for a new centre-forward after reluctantly allowing Robin van Persie to join Manchester United twelve months earlier. Liverpool didn't want to lose Suárez – especially not to a Premier League rival – but there was one minor catch. His contract contained a release clause that stipulated he was free to leave if any club bid more than £40 million. All of which made it rather awkward when Arsenal submitted an offer for Suárez in July for exactly £40,000,001.

By the terms of his contract, Suárez was free to leave Anfield. But Henry knew all about the value of contracts in football. He was fed up with being pushed around by players, agents, and Premier League rivals. So he resolved to take a leaf out of the players' manual. He would simply ignore the clause – and the contract – altogether. When Arsenal's offer arrived, Henry rejected it. 'What we've found is that contracts don't seem to mean a lot in England – actually, in world football,' Henry later explained. 'Since apparently these contracts don't seem to hold, we took the position that we're just not selling.'

The audacious move infuriated Arsenal and delighted Liverpool's supporters. When Henry tweeted about the developments later that day – 'What do you think they're smoking over there at Emirates?' – it infuriated Arsenal and delighted Liverpool's supporters even more.

But if Henry hoped his hard line would help to usher in the sort of binding contracts that exist in US sport, he would be disappointed. His stance towards Suárez – and later towards the Brazilian playmaker Philippe Coutinho, who was denied a move away from Liverpool in the waning days of the 2017 summer transfer window despite expressing a desire to leave – succeeded in keeping the player at Anfield. But in reality, it only delayed the inevitable. Both Suárez and Coutinho ended up joining FC Barcelona. Henry's quest for an edge in the transfer market went on. 'I don't believe you can find a more challenging enterprise than to try to win in English football,' he said.

Henry wasn't alone in believing there were market inefficiencies to exploit all over English football. As more American owners moved into the Premier League from US sport, where every team has an in-house analytics department mining data for opportunities to profit from, it was only natural they would pursue a similar approach with their football clubs. The only problem was no one seemed to be quite sure what they were looking for.

20

WHEN SHAHID KHAN, an auto-parts entrepreneur and owner of the NFL's Jacksonville Jaguars, took control of Fulham from Mohamed Al Fayed in July 2013, he became the sixth American owner of a Premier League team at that time. Like most of the others, he soon thought he'd identified an inefficiency in English football. This one was called Manchester United.

United had won the title the season before Khan's takeover, the club's thirteenth triumph in the Premier League era and the final championship of Alex Ferguson's twenty-seven-year tenure as manager. United's squad then was so deep, so stacked with high-priced, world-class players, Khan was told, that United could probably beat Fulham with its reserve team.

Which is exactly where Fulham decided to go shopping for players. First, the Cottagers recruited René Meulensteen, a Dutch assistant manager at Old Trafford, where he had worked on improving the skills of United's young players. Next, Fulham snapped up two of those young players, Ryan Tunnicliffe and Larnell Cole, to aid in their battle against relegation.

It's fair to say the double signing wasn't exactly hailed as a transfer coup when the United youngsters arrived at Craven Cottage on the final day of the January transfer window. Cole's lone senior appearance for United had come three years earlier, as a seventy-seventh-minute substitute in a League Cup win over Leeds while Tunnicliffe's United career encompassed a grand total of two first-team appearances – though that had been sufficient to win his father, Mick, a £10,000 payout thanks to a £100 bet he placed on his son's playing for the club one day. That was when Tunnicliffe was nine. But Khan wasn't looking for plaudits when he greenlit the deal. He was looking for value. And in the depths of Manchester United's reserve squad, he thought he'd found it. For all that the critics knew, Larnell Cole and Ryan Tunnicliffe could end up being the next David Beckham or Ryan Giggs.

Or not. Within three weeks of their arrival, Meulensteen was sacked and both Cole and Tunnicliffe were sent back to United, their loan deals terminated. Three months later, Fulham were relegated. The club's strategy of raiding the Manchester United reserves had backfired.

For Fulham, however, the search for a winning formula went on. Realizing that his own lack of Premier League expertise was a problem, Khan decided to delegate player recruitment to someone who knew a little more about football than he did. But not much. In 2017, Fulham announced that its director of football role would be filled by Khan's son, Tony, a former manager at a biodiesel company, whose primary qualification for a career in professional sport was that he'd kept score for his school basketball team. The following year, Khan earned the chance to test his data-driven approach to the transfer business where it really counted when Fulham were promoted to the Premier League – and backed it with £70 million worth of new players. They lasted all of one season before going straight back down.

Sunderland's Ellis Short, a private-equity manager from Missouri, was one of the few American owners who didn't come to English football explicitly looking for an inefficiency. But he discovered one anyway. Unfortunately, it was his own inefficiency at hiring managers.

In the ten years after Short took control of the Black Cats, thirteen different managers ran the team, a list that featured some of the most temperamental and tempestuous characters ever to set foot on a football pitch, from Paolo Di Canio and Roy Keane to Gus Poyet. Short, a keen cyclist, appeared to look for the same qualities in his managers as he does in his cycling partners. His favourite riding buddy when he goes to Hawaii is Lance Armstrong.

The last thing Randy Lerner wanted to do was Americanize Aston Villa.

He had no *Moneyball* plan for the club, no visions of outfoxing his rivals with an overwrought analytics model. He wasn't looking to create a revolution. A collector of art and a student of history, Lerner saw his mission differently: he would be a custodian of a once great institution. Something about Aston Villa awoke a nostalgia in him for an era of sporting stewardship that he'd never known.

When he acquired the club in 2006 for roughly £62 million, however, Lerner was clear-eyed enough to recognize that he was an interloper in England.

Sensitive to how fans would view him, he deliberately kept audio and video interviews to a minimum. Lerner had a better sense than most Americans of British attitudes towards foreigners – he'd studied at Clare College, Cambridge, and kept a home in Chelsea. And he knew that something about his American accent might offend the fans before he had a chance to restore their club to their former glory.

As it turned out, when supporters began chanting for his head a decade later, his accent would have nothing to do with it. By the time he sold Villa in 2016 after suffering massive losses, his best efforts at a club revival had long been obscured by miserable form on the pitch. His lasting impression of a decade in the English football ecosystem is one of unchecked lunacy among the people running it. Lerner's experience in the NFL had gotten him used to dealing with owners and executives, flawed as they might have been, who operated within a certain familiar business framework by an agreed-upon set of rules.

The Premier League, he discovered in 2006, could hardly have been more different as he found himself looking out at a Wild West, where he felt frauds and charlatans were allowed to roam freely. And by 2016, it was even worse. The Premier League appeared to be in the hands of the players and their agents – or was it the agents and their players?

'The intensity, the chaos,' he said, 'it either smokes some truth out of you, or you turn into one of them.'

That truth took years to dawn on Lerner. At the beginning of his tenure, he brought a giddy enthusiasm to the project he treated almost like art restoration. Enamoured with the authenticity of Villa and their history, he sought to put it on display wherever he could.

When they designed a mosaic for the stadium's famous Holte

End, he scrambled around Bloomsbury in London with an artist trying to identify precisely the right clarets and blues to match the club's colours. When they refurbished the Trinity Road stand, rather than dispose of an old stained-glass window, he had it shipped to his home on Long Island, where it still hangs today. And when he couldn't be in Birmingham to attend matches in person, Lerner would break his cardinal rule of never watching television and tune in from the States, plugging in the only set in his home before kick-off and unplugging it at full time.

'I have no problem being remembered as a sentimental putz,' he said in 2017, having withdrawn from the Premier League for good.

One of his earliest projects was restoring the derelict Victorian bar known as the Holte Hotel, which was across from Villa Park. That would be for the club's fans, his gift to them. The forty-four-year-old Lerner needed as much goodwill as he could afford. In those days, English football still got skittish around Americans stepping out of private jets into their local clubs with pockets full of dollar bills. What could a real estate and financial services billionaire possibly want with a team in the old heart of the West Midlands?

Truthfully, the trader in him liked the idea of holding a significant asset in a foreign currency. And the small-market NFL team owner enjoyed the prospect of adding a big-market club in one of England's largest cities. When he was asked to compare Cleveland and Birmingham, the soft-spoken Lerner had to admit he knew very little about the West Midlands – though he liked the echo of the American Midwest. Which is fair. Few Americans have ever heard of Birmingham. But even fewer Americans drop £60 million on a football team there, buy a farmhouse, and, while they're at it, also pick up a broken-down bar. To Villa supporters, the whole thing was dizzying. The pub was Lerner's peace offering. From 3,500 miles away, he made the call to brush out the cobwebs and fix the plumbing, put the rusty taps back in working order, and haul out the tree growing up through the floorboards. For more than twenty years, the Holte Hotel pub had been in tatters. Lerner was prepared to spend until it wasn't.

As for the club itself, the previous two decades were about as kind to Aston Villa as they'd been to the dusty bar. A team that had won a league title as recently as 1981 and been champions of Europe in 1982 were now solidly mid table. They had fallen behind the likes of Manchester United, Arsenal, and Chelsea during the ownership of Doug Ellis, a crotchety purveyor of all-inclusive Spanish vacations and very much of football's old school.

Lerner was in a different league of rich guy from Ellis. The son of a former US marine who went from selling furniture to running the credit-card giant MBNA, Randy was an Ivy League-educated professional investor. When his father died of brain cancer in 2002 at the age of sixty-nine, Randy inherited a philanthropic disposition and a share of more than $2 billion.

Keenly aware of his duty towards his father's legacy, Lerner felt his responsibility, above all, was to protect his fortune for the rest of the family and look after the properties he loved most, which included the Browns, never compromising their values for profit. Even as Al Lerner lay dying, he instructed Randy not to sell the naming rights to Cleveland Browns Stadium. Because of the NFL's revenue-sharing model, Lerner was quite literally costing the other owners money, but he stood firm. Never mind that the Browns were perennial losers. Between the time Al Lerner took over the team in 1998 and Randy's acquisition of Villa in 2006, the Browns had posted a winning record just once.

But unlike in English football, there is no penalty for terrible teams in the NFL, no threat of the financial catastrophe visited upon the Premier League's bottom three teams every season as they tumble down to the Championship. The Browns were free to play awful football for as long as they wanted, and their owners would still make money as members of the revenue-sharing NFL cartel.

Aston Villa, on the other hand, were a team of a certain pedigree. They weren't much in the Premier League or European trophy mix these days, but once upon a time they had been. More than that, Villa were a historic pillar of English football. Formed in 1874, they pre-dated Manchester United by four years and were nearly two decades older than Liverpool. In 1888, Villa carried enough clout to become a charter member of the Football League. And their stadium, Villa Park, had been the club's home since 1897. Lerner, a large donor to London's National Portrait Gallery, knew a museum when he saw one.

He'd caught Doug Ellis at the right time. Ellis had sacked thirteen different managers and outlasted an entire generation of haters. As the fans liked to say, Villa were the first club to enter the twentieth century and, thanks to Ellis, the last to leave it. But triple-bypass surgery did what the supporters never could, and pushed him out. In 2005, at the age of eighty-one, he started searching for a place to dump his shares.

By taking the plunge into the Premier League, Lerner was ahead of the curve. At the start of the 2006–7 season, only three other clubs were foreign owned. The rest of the league was still, for the most part, in the hands of home-grown magnates and small-time millionaires like Ellis.

And like the best of the old-school club custodians, Lerner believed. Really believed. So much so that he got a tattoo of the Villa logo, a rampant lion, on his ankle.

The pub and the stadium renovations were only the beginning. When the Aston Villa Supporters' Trust raised money for a statue of William McGregor, the club chairman who founded the Football League in 1888, Lerner pledged to match every penny.

Lerner was determined to earn the Villa faithful's trust by making an emotional connection, not just by selling them tickets and beer. The seduction was full of little gestures cooked up by Lerner himself. In November 2006, Lerner laid on ninety buses for 4,500 travelling Villa supporters making the four-hour round trip to London for a League Cup match against Chelsea. The following spring, he produced 40,000 claret-and-blue scarves for every fan who attended the final home game of the season, all emblazoned with PROUD HISTORY, BRIGHT FUTURE.

There would be grander gestures, too, moves that flew in the face of the Premier League's cash-hungry ethos. For two seasons, Lerner eschewed a major kit sponsorship worth several million pounds a year for a worthy cause. Instead of shilling for beer or airlines or shady online casinos, Lerner gave the real estate on the front of Villa's shirt to the Acorns Children's Hospice Trust. Only a bean counter made of stone could have criticized him. As Dave Woodhall, the editor of the club's fanzine, said, 'This was a club that was going places' for the first time in decades.

And among the people helping Lerner get there was a character who, by coincidence, had cropped up in Premier League history once before, General Charles Chandler 'Chuck' Krulak. A former Commandant of the US Marine Corps, Krulak was a veteran of Vietnam, Iraq, and Chelsea's preparations to face Liverpool on the final day of the 2003–4 season. But he popped up alongside Lerner at Villa because of a long-standing family connection to Lerner's father, whom he'd followed to MBNA.

If Lerner and the general were going to turn Villa around, all while bouncing back and forth across the Atlantic, they knew they'd need an effective way of keeping their fingers on the pulse. So the general waded into football's closest equivalent to a military quagmire: the Aston Villa message boards. Lerner begged him not to. But at least once a week, Krulak would engage with fans to take their temperature, hear their concerns, and address them in greater detail than any director in Premier League history.

His notes all began the same way, 'The General here,' and he signed off with the Marine Corps motto of *Semper fidelis* – always loyal. He fielded questions on everything from ticket prices to the brand of chocolate sold inside Villa Park and always, always about transfers. Lerner, too, got to know his constituents whenever he could, popping up in Birmingham pubs unannounced. He did his best to make the fans feel special because he wasn't just selling them a match-day experience, he was an outsider trying to figure out how to return their own culture to them. But, like Krulak, he understood there is no quicker way to a Premier League fan base's heart than spending money on players.

In Martin O'Neill, he found a manager who was more than happy to do that for him. A testy Northern Irishman who wore tracksuits on the touchline, grabbed his players by the collar to yell at them in training, and cultivated an expertise in crime and criminology (as a player, he occasionally travelled with homicide case files to pore over in hotels), O'Neill had been coaching in the top flight for a decade. In the first four seasons of spending lavishly on transfers and salaries, Villa splashed around £130 million in the transfer market, placing the club among Europe's most extravagant. But the strategy did yield some success. After an eleventh-place finish in the 2006–7 campaign, Villa finished in the top six for three straight seasons.

The only problem was that the Premier League equation for success – spend money, improve the team, never see that money again – went against every one of Lerner's investing instincts. This was not how his father had become a billionaire. And it was certainly not how Randy was going to stay one. It dawned on him that he was never going to recoup that money. He had to tighten the purse strings.

When O'Neill went upstairs for more money to spend on players in the summer of 2010, Lerner expressed some scepticism. He'd been baffled and frustrated by the type of players flooding into his club and drawing increasingly wild pay cheques. It seemed to him that O'Neill kept signing guys who were already in their late twenties on big wages with no resale value. They all seemed to be from the UK and Ireland, too, where they had learned to play direct football while the rest of the league developed a more sophisticated Continental approach. And what about promoting from the youth system? Lerner joked that the only reason O'Neill knew the club had an academy was because it trained on a neighbouring pitch.

With Villa more than £150 million in the hole, Lerner had no plans to dig himself any deeper.

It came to a head five days before the start of the 2010–11 season. O'Neill walked out on the club and left Lerner to fume. Villa hastily replaced O'Neill with Gérard Houllier, a Frenchman with chronic heart problems who 'was trying to make a soufflé with the wrong implements,' one former executive said. Even Houllier knew it. Looking at his squad, he told Lerner that none of the guys knew how to play football. But Lerner's problems only continued. O'Neill took Lerner to an arbitration tribunal to litigate the circumstances that led to his departure, and the proceedings dragged on for nine months.

Lerner exited the London arbitration hearing wondering what he had gotten himself into. He felt the arbitrators had little idea what they were ruling on. When the line of inquiry turned to Villa's transfer policy – the heart of O'Neill's gripe with the club – one person on the panel asked Lerner if he had consulted Villa's board about signing players. Lerner, stunned by the question, had to explain that because he owned 100 per cent of the club's shares, there wasn't a board. This detail, Lerner said, had somehow eluded the people making a multimillion-pound judgment on how he ran his club. Lerner ended up settling with O'Neill in 2011 on what the press described as 'amicable terms'. But the whole affair had spoiled Premier League club ownership for him. The frustration was no longer worth the narcotic effect that radiated through him in the beginning or in the years he owned the Browns before the violence of the NFL turned him off. The people who populated English football simply were not his sort.

Things that used to amuse him about this unique experience – hearing the roar inside Villa Park, an away trip to Scunthorpe – lost their lustre. Even when Villa reached the 2015 FA Cup final against Arsenal, Lerner couldn't wait to get out of Wembley. The awkward-ness of enduring small talk with Prince William, nominally a Villa fan, while the Gunners pummelled his team was too much for him. Lerner made a hasty exit after the game, thinking only of hopping in a car to his favourite pub in South Kensington.

Looking back, Lerner admits that he wasn't prepared for the everyday commitment it takes to run a successful Premier League club. At the time, it was one of seven or eight businesses he operated, and by comparison, football seemed like small potatoes. After all, Lerner was chairman of MBNA, whose market cap was greater than the value of all twenty Premier League clubs and all thirty-two NFL teams put together.

His other realization was that buying a Premier League club effectively meant buying it twice. NFL teams might be more expen-sive, but once you've bought one, there is almost no further spending except for free-agent players – operational costs are more or less covered by the league's revenue sharing and stadiums are paid for by the cities. In football, however, paying the list price on a club only guarantees that your chequebook will stay open. Villa's mis-adventures in the transfer market taught Lerner that much.

After 2010, a disenchanted Lerner let others run the club for him. With no continuity in the dugout, the club that had so recently become accustomed to top-six finishes were suddenly thrust into annual relegation battles. In March 2011, with Villa one point from the drop, times were so desperate that the general took things into his own hands and issued a rallying cry ahead of his unit's deployment to Everton's Goodison Park: 'When my Marines put on their uniforms and the emblem of the corps and went into battle and things got tough, they did not fight for their commander, they fought for their brothers-in-arms, the men wearing their uniform and emblem. When a player puts on a kit and wears the club badge, I would expect the same.'

Something clicked and Villa won four of their final eight games to avoid relegation. But it was only a temporary reprieve. The stress of O'Neill's exit and another relegation fight had taken its toll on Lerner, and he was determined not to put himself through it again. He decided to level with the fans.

'I have come to know well that fates are fickle in the business of English football. And I feel that I have pushed mine well past the limit,' Lerner wrote on the club's website. Like everything Lerner says and publishes, it was considered at length and laced with a carefully chosen reference. 'On a personal level it is time for me, like the Shunammite, to dwell among my own and get on with other aspects of my career, following a sale.'

The comparison to a character from the Old Testament's First Book of Kings went over most supporters' heads. But the message was clear: Lerner was ready to depart English football.

Lerner had, in fact, been prepared to dump Villa long before he clued in the fans. In the spring of 2014, he had a deal in place to sell to David Blitzer and Josh Harris. 'It was done,' said a person with direct knowledge of the agreement. Until it wasn't. The deal died on Aston Villa's training pitch when Belgian striker Christian Benteke, the club's best player, ruptured his Achilles tendon on a Thursday morning in April. Blitzer and Harris paused. Benteke was staring at six months on the sidelines, meaning he wouldn't play until deep into the following season, and with suitors lining up to pay north of £25 million to sign him that summer, he couldn't be sold. The done deal collapsed, and Blitzer and Harris landed at Palace instead.

Lerner said he also came close to a deal with a buyer in Abu

Dhabi, but that one fell through as well. In 2015, he was stuck. And the cycle of desperate short-term decisions that leads clubs to relegation had already begun.

The big things, the little things, everything was going wrong. The attention to detail that had won over the fans was a distant memory. In November 2015, when Villa unveiled their fifth manager in five years, the Frenchman Rémi Garde, the club couldn't even spell his name right. Villa made the official hashtag #WelcomeRemy. But like the typo, Garde became just one more *Zut alors!* on an ever-growing list. He lasted just twenty-three games.

Aston Villa were fighting a losing battle. The general tried to rally the troops again, this time drawing a parallel between Villa's predicament and his own experience in Iraq. 'Let's just look at Desert Storm,' he said, in an interview with the *Sun*. 'It was 4 a.m. and we were standing next to minefields separating Saudi Arabia and Kuwait. There were trenches filled with gas, massive artillery ready to rain down on us and the threat of chemical attack. My next in command looked at me and said, "How are we gonna get through this?" I said, "We're gonna do it, we're gonna go through this like a knife through butter."'

Having the might of the US Marine Corps at your disposal is one thing. Having the 2015–16 Aston Villa squad was quite another. Villa couldn't win away at Norwich, hardly a Premier League minefield. Things fell apart for good on 16 April, with a defeat at Manchester United. By then, Villa supporters were so deep into gallows humour that they chanted, 'Let's pretend we've scored a goal,' before belting out a rendition of 'We'll Meet Again.'

In the space of a decade, Lerner's custody had taken the club from rubbing elbows with the Premier League elite to being kicked out of the party altogether. And he had spent more than a quarter of a billion dollars for the privilege.

'How many seasons after all can one hold on and hope to slide through? That is not Aston Villa. That kind of desperate existence is totally unacceptable, unbearable and totally incompatible with Villa's glorious past,' he wrote on the club's website. 'That is not what, or why, I looked to get involved back then and it is why I've looked for some time to make a change. I can say certainly in good faith that I have tried to sell since my May 2014 announcement and put our beloved club in better suited hands – but that hasn't happened.

'I write to Villa supporters to make clear that this relegation lies at my feet and no one else's.'

One's man relegation was another man's bargain. In May 2016, knowing that Villa's immediate future lay in the Championship, Dr Tony Xia, a Harvard-, MIT- and Oxford-groomed billionaire from China, paid around £60 million to acquire the club and end Lerner's ordeal. The environment had become so toxic that right before the sale was announced Lerner received a call from law enforcement advising him maybe not to open his post for a little while.

Lerner bid farewell in a statement he titled 'Goodbye to All That', a reference to Robert Graves's autobiographical work on the legacy of the Great War and an England he no longer recognized. Devoured by the Premier League, Lerner hoped that his own legacy at the 'beloved old club' might have room for his refurbishment of the Holte End, his substantial investment in the club's facilities, and one of the very first gifts he'd given the supporters a decade before: the pub.

In that final note, Lerner also addressed 'the popular and dark pastime of wondering aloud how much was spent, or lost,' knowing too well that the catastrophic losses would colour his tenure for ever. The sum total of Villa's annual operating losses over the ten years came to more than £180 million. He had sold the Browns in 2012 for around $1 billion. Because Lerner's personal assets were so spread out – and because of the US tax code – he was able to offset many of those losses against profits elsewhere. But the surrender stung.

When it comes to assessing the personal toll of life in English football, Lerner paraphrased something he remembered George Harrison once saying about life in the Beatles: 'The Premier League cost me my nervous system.'

The tattoo, of course, is still on his ankle. The TV now stays unplugged. Yet, despite the losses, Lerner feels he was able to leave on more or less his own terms.

'It would be very easy to say the Premier League chewed me up and spat me out. But I like to think I put my finger down its throat, and said, "Now puke me up."'

21

Long before Lerner fell out of the Premier League, other American owners had become so spooked by the prospect of relegation – and the financial sinkhole that comes with it – that they lobbied the league to do away entirely with the century-old practice of dumping out its weakest teams.

'If you're looking at sport all around the world and you look at sport owners trying to work out how to invest and make money, you'll find that most of them like the idea of franchises,' Richard Bevan, the chairman of the League Managers Association said in 2011. 'There are a number of overseas-owned clubs already talking about bringing about the avoidance of promotion and relegation in the Premier League.'

But boarding up the trapdoor was never going to happen. The parties in favour of it were nowhere near the required fourteen votes to amend Premier League rules – and even then, the backlash from the rest of English football hoping to someday gain promotion would have been too ferocious to ignore. If eliminating relegation altogether was off the table, several American owners knew enough to go after the next best thing in times of crisis: the relegation doctor *par excellence*, Sam Allardyce. His charisma, his season playing for the NASL's Tampa Bay Rowdies, and his love of analytics ticked all the boxes for an American owner in a tight spot. Randy Lerner wanted him at Villa but could not get him. Ellis Short had him at Sunderland but could not keep him. Josh Harris and David Blitzer, the private-equity titans who bought into English football in 2015, snagged him at Crystal Palace, where he pulled off another of his famous turn-arounds in the final months of the season to save the club from a perilous position.

What Allardyce's popularity among those owners made clear – even if they were reluctant to admit it – is that the danger of relegation contributed to the thrill as long as they could pull out of the tailspin. Taking their chances with a high-stakes bet in a league without a safety net is precisely the kind of thing that appeals to the more cocksure, type A personalities that rise to the top of the business. It's no accident that the list of owners heading into the recent seasons included several hedge-fund billionaires, former corporate raiders, property speculators, and one professional gambler.

But perhaps no one in that bunch made a riskier wager than the Americans who were so eager to buy into English football in the summer of 2016 that they looked from Washington, DC, to south Wales and a seaside city of 250,000.

Since Swansea City were founded in 1912, the Swans had spent just seven of their 104 campaigns in English football's top flight. They began every Premier League season among the favourites for relegation, and the prospect of financial catastrophe was never far away. As recently as 2001, Swansea were sold for the princely sum of one pound. Not long afterward, the team's own supporters and former executives stumped up £300,000 to save the club from going bust.

So when Americans Steve Kaplan and Jason Levien plunked down £110 million for the club in June 2016, there were a few raised eyebrows in Wales. But Kaplan and Levien weren't worried. Like so many US investors before them, they looked at the Premier League's success, income, and prospects for growth, and convinced themselves they had gotten a steal.

At first, Swansea fans were sceptical. Then, after a few months, they turned downright hostile. Just nine games into their first season as owners, Kaplan and Levien were subjected to protests from the stands and one particularly catchy ditty: 'You can stick your fucking dollars up your arse!'

The animosity was partly due to a string of bad results, which left Swansea bottom of the table after twelve games. But that wasn't all. Swansea supporters could deal with poor results – they did it all the time. What really irked them was the decision that put them in that predicament: Kaplan and Levien's choice of manager.

Former US coach Bob Bradley, fifty-eight years old, had never worked in the top division of a major European league, let alone won a major trophy, before hopping into the dugout at Swansea. Even more offensive to the fans than his résumé, however, was his American accent. For an English football audience that had already witnessed a succession of American investors flail about in the boardroom, the prospect of a Yank giving orders in the dressing room was a step too far.

The supporters' crankiness reached a new high when, of all things, Bradley referred to a penalty kick as a 'PK' in a post-game interview with the BBC. He immediately caught himself and corrected it to 'penalty,' but it was too late. In the court of social media, Bradley was charged with the unforgivable crime of sounding American while talking about football.

No one seemed to care that more than fifty other non-British managers had paraded their accents through the English top flight before him to no great fuss. The sound of Bradley's New Jersey accent, despite his Princeton education, was hilarious, cringe inducing, and occasionally offensive to delicate British ears. All because he sometimes used a more American turn of phrase in the sport they invented.

The strangest part of the whole controversy was that Bradley actually used more of the game's British terminology than American. In more than four hours of televised press conferences and interviews during his time in charge of Swansea, he uttered the word 'football' seventy-seven times. He never once used the word 'soccer'. He also faithfully stuck to 'clean sheet' over 'shutout', 'training' over 'practise', and 'dressing room' over 'locker room'.

Ultimately, however, Bradley's lexicon was a sideshow to the disaster unfolding every week on the pitch. His tenure lasted only eighty-five days and eleven games, the second-shortest stint in Premier League history, producing just two wins and leaving Swansea mired in the relegation zone. 'Obviously, it doesn't always say too much about the overall ability to manage and coach,' Bradley said, after he was turfed out, 'because it's tested in a very different way in the Premier League.'

Forced to cast about for a new manager midway through the

season and with their team seemingly destined for the drop, Swansea's new owners were in a tough spot. They needed a manager to instil some discipline in the team and some confidence in the supporters.

Kaplan and Levien settled on Paul Clement, a long-time assistant coach whose most obvious quality was his English accent – and spells as an assistant at Real Madrid and Paris Saint-Germain. This time, their gamble paid off. Clement kept Swansea up with one game to spare.

'Even from the other side of the Atlantic,' the relieved owners wrote of their manager, players, and fans after the season, 'we could feel the connection and it was spine-tingling.'

'Spine-tingling' might not be the word Swansea supporters would use to describe a season in which their team recorded twenty-one losses, conceded seventy goals in thirty-eight games, and burned through three different managers. But it beat what happened twelve months later when Swansea finished eighteenth and were finally relegated.

Still, Kaplan and Levien were right about one thing. Success – even the kind challenged by local fans – would yield extraordinary returns to the owners who could navigate the Premier League's stormy seasons. The problem is that owners and supporters have rarely been on the same page when it comes to defining precisely what constitutes success.

Since American owners took control of Manchester United, Arsenal, and Liverpool, they have collectively won seventeen major trophies despite occasional lambastings. And the combined market value of the three clubs has increased, at a conservative estimate, by around $7 billion. For years, Malcolm Glazer was one of the most hated men in Britain after his leveraged buyout of Manchester United left the club with debts that ran into ten figures. But it's hard to argue that his clan's tenure has been the disaster many feared it would become when they first heard about the mountains of debt and an American family with no experience in football. In the first decade of their ownership, Manchester United won five Premier League titles compared with six in the previous decade, matched the haul of one Champions League trophy, and ran a tight-enough ship to halve the debt from its 2010 peak of nearly $1.2 billion. By the

2016–17 season, the club had returned to posting the highest revenues of any club on the planet on the back of the Premier League's broadcast contracts and United's own titanic commercial operation.

But stickers proclaiming LOVE UNITED, HATE GLAZER still remained stuck to folding seats all over Old Trafford.

United fans have at least this much in common with their counterparts from Arsenal to Swansea to Liverpool, where supporters are prepared to take to the streets with banners and chants anytime their own Americans appear to slight their clubs' traditions. There was something in particular about American owners, much like Bob Bradley's accent, that didn't sit well with fans.

Many United States-based owners reported the same strange phenomenon when they entered or left the marketplace for Premier League clubs: a cognitive dissonance among fans who see Americans as inauthentic but wouldn't mind a sugar daddy coming in to lavish money on their squads. If an American drops in to have a look around, he is treated one way. But if, for instance, an investor arrives from China, the Gulf, or Russia, English clubs seem oddly eager to roll out the red carpet. Something clicks and people fantasize about being the next Chelsea or Manchester City, with an owner prepared to set money on fire for a while. No one wants to be the next Manchester United, because in the minds of supporters, it comes down to this: clubs that are run according to rigorous financial plans involving leveraged buyouts and debt and loan repayments just aren't that much fun.

But for all of the flaws of American owners, they were welcomed with open arms by their Premier League counterparts and Richard Scudamore. They, at least, could see that the Yanks were useful in one crucial respect.

The American invasion offered the league a wide-open highway to the mother of all markets.

PART V

Britain's New Empire

'They have petrol and ideas.'
Arsène Wenger, Arsenal FC

22

THE PREMIER LEAGUE offices in London's West End are located mostly underground. This fact alone does not make them exceptional in the world of football administration – FIFA's lair in Zurich features five subterranean levels, including a sinister conference room ripped straight out of *Dr Strangelove*. But the Premier League isn't going for the futuristic bunker vibe. Nothing about it exudes Bond-villain hideout or military robotics lab.

What makes the place remarkable is its modesty. Premier League HQ feels more like the offices of a mid-size legal practice.

Blending into a row of elegant Georgian buildings with white fronts and black railings, the exterior of the Premier League offices at 30 Gloucester Place is marked only by a small silver plaque. Where it publishes its address, the Premier League points out that access is 'by appointment only'. The few people who ever stop to take pictures are the tabloid photographers working the sidewalk whenever the Premier League managers gather for their league-wide meetings – think photos of middle-aged men in ill-fitting suits emerging from black cabs.

When the league moved into the space in 2005, domestic TV rights had just cleared the billion-pound mark for the second successive cycle. Ratings were through the roof. Yet for the most popular league on the planet, the offices have none of the ostentation or scale of the NFL's, for instance, perched high above the corner of Fifty-First Street and Park Avenue in New York, or the NBA's, which live in a fifty-one-storey tower two avenues over. In part, that's because the Premier League has roughly ten times fewer employees than the NFL or NBA, with a head count hovering around 110.

Visitors to the home of the world's most popular league are

led downstairs to a small waiting area where the sofas are pointed at the Premier League trophy and a tea station. The atmosphere is of quiet, businesslike efficiency. Chief executive Richard Scudamore kept a spartan office here, as do the aides who make sure that contracts are up to date, partners are kept happy, and the league's extensive charity operations tick over smoothly. Scudamore, the Premier League's highest-paid executive, earned a basic salary in the low seven figures. Compare that to the $34 million that NFL commissioner Roger Goodell earned in 2016 or the roughly $20 million the NBA is believed to pay commissioner Adam Silver, and you wonder why the Premier League – for all of the cash flooding into its clubs – makes its brass look so small-time.

The reason is that the Premier League is a much smaller government than any of its American counterparts. It's first and foremost a media-rights-selling organization that happens to provide twenty clubs with a platform, referees, and a match ball. The organization has six league-wide sponsors – no more – in obvious categories such as Official Timekeeper, Official Snack, and a ball contract with Nike that has quietly hummed along since 2000.

The NFL, by contrast, had thirty-two league-wide sponsors in 2015, including an Official Soup of the National Football League.

The most profitable sporting organization to come out of England isn't in the business of peddling merchandise either. They won't sell you a baseball cap or scarf. They leave that entirely to the clubs. In fact, the Premier League's website does not even have an online shop. That's why the whole operation can be happily contained in a single office that almost nobody knows is there.

But ever since 2005, that humble residence at Gloucester Place has served as mission control for the Premier League's quest for global domination.

The first time English football conquered the world was back in the late nineteenth century when it exported the laws of Association Football to the four corners of the globe. Overall, it went down as a qualified success. The rest of the world quickly learned how to play this game with a ball and a net. And then it got a bit too good at it. Before long, England's position as undisputed master of the sport it invented was being called into question, then overtly challenged, then ruthlessly debunked as the country's finest players suffered humbling defeats at the hands of Hungary, the United States, and, of course, Germany. Thereafter, English football came to view the game beyond its shores rather sceptically, like a cup of Earl Grey prepared by an American. As late as 1992, when the Premier League was formed, its clubs had a grand total of thirteen foreigners on their books. The rest of the world tuned in to watch English football, but English football still didn't care much about the rest of the world.

On the pitch, that slowly began to change with the arrival of foreign players through the mid 1990s. In the corridors of English football power, the turning point is clearer: 1999, when the Premier League hired Scudamore, its third chief executive and a former employee of the Yellow Pages.

Smartly dressed, with a lean frame and thinning grey hair, Scudamore didn't look much different from the two men who had previously occupied the position of Premier League CEO. But unlike Rick Parry, a former accountant, and Peter Leaver, who returned to his legal practice after two years as chief executive, Scudamore brought some serious commercial chops to the league office. His background was in sales, and over the course of the next two decades he would package the Premier League as one of the most attractive sports products on the planet and devise new ways of wringing out every penny available to English football in nearly two hundred countries.

Little of his professional experience until that point explicitly prepared him to run a global operation for such an addictive product. Long before selling football, for instance, he sold phone books. Scudamore landed in advertising sales at the Yellow Pages in 1980, having studied law at the University of Nottingham and realizing he hated the subject. He climbed the corporate ladder, earning eight promotions in eight years, and reached the position of sales director. When he decided it was time to try pushing something a little sexier than telephone directories, Scudamore joined Thomson Newspapers in 1989 as a sales and marketing director in the UK before moving to New York to serve as the company's senior vice president, responsible for its newspaper operations in the southern and eastern United States. For a reserved, soft-spoken Brit, Scudamore thrived in America's corporate culture, relishing its competitiveness, efficiency, and openness to innovation. He was soon overseeing a £560 million corporate and advertising turnover and more than two hundred newspapers in forty US states.

By 1997, however, he and his wife, Catherine, were eager to return home. It was while taking a trip back to Britain that Scudamore spotted an ad in *The Times* for the chief executive's job at the Football League, the organization that oversaw the three levels of club football below the Premier League. Scudamore applied, won the job, and quickly built a reputation as a sharp, savvy operator unlike the stuffed shirts who usually passed for top administrators in English football. So it made perfect sense when the Premier League knocked on his door after he'd been in the job for only two years. In many ways, Scudamore was ideal for them. His commercial experience already set him apart from the majority of candidates, but his personal background also helped him stand out. For one thing, he was a qualified referee, a useful attribute when it came to mediating heated discussions between the twenty billionaires and multibillionaires who would soon become his bosses. Then there was the detail of his home town. Scudamore was born and raised in Bristol. 'My CV did not say I was from either London or the north-west, the traditional centres of football power,' Scudamore later told the trade magazine *Management Today*. 'In football dogma, I was regarded as a neutral.'

Scudamore may have been perfectly cast for the role of head of the Premier League, but once he was in the job, it was left up to him to draw the contours of that role. Over the course of the next two decades, as English football dealt with rapid global expansion, massive foreign investment, and issues ranging from racism to shady agents, Scudamore would have the chance to define the job of Premier League chief executive as a sort of outward-facing ambassador for the highest level of English football.

In the end, however, he chose a narrower definition. What Scudamore really wanted to be was the league's permanent salesman.

By the time Scudamore was introduced as chief executive, he could tell the Premier League was already well on its way to becoming a domestic juggernaut. Sky had renegotiated its contract for UK TV rights the year before, agreeing to pay £670 million over four years, more than double the price of its previous deal. When Scudamore looked at the international revenues, though, he saw a world of untapped potential. The league's overseas broadcast rights had sold for just £98 million in 1997, a figure Scudamore regarded not merely as disappointing but borderline disrespectful. In his mind, the Premier League was the most exciting football competition on the planet. It was time they got paid like it.

First, Scudamore set about overhauling the way the league sold itself abroad. Until now, the league had auctioned off its overseas rights package en bloc for a fixed fee, with the winning bidder then free to unpackage those rights and resell them in different countries and territories as they saw fit. In 1997, a joint bid from IMG and Canal+ had won the tender for the whole bundle. The next cycle saw a consortium of four agencies acquire the rights for £178 million in 2001. Still, Scudamore saw a fundamental problem: the Premier League was effectively choosing the most convenient way to sell itself internationally instead of the most profitable.

He wanted to cut out the middleman and negotiate with broadcasters himself. Scudamore was a man who liked to be in the room.

Scudamore told the club owners that they stood a better chance of finally raking in what they were worth by breaking up the overseas rights into separate territorial packages and dealing face to face with the TV companies. Convinced by his commercial background, the owners signed off on Scudamore's proposal. They would try it his way.

The scheme paid off immediately. In 2004, the league's international rights sold for £325 million, an increase of 83 per cent over the previous cycle. In 2007, the total jumped to £625 million while the 2010 cycle saw the sale of the Premier League's overseas rights fees fetch £1.4 billion, eclipsing the billion-pound mark for the first time. In just nine years, Scudamore had driven a staggering 687 per cent increase in overseas broadcast revenue. The single deal the league used to have for overseas rights had mushroomed to 80 agreements covering 211 countries and territories.

English football aficionados around the globe consequently wound up with more comprehensive Premier League coverage than the fans back home, where a long-standing agreement between the football authorities prohibits broadcasters from televising live matches between 2.45 p.m. and 5.15 p.m. on Saturdays in order to safeguard the attendances of the country's thousands of professional and semi-professional teams. As Scudamore criss-crossed the planet selling rights to the league's games, none of those decades-old restrictions about time slots and television scheduling stood in his way. International broadcasters could carry the whole shebang, every single Premier League game live. All they needed was enough channels to show it.

What wasn't in question was the appetite for Premier League football around the world. As Scudamore gradually shaped his role into that of a globetrotting executive, making visits to key markets including India, Thailand, Singapore, and the Middle East during each new season, he realized that the Premier League product was equipped with a host of built-in advantages. These factors, so obvious in retrospect, meant that fans around the world were predisposed to the Premier League even before they realized it. Best of all, those advantages were a total coincidence. The league had nothing to do with their existence.

The first – and most forehead-slappingly simple – is that this whole show takes place in English. While Italy's Serie A and Germany's Bundesliga must first help viewers make sense of names like Sampdoria and Borussia Mönchengladbach, one-quarter of the world's population can tune in to a Premier League and immediately understand what's happening – even if it means occasionally wading into the absurdly tedious soccer vs football debate. (For the record, 'soccer', like 'football', is an originally British term short for 'association football'.) Beyond the language, the league also benefits from its location. As countless London firms have discovered through the years, the fact that the British business day overlaps with both Asian and American daytime hours gave the league a leg up on rival sports organizations, including the NFL and the NBA. A Premier League match that kicks off in the early afternoon can be consumed both as prime-time Saturday-night entertainment in Singapore and over a bowl of Cheerios on a Saturday morning in Brooklyn. On top of all this, it was obvious to Scudamore that overseas viewers had a sort of natural Anglophilia and were gravitating to the heritage and culture of English football, its authenticity. In short, they craved the Britishness of it all.

'Being British is the essence of what we are,' Scudamore told *The Times* in 2013. 'It's a bit like being the Queen or the BBC.'

By the end of his first decade as chief executive, Scudamore had parlayed that head start into a tenfold increase in the value of the league's international TV rights. Now he had to add some creativity of his own. To keep global rights fees rising, it was no longer enough simply to cut out the middleman and deal with international broadcasters directly. He needed to convince them that the Premier League rights they had just paid through the nose for were indispensable to their business model. And to do that, Scudamore developed two clear strategies.

The first relied on Scudamore's own talents as a salesman. Or to be more specific, what one Premier League owner described as his talent for 'creating tension' at the negotiating table, never letting buyers get too comfortable. If that gives the impression of Scudamore as a sales shark sniffing out weaknesses and exploiting them to push his product, the reality could not be more different. In fact, Scudamore created the most fiendish auction process in world sports by running the league's sales department with the sort of folksy, homespun charm of a neighbourhood post office. He purposely kept his sales team to roughly a half-dozen employees so that broadcasters felt a personal connection when they rang Gloucester Place. And the mantra they lived by was less 'always be closing' and more 'always be courteous'. Scudamore's unshakeable sense of decorum taught him that politeness was the key to preserving customer relationships. At the end of every season, he personally emailed thank-you notes to the league's eighty international broadcasters and sent special goodbye messages to those whose contracts with the league had expired.

Scudamore also began to accompany the prime minister on trade missions, taking the Premier League trophy with him. 'Everyone who sees the trophy will say, "Wow"', he explained. 'Heads of state, prime ministers – they all want a photo with the trophy. It's what we like to call soft power.'

All of which may sound a little quaint but for the fact that Scudamore's schtick brought a steady stream of bidders clamouring for a seat at the table. In nearly every territory on the planet, Scudamore could guarantee that the league's rights auctions remained furiously contested every time they came up for renewal.

Take Hong Kong, for example. In 2010, the i-Cable subscription-TV network won the Premier League rights for roughly £100 million, an increase of around 30 per cent over the league's previous deal with a broadcaster called Now TV. When the i-Cable deal came up for renewal in 2013, Scudamore was able to coax Now TV back to the table, with the network paying £130 million this time to reacquire the exclusive rights to Premier League games. But when that agreement expired three years later, Scudamore seemed to be out of options. Now TV and i-Cable had spent the best part of a decade outbidding each other in a high-priced arm wrestle for Premier League rights and neither of them was interested in another costly bidding war. This time, the broadcasters decided they wouldn't play Scudamore's game and he would have to negotiate on their terms. Or not. As it turned out, Scudamore had another ace up his sleeve: he'd quietly been in discussions with a third bidder the entire time. In 2016, Chinese broadband provider LeTV snapped up the rights to Premier League games in Hong Kong – population 7 million – for a staggering £260 million, which was more than double the previous price and the league's biggest overseas TV rights deal at that time. All because Scudamore never lost sight of the whole field. 'We've spent twenty years building in these local markets not just relationships with those who've got the rights, but relationships with people who haven't got the rights,' Scudamore said. 'Some of our best friends are our non-licensees, because they might become our licensees one day.'

But those friendships could do only so much. Even as international rights fees began to rise, and the Premier League began to administer its international rights by closed secure online auctions

– sometimes as many as two or three a week during the renewal period – Scudamore knew that for English football to really unlock its global income he was going to need an assist from the biggest stars in the game: the twenty Premier League clubs themselves.

23

IT WOULD BE wrong to describe Premier League clubs as committed isolationists before Richard Scudamore joined became chief executive in 1998. A few of them had begun to explore what the wider world had to offer. As usual, Manchester United led the way. The year before, United had embarked on a three-match pre-season tour of Asia, seeking to export all that new merchandise to their fans in Thailand, Hong Kong, and Japan.

But for most of the league's teams, the closest they got to international outreach was an annual pre-season training camp on the Continent – France, Austria, or Switzerland, say – where they could undergo a couple of weeks of fitness training in the bucolic Alpine air – and perhaps indulge the residents by playing a friendly against the local amateur team or trashing the nearest nightclub. The whole endeavour was conceived purely as a way to break up the monotony of the pre-season. Commercial considerations didn't come into it. That perception was so ingrained that the *Guardian* called the United–Sporting Lisbon match in 2003 – the one where United signed Cristiano Ronaldo – a 'meaningless friendly'.

Even those clubs that did appreciate the branding possibilities of pre-season still treated the matches on those trips as glorified walk-throughs. But as Scudamore began to focus on international markets as a way to boost the league's revenues, he came to realize that he could do for the Premier League pre-season what he had done for TV. If they packaged it the right way and took it directly to the league's key international markets, the pre-season could help the league engage with its overseas fans on a new level, raising its global profile and, by extension, its global profits.

The first step came in 2003 when the Premier League launched its first officially sanctioned overseas competition in Malaysia, the four-team Asia Cup. The motley line-up was Chelsea, Newcastle, Birmingham, and, oddly, the Malaysian national team. By 2005, when Bolton, Everton, and Manchester City travelled to Thailand for the second edition of the tournament, it was known as the Asia Trophy, and two years later, when Hong Kong served as host, it proved so popular that every game sold out and Barclays bank came aboard as a title sponsor.

It wasn't long before the clubs started to see the impact of Scudamore's approach. Sponsorship income swelled as overseas companies targeted Premier League teams as a way to reach customers in Asia. At the Emirates in London, for instance, ads by the pitch began cropping up in Vietnamese. In 2009, the online-gambling firm 188BET sealed shirt sponsorship deals with two Premier League clubs – Bolton and Wigan. 'The reason we chose to be involved has nothing to do with the UK,' the company's chief executive said at the time. 'We're an Asia-facing business. It's about the global reach.'

But while the league's official competition focused on its key markets in Asia, where the popularity of English football remains unrivalled, others trained their sights in the opposite direction towards a land of opportunity, a sport-crazy country where fans had dispos-able income to burn and six TVs in every home.

All they had to do was convince America that football wasn't the enemy.

In 2001, United had opened the modern US frontier by signing a bilateral marketing agreement with the New York Yankees. Two of the most famous teams on the planet pairing up – on paper, at least – seemed like a sure-fire way to cash in on something. Except no one knew exactly what that something was. Manchester United legend-turned-director Bobby Charlton barely had a grasp on what the deal *wasn't* for. 'We don't want to for one moment think that Manchester United is going to produce baseball teams,' he said. 'We don't expect the New York Yankees to produce soccer teams.'

At least they had that covered. The dream was to sell Yankee caps at Old Trafford and United kits at Yankee Stadium. But the whole thing was a false start. United made much more progress in 2003 with a barnstorming pre-season tour of exhibition games in Seattle, Los Angeles, New York, and Philadelphia that sold more than 300,000 tickets.

It didn't take long for other clubs to follow them across the pond. In 2005, Fulham accepted an invitation from Major League Soccer to play in their annual All-Star Game. Chelsea made the trip the next year, and West Ham took its turn in 2008. If the matches themselves weren't always thrilling spectacles, there was at least evidence that English clubs were treating them more seriously. West Ham's supporters lent a sheen of authenticity to the whole thing when they engaged in a brawl with fans of the Columbus Crew, an unlikely outbreak of violence at a so-called friendly game that ended only when police administered pepper spray to both sets of supporters.

By 2009, a jet-setting pre-season tour was no longer a novelty. It was an essential exercise for any self-respecting Premier League club that viewed itself as a global brand. Which meant that Manchester City couldn't resist. As usual, the club's first instinct was to cast their eyes across town and study what Manchester United were up to. That's when Garry Cook came up with an idea. If authenticity was what overseas fans craved – along with a chance to see English clubs play in a game with at least something at stake – why not offer them the one match-up that would mean something to the club's supporters whether it was played at home or away, in Asia or America, or even on the dark side of the moon. Cook wanted to export one of English football's oldest intra-city rivalries, the Manchester derby.

But when Cook proposed taking City vs United on a tour – one game in Beijing, maybe one in New York – to United chief executive David Gill during one of their regular meetings that year, he discovered that the Old Trafford club were less enthusiastic about the plan. 'It's a great idea,' Gill told him, 'but our guys will not go for that.' Gill was aware that agreeing on an economic split with a club the size of City would've been a tough sell in those days – and that was before anyone told Alex Ferguson about it. Cook's plan was dead in the water. It took nearly a decade to revive it, long after Cook and Gill had both left the scene.

In the summer of 2017, Manchester United and Manchester City squared off in a pre-season game in Houston, the first Manchester derby to be staged outside of the UK. It drew more than 67,000 people.

So what changed in those eight years? The answer lies deep inside Manchester City's offices, where a revolutionary strategy had been bubbling away for years. In their bid to become a global powerhouse, City were also turning itself into the world's foremost exporter of the Premier League.

By winning the title with the last kick of the 2011–12 season, they had already gifted the suits at 30 Gloucester Place the ideal highlight reel to whet the appetites of international broadcasters as they prepared to blow fortunes on the next cycle of rights that autumn. Agüero, the ninety-fourth minute, one perfect sports moment. The Premier League immediately showed clips of it to potential bidders from abroad. The next phase, having conquered England just four years into the Abu Dhabi era, was for Manchester City to embark on a one-club mission to build a global empire.

But before they could start looking outward, they had to do a little more importing first.

City's wholesale appropriation of football cultures they admired continued unabated. The same way they had looked enviously at the success of Manchester United across town – a daily reminder of what greatness looked like – and then signed players in packs from Arsenal and other teams with a strong football identity, they now fixed their gaze on the most successful club on the planet since 2008: Barcelona.

City couldn't pry away Lionel Messi. They had tried that already – albeit by accident. And in 2012, Barça's revolutionary young manager, Pep Guardiola, wasn't interested in a move to the Premier League. The club took a different tack. If it couldn't poach the best and brightest from Barça's starting line-up or its dugout, it would pluck them from Barça's boardroom.

City started with Omar Berrada, a commercial whiz, to be the club's new chief operating officer. Then they set about luring Berrada's old boss, former Barcelona money man Ferran Soriano. The son of a hairdresser in Barcelona, the six-foot-three polymath with an MBA had distinguished himself early on for his shrewd understanding of football's business landscape. He became a fervent believer in a piece of research by a University of Michigan professor who found a near-perfect correlation between team wages and league positions. It was uncanny. Sort the twenty payrolls in La Liga or the Premier League or the Bundesliga on day one of the season and you could fashion a pretty good idea of how the tables would look ten months later. Football, Soriano realized, was not a complicated game. Success could be bought. The hard part was making enough money to pay for it.

Soriano spent his five years as Barça's finance director from 2003 to 2008 trying to solve that problem. He laboured to grow the club's name outside of Spain. He shopped aggressively for commercial partnerships. In short, he did what he had seen the likes of Manchester United do to such devastating effect the decade before, opening up a revenue gap on its rivals that no one could close without a bene-factor owner. During that period, Soriano grew Barça's annual revenue from €123 to €309 million. More than that, his ideas about how the club should market itself were as clear as Guardiola's about how the team should play.

City courted him like he was a Brazilian striker.

Soriano left Catalonia abruptly in 2008 when the political tide within the club turned against the Barcelona president and took flight to the airline industry. But following Garry Cook's exit as City chief executive in 2011, Soriano started getting regular calls from Marty Edelman, the high-powered New York lawyer on Manchester City's board. They met in London, Paris, and Abu Dhabi over the course of several months as Soriano refused to dive back into football. But Edelman finally wore down his resistance sometime after City won its first Premier League title. That summer, he snuck Soriano into the Lowry Hotel in Manchester – a favourite spot of City and United alike for closing deals – and brought him on board.

Until that point, Soriano had always been on the other side of Abu Dhabi's free-spending entrance on the football stage. He even reserved a special place for it in his 2009 book about how to run a football club, *Goal: The Ball Doesn't Go In by Chance*. 'They were threatening to buy up the best players,' he wrote, 'at whatever price, creating another wave of inflation.'

Soriano knew this first-hand, since he had once used City's largesse to open negotiations over the Brazilian wizard Ronaldinho in 2008, not with any intention of selling him to Manchester but simply to inflate the asking price in his parallel talks with AC Milan.

Later that year, Soriano hired Txiki Begiristain as sporting director. A former winger on the Barcelona Dream Team of the early 1990s, he was steeped in the pass first, play beautifully philosophy of that side's manager, Johan Cruyff. It was Cruyff, as a player and then a coach, who first preached the gospel of the free-flowing football that Barça came to embody. And Begiristain and Guardiola became his disciples.

City wanted to import some of that holiness for themselves.

With Soriano and Begiristain in place, the wholesale appropriation of Barcelona's on-pitch heritage and off-pitch strategy could begin. In fact, they wanted to take things even further than Barça ever could.

Abu Dhabi's money and the laissez-faire approach of the Premier League combined with City's relatively recent arrival to the big time meant that Soriano was staring at a blank slate. The club could continue to spend lavishly and reel in talent from all over the world – the approach that had built the 2011–12 title – but dominating England was no longer enough. City were going to redefine what it meant to be a global football club.

'What about doing this other thing,' Soriano said in his first meeting with the owners, 'creating the first multinational of football?'

The vision had first appeared to Soriano at Barcelona. He dreamed of establishing a US branch for the Catalan club, a sort of Barcelona USA, that would compete in Major League Soccer and wear the famous blaugrana colours. He wanted to bundle up everything that drew fans from around the globe to his club and find a way to take it directly to them. Not on a summer tour and not through merchandise. He had been struck by how many fans in Japan bought Barcelona memberships even though they couldn't use any of the perks from 6,500 miles away – they felt connected simply by carrying their numbered *socio* cards. Now Soriano wanted to give fans abroad a Barcelona to call their very own.

The trouble was squaring that vision with the deeply parochial traditions of the club back home. How could he convince the 143,000 voting members of Barcelona – technically the club's owners – that it was in their interest to let a franchise in New York borrow their history in the name of commercial expansion? And what if the team were awful? Soriano couldn't justify it. 'There was a sense at the time that FC Barcelona was a club for Barcelona,' Omar Berrada said. 'The only true FC Barcelona had to be in Barcelona. It didn't fit with the perception of the members of what the club was that there could be an FC Barcelona in the US.'

Others had attempted to execute similar plans to command attention far beyond their own front lawns. Since 1999, Ajax Amsterdam had run a club of their own creation in South Africa called Ajax Cape Town FC to expand their scouting network. And in MLS, southern California's Chivas USA enjoyed a decade-long existence as a cross-border affiliate of the Mexican team Chivas Guadalajara before folding in 2013. The energy-drink company Red Bull, meanwhile, had built up a portfolio of five identically branded clubs beginning with Red Bull Salzburg in Austria and later the New York Red Bulls of MLS but had so far failed to break into the absurdly pricey Premier League market.

No one dared try it on the scale Soriano imagined.

'We reached the conclusion that in the football industry there was a startling gap between the clubs that had become entertainment providers with global brands and the other clubs who were limited to their local markets,' Soriano wrote.

City would have to be one of the former. So he picked up right where the Barcelona idea had left off: New York. On his second official day of work at City, Soriano landed in the United States, where Edelman whisked him off to a meeting with the New York Yankees. In a matter of minutes, the owners agreed to take a 20 per cent stake in whatever future club Man City set up there once it had settled the $100 million required by MLS to add a new club to the league. (Times in the City universe were changing fast – that was around half of what Sheikh Mansour had paid just four years earlier to buy into the Premier League.) 'It was quite scary, really, because it was only the infancy of our success,' said Brian Marwood, who was put in charge of running the football side of what the club now called the City Football Group. 'So how can we go and do this elsewhere?'

In May 2013, City announced the creation of New York City FC. Like Manchester City, the team would wear sky-blue shirts with the Etihad Airlines name splashed across the front. It would try to play attractive, stylish football. And it would belong to New Yorkers. The idea, Berrada said, was to create an ambassador, a full-time presence 'with its own identity' in City's orbit that could be an everyday 'living, breathing point of connection' independent from whatever was happening in north-west England. City's brass back home would later notice a weird phenomenon of US-based Liverpool fans adopting NYCFC as their preferred MLS team – presumably due to a mutual loathing of all things Manchester United.

But as with everything else in the Manchester City empire, there was a larger mission behind this move. Above all, New York was a delicate, ambitious exercise in international publicity for the emirate – a public relations ploy that was shinier and more vibrant than anything the Abu Dhabi Tourism Authority or Etihad Airways could cook up. Football, as always, was the delivery mechanism. And City's efforts to find a home in New York made that eminently clear.

Hoping to avoid the mistake made by the Big Apple's other MLS franchise, the Red Bulls, who landed in the post-industrial wasteland of Harrison, New Jersey, Manchester City were adamant about planting their flag within the five boroughs of New York City. From a list of twenty-four potential sites, including a pier on the Hudson River, they narrowed it down to one where they could build a glittering new football-specific stadium: Flushing Meadows–Corona Park in Queens. Their neighbours would be the New York Mets, who play at the 42,000-capacity Citi Field, and the USTA Billie Jean King National Tennis Centre, home of the US Open. Like any New York construction project, nothing about it was easy. Manchester City executives, led by Edelman and Simon Pearce, would need to convince City Hall and others that a stadium for New York City FC would represent an appropriate use of public parkland.

Edelman was a master at dealing with the ins and outs of real estate in this town. He had plenty of political suction, too. But the hold-ups still dragged on for months. Local groups in Queens protested loudly and often. The Mets and the USTA also came out against the project. By the spring of 2013, it was no longer clear that City Football Group would be able to make the stadium project happen at all. In a series of emails that copied in the UAE's ambassador to the United States, Yousef Al Otaiba – and leaked after a hack in 2017 – the club brass considered its options.

'Is MCFC/CFG/UAE/AD prepared to weather storm of controversy and scrutiny for achievable but uncertain stadium approval?' Pearce, the former PR guru, wrote to Edelman and Soriano as they prepared to brief City Football Group chairman Khaldoon al-Mubarak. 'Is this the issue on which UAE/AD is prepared to put at risk hard-earned and limited US political capital and public goodwill?'

The briefing note went on to list CFG's assets and liabilities, because, as Pearce put it, they would be '"tooling-up" for a very public fight'.

'AD/UAE vulnerabilities put in play: gay, wealth, women, Israel,' he wrote. That would be Abu Dhabi's criminalization of homosexuality, its vast and ostentatious wealth, its limitations on women's rights, and its decidedly pro-Palestine positions.

After more than a year of trying, City walked away from the stadium altogether and NYCFC took up residence on a makeshift pitch jammed onto the baseball field at Yankee Stadium in the Bronx. A stadium could wait, putting out a team couldn't. The new outfit kicked off life in MLS on 12 March 2015. David Villa, the ex-Barcelona star, scored the opening goal somewhere along the first-base line.

By that time, however, the City Football Group was already conquering new territories as quickly as it could grab them. The original plan called for the empire to expand to three clubs – Manchester City, New York, and one other. The dream was to add one in China, but the realities of doing business in the league there at the time proved too chaotic. Then an alternative cropped up in Australia. When the strategy proved it could work, they thought about adding even more. Within four years, City Football Group had expanded to six clubs on five continents.

'The strength of the Premier League internationally was so much more powerful than anything you found in European football leagues,' Berrada said, acknowledging the commercial and broadcasting groundwork laid by City's rivals over the previous two decades. 'So we were able to move quicker than if we'd been in La Liga or Ligue 1 or Serie A in Italy.'

City took over a club called Melbourne Heart in Australia and immediately gave it the full sky-blue makeover. Melbourne Heart became Melbourne City. Their shirt sponsor became Etihad. And, of course, the team's colours simply couldn't remain red and white stripes – much to the chagrin of the already sky-blue Sydney FC, who objected to having two clubs wearing identical colours in a league of just ten teams.

In Japan, City saw a branding opportunity and brought Yokohama F. Marinos into the fold, acquiring a 20 per cent stake. Yokohama were allowed to keep their royal blue colour scheme because this was more of a commercial play for City rather than a full-on take-over – City and Yokohama shared a mutual interest in partnering with the car manufacturer Nissan.

And then, in 2017, City added two more teams, this time for actual football purposes. They were going to take a stab at solving a couple of problems that had perplexed top Premier League clubs for years. How do you gain an edge in spotting the best teenagers on the planet when everyone is working off the same information? And even if you're lucky enough to snag one of those teenagers, how do you prepare him to play in the Premier League?

Even the highest levels of youth football had long been a frustration for clubs because players were kept in narrow age groups. The same occurred with reserve-team football, which imposed strict limits on fielding players over the age of twenty-three. All of which meant that young players never faced more mature, battle-worn competitors. In other words, their experience was worthless. One solution was to send youngsters out on loan to a network of clubs in smaller leagues, such as the English second division or the Dutch or Belgian leagues, to gain some experience, but in those cases, the parent club lost all control over their technical development.

Manchester City decided it shouldn't have to compromise. They acquired a small Uruguayan team named Torque as a way of stealing a march in the talent-scouting game. Uruguay, a country of 3.4 million, is one of the top pound-for-pound football nations on the planet – it has won the World Cup twice and produced stars such as Luis Suárez and Edinson Cavani. City wanted a piece of that. Not only did Torque give the club access to a scouting pipeline in South America, but it also gave City a place to stash any South American players it discovered.

Acquiring a minority stake in Girona FC, a second-tier Spanish club from Catalonia, offered much the same advantages. And, because they played in a European league of a decent standard, they also provided one more spot for City loanees to hone their skills until they were called back to the mothership in Manchester – or sold at a profit.

Once again, City were taking an idea that existed in football and carrying it to its most expensive, most logical extreme. And all of it proved more innovative than keeping developing talent in the coddled environment of youth football, where City's loaded academy teams can usually win games without getting out of second gear. 'Our win rate is extremely high,' Marwood said. 'We have a lot of young players who just get used to winning every week.' Dropping them into foreign leagues as full-time professionals, where the team may not be quite so good, was a way for them to gain some meaningful experience and taste a little bit of adversity.

As it happened, there wasn't a huge amount of adversity available to City's clubs once the mothership started pumping money into them. Melbourne went from bottom of the league to the semi-finals of the A-League play-offs, Girona were promoted to La Liga, and Torque won the Uruguayan second division in their first season as a City subsidiary.

Spending money like it was going out of style was never going to earn Manchester City many friends. Spending money like it was going out of style and also winning made them Public Enemy No. 1. Even football's existing superrich had to complain. Juventus chairman Andrea Agnelli, whose family had liberally ploughed money from their Fiat empire into the club, accused City of 'financial doping'. Never mind that in 2012–13, Manchester City had ceased being a money-losing operation.

The club had long attracted the attention of the European football authorities, who were hoping to crack down on clubs that warped competition by pouring money into the ground – in other words, what City were doing now and Chelsea had done for nearly a decade. UEFA's tool was its new Financial Fair Play Regulations, which prohibited a club from averaging annual losses of €35 million over a three-year period. Abu Dhabi had blown about £1 billion in the first five years of its stewardship. 'If you look at the grand plan, this made sense. It was a good idea to over-invest in that period,' Soriano said.

UEFA – and City's rivals – were also suspicious about the club's arrangement with their main sponsor, Etihad Airways, which happened to be owned by members of Abu Dhabi's royal family. The sponsorship deal was widely reported to be worth $400 million over ten years, far exceeding the world-record, $300 million, ten-year deal agreed to by JPMorgan Chase and Madison Square Garden. And yet, since their formation in 2003, Etihad had never posted a profit. Critics alleged that Abu Dhabi had manufactured a sponsorship deal far above normal market value so it could freely move money into Manchester City and minimize their accounting losses. City denied any wrongdoing.

Still, no one was particularly surprised when UEFA imposed FFP sanctions on City in 2014 that included a €20 million fine and a reduction of their squad from twenty-five players to twenty-one for that season's Champions League. City tried to argue that they shouldn't be punished because, while the club did post losses, it had no debt.

UEFA didn't buy it. Of course City didn't have any debt. It had an owner worth $20 billion instead. And his club had far bigger fish to fry than UEFA. The Catalan-led revolution at City was taking the second-best club in Manchester and turning it into a global entertainment powerhouse.

'I'm not saying that we're Disney, but if you think about it, it's not that dissimilar,' Berrada said. 'We have characters – which are players – that our fans relate to; we put on a show every three or four days. And then we take that show around the world in the summer. In that sense, we are part of the entertainment industry.'

24

FOR CLUBS WITHOUT a global empire, the best way to hawk their wares abroad was still taking the Premier League show on the road every summer. And here again, the league got their timing just right. When English clubs first started exploring the possibility of playing games across the Atlantic, they found a kindred spirit for their budding international enterprises: a motor-mouthed New Jersey Italian who had put on a few pounds since his soccer-playing days at Princeton and been drummed out of his role as the first general manager of Major League Soccer's New York/New Jersey MetroStars. His name was Charlie Stillitano.

In the early 2000s, he mortgaged his house so he could fund his sport promotion business and invite the world's biggest clubs to play summer friendly matches in the United States. Within ten years, Stillitano became one of the few Americans on the planet who could pick up the phone and ring Alex Ferguson or José Mourinho at any time of the day or night. Even the Glazers don't always have that kind of access.

In the early days, Stillitano found the Premier League clubs he dealt with to be practically clueless. He could pay them $500,000 a game and retain all of the television rights. 'They weren't thinking of this as a serious thing,' he said. 'They wanted a few bucks.' Only United knew to demand something more sophisticated, with Peter Kenyon and David Gill working out a revenue-sharing arrangement with Stillitano's company. They could see the potential. More than 80,000 fans would pack into Giants Stadium in New Jersey to watch the European heavyweights in the flesh – even if United disappointed them in 2003 by selling David Beckham to Real Madrid right before the tour.

The players liked coming over, too, as Stillitano made sure everything about the visit was first class, from dinners at Le Cirque and shopping on Manhattan's Fifth Avenue to NFL-grade training facilities. For squads used to the wooden benches and mildewed tiles of shoebox European dressing rooms, treading the plush carpets of an NFL locker room the size of a penthouse flat was an edifying experience.

Stillitano's biggest challenge – besides his company going briefly bankrupt in the mid 2000s – was getting the likes of United and Real and Liverpool to play each other. For years, they were convinced that actually exerting themselves on one of these American junkets would ruin their seasons. Until Chelsea and Inter Milan finally gave Stillitano the ammunition he needed in 2009. Carlo Ancelotti's Chelsea and José Mourinho's Inter went on to win their domestic leagues and domestic cups while the Italian side even added the Champions League to their haul. Now, there was no reason for any club to stay home. From begging teams to come over just a few years before, Stillitano could afford to be picky.

'The commercial departments went from (forgive me) knuckle-heads to brilliant people, led initially by Manchester United,' he said. Some even offered to come over for free. Stillitano's status, with one large foot in the world of European football and another in American sport, put him at some interesting crossroads of the inter-national sports world. Suddenly, he had access to the most popular teams in the most popular sport *and* the power players in the market they were all desperate to capture. After all, where was Stillitano finding his venues but the NFL?

So his 2004 lunch on Roman Abramovich's yacht – 'This one had a helicopter and a sailboat on the boat' – was not an uncommon event. It was there, while docked in the Port of Philadelphia, that Stillitano introduced Abramovich to Jeffrey Lurie, owner of the Philadelphia Eagles. Speaking businessman to businessman, Lurie asked Abramovich what his EBITDA (operating performance) was for Chelsea. The answer left Lurie aghast: Abramovich told him the club had lost more than $200 million the previous year trying to vault themselves into contention. Still, Lurie liked the product. He could smell that there was money to be made if English football would just become a little more like his own business. NFL teams make money pretty much every year, win or lose.

'I've got an idea,' Lurie said. 'Why don't my partners and I' – meaning the other thirty-one NFL owners – 'buy the Premier League?'

No one could be quite sure whether or not he was joking. But Lurie never followed up.

The NFL owner who did get involved lived further south. Stephen Ross, owner of the Miami Dolphins and pals with Manchester City's Marty Edelman, became intrigued by Stillitano's summer roadshow after attending a game in 2011. Though he didn't know a thing about football, Ross thought it might be a good way to fill his empty stadium in Miami in the summer. He soon bought out Stillitano's whole group from Creative Artists Agency and decided to make the World Football Challenge, as it was called, more than a tournament-planning organization. They were going to grow the international television rights side of the business, too. In 2013, Ross and Stillitano launched a summer event they dubbed the International Champions Cup, a twelve-game extravaganza featuring eight clubs and venues across seven cities, including Phoenix and Los Angeles. The final, of course, was in Ross's back garden, Miami.

By 2016 and 2017, the tournament expanded to include venues in China, Singapore, and Australia; Stillitano would secure participation from five top English teams every summer – a quarter of the Premier League. Chelsea, Man United, Everton, Leicester, Arsenal, Man City, and Tottenham have all taken part.

But as early as 2008, it was already clear to anyone paying attention: the summer tours had tapped into a well of sleeping Premier League football fans in the United States who were quietly waiting for someone to deliver them more than friendly games. If you gave America more football, they were ready to drink it up.

All of which paved the way for what may be the most significant TV rights deal in English football since Rupert Murdoch picked up the phone one morning in New York in May 1992.

As it happens, the man responsible for that deal wasn't much of a football fan, either. In fact, Jon Miller, a long-time executive at NBC, was more of a golfer.

Which is why every Saturday morning, Miller would wake early at his family home in New Jersey, creep downstairs, and quietly slip out the back door to shoot eighteen holes before lunch. On those morning drives to the course, he might catch a glimpse of a deer or a red fox on the quiet, tree-lined streets that led to the nearby Rockland Country Club. But one particular morning, Miller caught sight of an even rarer creature, one seldom encountered in the still, purple hours before daybreak: his teenage son.

Wrapped in a blanket on a couch in the family room a little more than a couple of hours after returning home from a night out, Robby Miller was already awake, alert, and staring intently at the TV. For his father, this was a deeply troubling sight.

'What are you doing up?' Miller enquired apprehensively, poking his head around the door.

'Dad,' came the exasperated reply, 'it's Arsenal–Tottenham.'

That didn't entirely answer Miller's question. He had no idea what an Arsenal was, much less a Tottenham. He was even more confused when he pulled his car around to the front of the house moments later and spotted four or five other kids from the neighbourhood marching up his driveway towards the front door, blankets tucked under their arms. And when he returned home several hours later and found those same kids still camped out at his home, transfixed by the action unfolding 4,000 miles away, he was completely bewildered. But Miller was also curious.

'I learned a long time ago that you cannot ignore what your kids are watching,' Miller said.

Miller did more than not ignore it. In the spring of 2012, he sat himself down across from Richard Scudamore in a Manhattan office to discuss a possible bid for the US TV rights to Premier League football. Fox had held those rights for the better part of two decades. Its most recent deal, a three-year, $70-million agreement covering the 2010–11 season through 2012–13, had delivered solid audiences as the Premier League's annual pre-season trips across the Atlantic slowly began to pay dividends. The previous season, an as-live delayed broadcast of Chelsea's November contest with Liverpool had drawn a US-record 1.7 million viewers on Fox's free-to-air channel.

Miller thought the Premier League could do better. In his view,

English football in America remained an 'underappreciated, under-marketed, and certainly an underexposed product'. And Miller was now in a position to do something about it. A year earlier, he had been named head of programming for the newly acquired NBC Sports Network, a twenty-four-hour cable channel that produced roughly 9,000 hours of weekly sport programming. To fill that airtime, the company had already acquired rights to NHL ice hockey and Formula One. But Miller felt it still lacked a marquee property. The answer, he told Scudamore, was Premier League football.

In the autumn of 2012, Miller had all the sign-offs for NBC to submit a three-year, $250-million bid for the Premier League's US broadcast rights, more than tripling the rate of $23 million per year that Fox was paying.

Despite the colossal bid, no one really expected NBC to win. Not only were Miller and his team competing with rivals CBS, Fox, and ESPN, but they were also up against a joint Fox–ESPN bid. Even when NBC advanced to the final round of bidding, few people inside or outside their building gave the network much of a chance of stealing the rights. Until one morning on the last Friday in October when the telephone rang outside Jon Miller's office.

Miller didn't usually receive calls to his office himself. But on this particular Friday morning, Miller's assistant – like most of the rest of the staff in his department – was out of the office. Hurricane Sandy was due to hit New York that weekend and many of the NBC employees had skipped town.

He picked up. 'Jon Miller.'

'Jon Miller,' came the businesslike reply, 'this is Richard Scudamore.'

Miller's heart began pounding in his chest. He knew that interested parties were due to hear from the Premier League within the next week or so. But like always, he had tried not to get too emotionally invested in the outcome. Now, with the Premier League's chief executive on the other end of the line, he was emotionally invested. In fact, he could barely get out a sentence.

'Richard, hi,' Miller uttered. 'How are you?'

'Well, I'm fine,' Scudamore answered. 'But I'm not nearly as good as you are.'

'What does that mean?'

'Well, I'm calling to congratulate you because you are the new home for the Premier League in the United States for the next three years.'

The conversation continued, but by now Miller could barely concentrate, so the two men wrapped up, promising to talk more in the coming days. When he put down the receiver, Miller closed his eyes and let the moment wash over him. 'I've had my wedding, the birth of my kids, and a few other things,' he said, 'but never did I feel as excited or as happy as I did when those words came out his mouth.'

There was only one problem: he had no one to share it with.

Miller's office was basically empty. His boss, NBC Sports' chief executive Mark Lazarus, was midway across the Atlantic, returning home from a trip to Sochi, where NBC were scouting ahead of the 2014 Winter Olympics. Miller tried to call his wife to tell her the good news, but there was no answer. So as he left the office and began walking down Sixth Avenue, Miller decided to call the one person he knew who would appreciate the enormity of what he'd just learned.

Robby Miller was on the treadmill at home when his dad called to inform him that he had won the rights to the Premier League. 'He paid me one of the greatest compliments that a son can pay a father,' Miller recalled. 'He said, "Dad, you're an animal."'

Lazarus was almost as effusive when he called Miller on his way home from the airport later that day. The other NBC executives were also ecstatic. But it turned out that there was one important constituency that wasn't quite so thrilled to learn that NBC had won the US rights to Premier League games: the Premier League owners.

Even with a sizable contingent of Americans now among their number, the league's twenty team owners remained a surprisingly parochial bunch, with little knowledge of the US TV landscape. The one thing they were certain of was that ESPN was the most famous sports network on the planet. For many of them, the prospect of abandoning that platform for a rival network still best known in Britain as the home of *Friends* didn't sound like a commercial masterstroke. At least not until Scudamore got to work on them.

Over the following weeks and months, Scudamore worked tirelessly to quell those doubts and convince the owners that NBC was the right partner for the league. He made personal visits to several clubs and a series of phone calls to a handful more to present the case for NBC. His pitch wasn't purely financial, though the terms of the NBC deal far outstripped the league's previous US TV deal. It was about growing the brand. Under the terms of the deal, Scudamore explained, NBC had pledged to show twenty-five matches per season on its free-to-air network, marking the first time English football would be shown live on broadcast television in the United States. (Previously, live games had aired exclusively on cable or occasionally on tape delay on Fox's broadcast network.) Scudamore raved about NBC's production values, its successful history of covering the Olympics, and its commitment to innovating with its Premier League coverage. 'The plans these guys have are a big step for us,' Scudamore promised. His comforting and cajoling quickly paid off. By the time NBC came to sign their contract with the Premier League, he had established a consensus among the twenty owners that the move to abandon ESPN was the right one.

It didn't take long for NBC to vindicate Scudamore's faith. In the first three seasons, NBC aired eight of the ten most watched live Premier League matches in US television history.

The increase under NBC was partly due to timing. Its first season came on the heels of the 2014 World Cup, which provided a natural spike in interest if not a great advertisement for English football. The network also offered unparalleled access to Premier League matches through multichannel broadcasts and a digital service that carried every single game live.

But the surge in ratings was also due to NBC's coverage. What the network realized early on was that its new audience wouldn't tolerate an inauthentic product. Though Fox had built a decent viewership during its three-year stint as the league's US broadcaster, there was a sense that it never got the tone quite right from its studio in Los Angeles, some 6,000 miles from the nearest English boozer.

By contrast, NBC set out to make its coverage feel so legit you could almost taste the half-time beer. They recognized that Americans tuning in to English football expect to hear English commentators, that colloquialisms like pitch, kit, and clean sheet are part of the Premier League's transatlantic appeal. NBC had struck the delicate balance between speaking directly to an American audience without sacrificing its English accent.

While it didn't show up in ratings or ad buys, a subtler shift was also taking place. Far from its violent, working-class roots in England, Premier League fandom in America was becoming something of a status symbol. Anyone could cheer for the Dallas Cowboys or the Golden State Warriors, but it took a certain worldliness to care about a team of eleven guys from a place you'd never heard of. Wearing a Premier League kit turned into a way to tell your friends in Brooklyn or San Francisco that you were sophisticated, curious, and sometimes drunk in the morning. Even American celebrities tuned in. The NBA's Kevin Garnett became a proud Chelsea fan just like the actor Will Ferrell. Jay-Z claimed to be an Arsenal supporter. And LeBron James outdid them all by buying a small stake in Liverpool.

But perhaps the Premier League's simplest appeal was its convenience. The game's ninety-minute format made it the most easy-to-watch sport on American television. You could sleep in on a Saturday morning, watch a game at 10 a.m., and still have the rest of the day to live like a functional human. Or, if you happened to be up at 7.30 a.m. with a bouncing five-year-old, you could at least have some live sports with your coffee before the cartoons took over. And if you wanted more, you could take in a whole double-header in the same time it takes to slog through a single college football game, with 80 per cent fewer adverts for pick-up trucks.

The NBC executives could see all this. They looked at their audience numbers, the growing engagement with football across America, and they doubled down. When the network's initial three-year deal came up for renewal in 2015, they decided they didn't want merely to extend their coverage. They wanted to expand it. 'We decided to go really bold,' Miller said.

The next time Richard Scudamore called with some good news, it wasn't to say that the Premier League was sticking with NBC for another three years. This new agreement would stretch over six years, through 2022, and it would be at twice the rate NBC had been paying per season. For the first time in Scudamore's tenure, the Premier League had deviated from its policy of awarding international contracts on a rolling three-year basis. But it wasn't hard to understand why. The new deal would be worth $1 billion – more than ten times richer than the Fox deal five years earlier.

The English owners who'd rebelled back in 1992 had never dreamed of such success. They only wanted to imitate America. They had no idea that twenty-five years later their break-away league would be America's hottest import.

As they looked across the Atlantic at the millions of eyeballs in the United States now fixed on their game, the Premier League owners realized that they had finally arrived. And as those eyeballs looked back at them, the Premier League again demonstrated its knack for timing. The audience was in place for English football to unspool the most dramatic season in its history.

25

UNTIL THE BEGINNING of the 2015–16 season, Leicester City had been one of the rotating cast of clubs just making up the Premier League's numbers. The Foxes didn't contend for titles. And they didn't contend for European places. They just kind of . . . existed. That is, when the Foxes were in the Premier League at all. A yo-yo club usually found bouncing between the top flight and the second tier, Leicester had spent the majority of the Premier League era outside of the Premier League.

The club's life before that era began in 1992 hadn't been much happier. As the city of Leicester declined with the unthreading of the British textile industry, the Foxes tended to reflect its fortunes, languishing in the East Midlands while bigger cities took over the reins of both the economy and the national game. In the twenty years since Blackburn had become Premier League champions, every single title had landed in the trophy cabinets of clubs in London or Manchester. Compare that to the two decades before Blackburn and Uncle Jack upset the hierarchy – when championships passed through Derby and Nottingham and other out-of-the-way places – and it was clear that the era of small-town contenders was over. Top-level, supercar-driving foreign players didn't want to move from Milan or Barcelona to the East Midlands. And top-level, trophy-lifting managers didn't want to work in a place that might never see European competition.

The way the football world was moving, Leicester City's 152 years of existence without a championship might as well have extended another 20, 50, or 152 years into the future.

Not that Leicester's pedestrian outlook discouraged investors. In 2010, with the club in the Championship, the Foxes were acquired by a consortium led by a polo-playing, duty-free retail baron from Thailand named Vichai Srivaddhanaprabha. Like others who sought to buy into English football and were perhaps put off by the prohibitive cost of a Premier League club, Srivaddhanaprabha realized that there was a much more profitable way to make money in this game. It just required a little more patience. The plan was to pick up a club in the second tier and finance it to make the jump into the Premier League's land of milk and honey.

Srivaddhanaprabha's timing couldn't have been better. If Leicester could earn promotion in the next few years, it would reach the Premier League in time to ride the upcoming wave of improved television money. Which is exactly what the Foxes did. They secured a place in the top flight in 2014, prompting their new owners to pledge another £180 million to crack the Premier League's top five within three years.

The old hands inside the club, however, were inclined to be a little more cautious. They had seen this movie before. Small club with big dreams spends a foreign investor's money. Results don't live up to expectations. Investor yanks the rug out from under them. Hello, relegation, administration, and relegation again.

So even with the extra cash available, Leicester's 2015–16 squad were assembled on the cheap by Premier League standards. Cobbled together by chief scout Steve Walsh, a heavy-set northerner with sparse grey hair who looked every bit the part of a man who'd spent the bulk of his career zipped into a puffer jacket in the windy stands of obscure stadiums. Thirty years in the game, with stints at Newcastle, Hull, and Chelsea under José Mourinho, had taught him how to spot a player who could cut it in England. What Walsh did better than anyone else was spot a guy who could do that for next to nothing.

Over the course of three seasons, he quietly assembled a collection of misfits and cast-offs for around £60 million. (Arsenal's squad at the time cost around five times that, and Manchester City's was eight times more expensive.) Only Leicester's goalkeeper, Kasper Schmeichel, was already in place. Walsh's first two signings – Jamaica defender Wes Morgan and United academy washout Danny Drinkwater – cost the Foxes under £1 million each. From the French second division, he plucked Riyad Mahrez, an undersize Algerian who loved to dribble just a little too much, for £500,000.

And then there was Jamie Vardy, the whippet-thin striker, cut from Sheffield Wednesday's academy for being too small, who seemed to have no business in the top two tiers of English football. His now legendary rags-to-riches story had seen him begin his career seven levels below the English Premier League at Stocksbridge Park Steels, a semi-pro outfit that paid around £100 a week. Bigger clubs checked in on him, but all they saw were red flags – a string of red cards and Vardy's conviction for assault following a brawl in a pub. He was living under a court-ordered curfew and had to wear a monitoring tag on his ankle even during games. On longer away trips, Stocksbridge would substitute him before full time and stick him in a car so he could make it home in time.

A couple of clubs in the lower reaches took chances on him – Halifax Town, then Fleetwood Town. That was as high as Vardy ever thought he would go until Walsh spotted him in 2012. Vardy was already twenty-five years old, a late bloomer for sure, but he was banging in the goals. Plus, he had another quality that Walsh thought Leicester could do something with.

'There was no great secret to Jamie,' said Andrew Pilley, who signed Vardy in 2011 for Fleetwood Town, then in the fifth tier. 'He was ridiculously quick. It was almost like cheating.'

There was no sign early on that Walsh's bargain bunch had anything special about them. The Foxes were promoted to the Premier League for 2014–15, and the normal rules seemed to apply: you are what you spend. Leicester spent less than nearly everyone else, so it made perfect sense when they began 2015 dead last.

The bookmakers made them as prohibitive seven-to-ten favourites for relegation. It would not be the first time they were wrong about Leicester.

The Foxes won six of their last eight games that season to pull off one of the unlikeliest escapes in Premier League history. That did nothing, however, to convince anyone that they would survive again the following season. The Foxes had sacked the manager who'd saved them, and their squad was still a bargain-priced collection of spare parts – an IKEA dresser with all the wrong screws. When

Leicester kicked off the 2015–16 campaign, the club were back among the bookies' favourites for the drop. (They didn't much care that Leicester's owners had brought in Buddhist monks to bless the field and the team.) But because bookies do it for everyone, they also set a line on Leicester winning the Premier League: 5,000 to 1. It was basically a novelty bet. Those odds were on a par with what they offered on San Marino winning the next World Cup, David Beckham starring as the next James Bond, and Elvis Presley being discovered alive. Making the whole thing even more far-fetched for the Foxes, their new manager was Claudio Ranieri, the jokey Italian last spotted in the Premier League getting summarily fired by Chelsea eleven years earlier. In the meantime, he had managed seven other sides, including the Greek national team for all of four games – a calamity that ended after a home defeat against the Faroe Islands, then ranked 187th in the world.

Even Gary Lineker couldn't contain his surprise – or vague disgust. 'Claudio Ranieri?' he tweeted after the announcement in mid July. 'Really?'

That summer, Walsh kept hunting for talent in Europe's pound shops, spending just £45 million on nine players. Only when he sought to add a five-foot-six midfielder from the Paris suburbs named N'Golo Kanté did he encounter any resistance. Even though Kanté had been toiling in the third division of French soccer just two years earlier, Walsh thought the kid might be useful. If nothing else, he could run and run and run. Ranieri wasn't interested. 'I had to beg Claudio to take him,' Walsh said.

For days, Walsh would brush past Ranieri in Leicester's offices whispering, 'Kanté, Kanté, you must sign Kanté.' Ranieri still protested. Like everyone else, he deemed the player too slight for the rigours of English football. Besides, Ranieri couldn't see a spot for him in the team.

'He'll play anywhere,' Walsh told him. 'I know he's only a midget, but he'll play in goal!'

Walsh's badgering worked. And pretty soon, with Kanté at the heart of the side, Ranieri molded the squad he was dealt into one of the surprises of the autumn. Not only were Leicester holding off an immediate return to the relegation zone, they were pretty solid.

The Foxes didn't do anything flashy, but it worked. Unburdened by the expectations of bigger clubs to play entertaining, attractive football, Leicester were content to sit back and nail opponents on the counter-attack. Mahrez danced up and down the wing. The defensive pillars were so robust that their play bordered on illegal. And Vardy could chase balls knocked over the top for days. He scored so much that he found himself closing in on the record for goals in consecutive games by December. When he broke it, setting the new mark at eleven, Leicester finally understood what had been so obvious to Fleetwood Town years before: putting Vardy in your team really was almost like cheating.

At the same time, the sixty-four-year-old Ranieri was waging a charm offensive in all of his press conferences. His cheerful Italian accent and smiling demeanour infused everything he said with grandfatherly disbelief. He compared his squad of speed demons to the Royal Air Force. 'It's fantastic. Whoosh! Whoosh! I love it,' he giggled. Then he decided that the more apt analogy for Vardy was a 'fantastic horse'. Ranieri also brought in revolutionary coaching techniques, such as giving his team two days off each week instead of the customary one and promising to buy the whole team pizza whenever they posted clean sheets.

Everything anyone knew about the Premier League told them that Leicester would cool off. This just didn't make any sense. Leicester didn't have expensive players or a manager who had ever won a league before or the patina of seriousness. But when people looked around for someone to knock the Foxes off their perch, the usual suspects were too busy falling apart. The constant tension bred by José Mourinho at Chelsea, which had produced a title the season before, now threatened to melt down his dressing room. (The Chelsea disaster came to a head in December – after a defeat to Leicester, incidentally – when Mourinho accused his players of not trying hard enough and was sacked days later.) In Manchester, United were sputtering under David Moyes's successor, Louis van Gaal, and City were looking listless under Manuel Pellegrini. Arsenal and Tottenham both seemed steeled to mount a real challenge until they, too, spun off into inconsistency.

Not only did the Foxes happen to catch the league's biggest clubs all having a down year at the same time, but they also reaped the benefits of a larger shift that appeared to be unfolding in the Premier League. The new round of broadcast deals – Richard Scudamore's latest success – meant that simply by virtue of playing in England's top flight Leicester were suddenly among the richest clubs in Europe. And the effect was always going to be greater for a club like Leicester than for one like Manchester United – an extra £10 million made a much bigger difference to the Foxes than it did at Old Trafford. All of a sudden, the middle-class clubs could acquire better players, pay them higher wages, and hang on to them for longer. Gone were the days when a player would come to England with a mid-table club only to be snapped up by Manchester United after one good season.

'If you are clever with more investment you can keep those players,' said West Ham manager Slaven Bilić, whose side had the best record in the league against the top four that season.

On 1 January 2016, at the halfway point of the campaign, Leicester were tied for first with the Gunners. A month later, the Foxes were top with a three-point cushion between them and Manchester City. They were ticking along, using fewer players than any other team in the league, and the Premier League began to realize that this thing could actually happen. Even as Ranieri refused to admit that his team were in a title race, the whole season took on a surreal vibe. Leicester kept winning. And no one could quite explain why.

There were those who thought there was someone more important to the Foxes' run than Ranieri or Vardy or anyone else in a blue jersey. The more superstitious members of the Leicester faithful chalked it up to an MVP who'd been dead for five centuries: King Richard III, slain by multiple axe blows to the head at the Battle of Bosworth Field.

The story of how the cadaverous monarch came to turn around Leicester's fortunes began some 527 years after he met his grisly end. He spent that time rotting in a shallow grave, the location of which was forgotten until archaeologists from the University of Leicester discovered the bones in 2012. The king was under a car park.

After Richard's grand reburial in Leicester Cathedral – the first funeral for a British monarch in more than sixty years – something strange happened to the team. The Foxes won twenty-eight of their next forty-two matches, losing just four, which spanned their miraculous escape from relegation and their surge to the top of the Premier League.

The final weeks of the season turned into a flood of feel-good stories around the club, even if Ranieri was the last man in England to admit that Leicester were legitimate contenders. (They had a five-point lead in April before he said so publicly.) 'Okay, now we can do!' Ranieri told his players. 'Because never [again] could it happen.'

It was around that time that Ranieri got a mysterious phone call. He knew that a dead king was pulling for his team, now there was a blind tenor.

'Claudio, I feel something,' the Italian opera singer Andrea Bocelli told his countryman. 'There is a good atmosphere. I want to come there.'

Ranieri arranged the visit for Leicester's final home game. And when he lifted the trophy to complete the most improbable title run in English football history, the opera singer was on the pitch next to him. Because why not? The situation was already so crazy that it wasn't like adding the most famous tenor in the world singing 'Nessun dorma' to the mix would make this Sunday afternoon in Leicester any more surreal.

From narrowly avoiding relegation to champions in the space of a year was not anything that was supposed to happen. It ran counter to everything the Premier League had built over the previous twenty-four years. Champions needed to pay high salaries, spend fortunes in the transfer market, and dominate their opponents. Leicester pulled off their miracle with a fraction of the major clubs' wage bills and possessed the ball in matches less than any other champion in the Premier League era. The fairy tale earned the players national celebrity, an open-top-bus parade through the city, and a fleet of BMWs as a gift from their owner.

Never mind the season's not-so-Disney details. Like the incident in the summer before the season that saw a drunken Jamie Vardy use a racist slur towards an Asian man in a casino. Or the fact that Ranieri landed in the Leicester job only because his predecessor was sacked following the emergence of a sex tape involving several Leicester players on a pre-season tour of Thailand, one of whom was the former manager's son – a spectacularly tawdry tale even by English football standards. So there were at least a couple of reasons why the Leicester City miracle was not altogether a feel-good story.

And on this point, there was at least one group inclined to agree, but not because they cared about what Leicester players got up to in casinos or on pre-season tours. This group in particular was offended by the simple fact of Leicester's success. They were the Premier League's Big Six.

26

To MANCHESTER UNITED, Manchester City, Chelsea, Liverpool, Tottenham, and Arsenal, an upstart like Leicester was completely unacceptable.

Not because they had no room in their blackened hearts for an underdog story – though that was possible – but because the upper reaches of the Premier League were already feeling too crowded. The most powerful group of clubs, once known as the Big Five and later as the Big Four, had now expanded to six. There were more rich, ambitious teams than there were spots available in the Champions League. And for the likes of the Manchester clubs, Chelsea, and Arsenal, Champions League qualification wasn't just an annual luxury. It was a central column of their business models. The mere act of turning up to the 2016–17 Champions League was worth €12.7 million to each competing team even if they lost all six group-stage games. Premier League teams, which could reasonably expect to advance to the second round, were looking at a minimum payout of roughly €25 million. And if one of them caught fire and won the whole thing, they would cash in to the tune of €57 million.

Far too good for the likes of Leicester. The Big Six couldn't let an outsider snatch away one of those golden tickets again – not to mention win the whole damn league while they were at it. In the summer of 2016, they needed to rearm. Amid a league-wide wave of frenzied spending, Manchester United became the first English club in twenty years to break the world transfer record. Their target was French midfielder Paul Pogba . . . who had left the club as a nineteen-year-old four years earlier. The deal was orchestrated by Pogba's agent Mino Raiola, a man who is quite possibly the richest *pizzaiolo* on the planet. An Italian who emigrated to the Netherlands as a child, Raiola spent his teenage years working in his father's pizzeria before earning a law degree and ingratiating himself to Dutch footballers who wanted to move to Italy. But Pogba was his biggest coup. In 2012, Raiola was the one who had convinced him to flee United for Juventus, and in 2016, he was there again to set up Pogba's return for an unprecedented £93 million. The deal personally earned Raiola around £15 million plus some high praise from none other than Sir Alex Ferguson. He called Raiola a 'shitbag'.

The Pogba deal was only the headline in a summer of insane extravagance from Premier League teams. For the first time in their history, they combined to shell out more than £1 billion.

But as they carpet-bombed the European transfer market with blank cheques, the top English clubs had to admit an uncomfortable reality. The Premier League, for all their talk of being the richest, most competitive, most watched league in the world, simply couldn't buy football's superelite any more. It wasn't lost on them that for the better part of a decade the era-defining rivalry between Cristiano Ronaldo and Lionel Messi had unfolded in Spain, not England. Luis Suárez, after nearly carrying Liverpool to the title in 2014, had bolted to Barcelona two years after Gareth Bale electrified the Premier League and fled to Real Madrid. And when the time came for the Brazilian superstar-in-the-making Neymar to jump from South America to Europe, he turned down all the English suitors in favour of – you guessed it – Barça.

From a player's perspective, choosing one of the two Spanish giants over any of the Big Six is perfectly reasonable. There's a lot to like about playing in La Liga. Spanish football is less bruising than in England, where the referees are lenient, the conditions are worse, and the fans still cheer a crunching tackle. And off the pitch, the Spanish tax code has more holes for Europe's football-playing millionaires to exploit than a third-division defence. (When Liverpool player John Arne Riise's pay stub leaked out in 2007, for instance, it showed him straightforwardly paying the standard high-bracket tax rate of 40 per cent. Ronaldo, Messi, and Neymar, meanwhile, were all caught allegedly pushing their luck with the Spanish tax authorities.)

And then there's the small matter of the weather. The clichéd test of quality for flashy foreign players landing in England is whether they can cut it on a wet, windy night in Stoke. But why would they bother when they can live in Madrid, maintain a permatan, and golf four days a week?

So the Premier League needed something to seduce the superelite players besides outrageous salaries (Spain, Italy, and Germany had those, too), a self-appointed distinction as the 'best league in the world', and the charms of a windy night in Stoke. Consciously or not, it settled on another, more grizzled class of football men: the superelite managers, the larger-than-life coaches who stamp their identities on a club and come with such gravitational pull that top players join for the privilege of playing under them.

For a chunk of the Premier League's history, the only managers in England with that kind of magnetism were Alex Ferguson and Arsène Wenger. In the mid 2000s, José Mourinho was added to the mix. But that was pretty much it. Then, in 2013, Ferguson finally retired. Through sheer force of will and a reliance on Robin van Persie's goals, he had won his thirteenth Premier League title and rode off into the sunset.

The sheriff leaving town was always going to leave a vacuum. His aura — and his barrage of thinly veiled insults — had shaped every title race in the Premier League era, even those he didn't win. A Ferguson United team was always a factor, its very presence a distraction, much in the way that golfing next to Tiger Woods might rattle your short game. It's hardly a stretch to say that the Leicester City miracle might never have happened had Fergie stuck around. Some combination of his bullying on the back pages and the form his sides habitually used to uncork in the second half of the season might have squashed them. More accomplished teams than the 2015–16 Foxes had folded with United breathing down their necks.

But just as the end of the Liverpool dynasty of the 1980s gave way to a reordering at the top of English football, with title challenges from the likes of Norwich and Leeds United plus three different champions in the three years between 1990 and 1993, the post-Ferguson era created a shake-up. Leicester's title was only the most dramatic example.

One by one, as the establishment clubs attempted to consolidate their places in the top six, they handed the keys to their teams to European supermanagers. If Ferguson, Mourinho, and Wenger had taught them anything, it was that the most important employee at the club was the guy frantically chewing gum, or fiddling with the zip on his puffy coat, or muttering swear words in Portuguese on the sideline.

In the autumn of 2015, John Henry's Liverpool won the football-hipster lottery when they hired the bearded, bespectacled Jürgen Klopp after he left Borussia Dortmund, a club that had earned admirers all over Europe for its exciting style of football, its commitment to young talent, and its rabid fan base. Although Dortmund supporters were perhaps not as rabid as Klopp himself, whose ranting and raving and fist pumping on the touchline had made him the most viral manager in the world – a football coach for the Twitter set. A former player with what he called 'fifth-division skills but a first-division brain', he rose to prominence for his own brand of 'heavy-metal football', all pressing, passing, and counter-pressing all the time. Klopp used it to break big bad Bayern Munich's stranglehold on the Bundesliga in 2010 with back-to-back German titles. Until that point, Bayern had won eight of the previous twelve championships. When the two German sides met in the 2013 Champions League final, won at the last minute by Bayern, Klopp compared his Bavarian nemesis to a James Bond villain.

That's not to suggest that Klopp was any kind of James Bond – a tuxedo would cramp his style. While Arsène Wenger sported Lanvin suits in the dugout and José Mourinho favoured a puffer jacket designed by Porsche, Klopp was firmly a tracksuit manager who dressed as if he were about to board a fourteen-hour flight. The Puma tracksuit bottoms-and-hoodie combination he wore for one Champions League clash between Dortmund and Arsenal could be purchased from the club shop for under £100.

When the forty-eight-year-old Klopp arrived in England, the growing faction of Arsenal fans that wanted Wenger out after two decades saw a missed opportunity. *We should've gone for him.*

Klopp was the first of the Premier League's new supermanager wave. At Chelsea, Roman Abramovich hired the twelfth manager of his tenure, the dapper Italian, Antonio Conte. A former star for Juventus and Italy, Conte had developed into one of the most tactically savvy managers on the planet – and appeared to have grown a healthy new head of hair since his days as a balding midfielder. He lifted three consecutive league titles at Juventus before moulding what he admitted was the least talented Italy squad in a generation into a 'small war machine' and impressing at the 2016 European Championship. And like anyone else who has ever sat in a dugout for Abramovich, he was fully aware of the risks. The Russian owner had the quickest trigger in the league. The moment results started to slip, his first instinct was to make a change in the dugout. In the first thirteen years of his ownership, Abramovich had terminated World Cup winners, Champions League winners, Chelsea heroes, and José Mourinho twice. Not including one- or two-game caretakers, Abramovich made eleven changes in the dugout at a rate of one every fourteen months.

So why does a manager subject himself to the potential indignity of running afoul of Abramovich – as managers almost always do? For one, there is the simple fact that Chelsea are among the most ambitious and successful clubs in the world. And, just as important, managers know that they will be compensated for the risk. Like any dangerous gig, this one comes with hazard pay. Since 2003, Chelsea has spent more than £60 million in severance to various managers according to the club accounts. A 2011 analysis by Deloitte, for instance, revealed that the club's staff costs for the previous year included around £15 million in termination payments to managers and coaching staff plus an additional £13 million in relation to what Deloitte called 'changes in the first team management structure'.

In other words, firing people was fast becoming Abramovich's most expensive habit that wasn't related to floating his superyacht around the Mediterranean.

Still, Conte was eager to join the fray. His tactical rigour and maniacal work ethic seemed perfectly suited to the Premier League. And when the forty-six-year-old Italian arrived in England in July 2016, the 'Wenger Out' brigade across London again wished their club had considered a change. *We should've gone for him.*

That same summer, José Mourinho's third act in England kicked off at Manchester United seven months after he was booted out of Chelsea. The move had seemed preordained for years – Alex Ferguson was the only manager Mourinho spared from his various broadsides. In fact, Mourinho was United's top choice to succeed Ferguson in 2013, but he returned to Chelsea instead. The club instead settled on David Moyes, hand-picked by Ferguson. Only the 'Chosen One', as they called him, had been nothing short of a debacle. His ten months at Old Trafford set United up for a seventh-place finish and turned him into a national punchline. As the rapper and United fan Stormzy put it in one song, 'I come to your team and I fuck shit up / I'm David Moyes'. The two seasons that followed under Dutch manager Louis van Gaal, a man who seemed convinced he had never been wrong about anything ever, were only marginally better.

So when fifty-three-year-old Mourinho returned to the Premier League in 2016, that was another high-calibre manager crossed off the list of potential Wenger successors. But this time, even the most ardent 'Wenger Out' fans stayed quiet about the man who'd been picking fights with their club for the better part of fifteen years. *We should have gone for someone . . . just not him.*

Rounding out the Big Six were the pair in north London at opposite ends of their Premier League careers. At Tottenham, Mauricio Pochettino, the forty-four-year-old foul-mouthed ex-defender from Argentina, suddenly had a shine about him for turning Spurs into a high-octane contender. His training sessions were notoriously brutal for their endless running. His summers involved two and sometimes three gruelling fitness sessions a day. But there was a method to his taskmaster madness. When Pochettino arrived in England from Spain, it dawned on him that Premier League games felt somehow longer than any matches he'd been involved in elsewhere. They all lasted ninety minutes, of course, but Pochettino worked out that England had fewer stoppages due to fouls or the ball going out of play. Games packed in up to ten more minutes of live action or, as he saw it, ten more minutes that required flat-out effort. Players who weren't prepared to run like they were constantly on fire weren't going to play for Pochettino.

That approach put him on the radar of any major club looking for a manager with a long future. He had yet to win a major trophy in England, but he'd earned his place among the Premier League's supermanagers by the company he kept: United took a hard look at him before they landed Mourinho, and Real Madrid were later rumoured to have him atop their shortlist. It was clear Pochettino was going places.

His north London counterpart, meanwhile, seemingly wasn't going anywhere. With Ferguson retired, Wenger was the last of the old generals. In 2016, his twenty years in charge of the Gunners exceeded the combined tenures of the Premier League's nineteen other managers. But one question was consuming Arsenal's fan base: *Was Wenger the right man for the job?* Arsenal hadn't won a league title under him since 2004, nor had they really been in the hunt late in the season since at least 2010. And with 2016–17 shaping up to be what Wenger called a 'world championship of managers', could the sixty-six-year-old Frenchman keep up with a set of coaches more than ten years his junior?

The debate would reach an absurd altitude later that season when warring sets of Arsenal supporters each hired aeroplanes to fly banners over a single game. NO CONTRACT #WENGEROUT read the first. Minutes later, another plane flew over the stadium with a conflicting message fluttering in five-foot letters: IN ARSÈNE WE TRUST #RESPECTAW. The only winner that day was the owner of a small banner-flying company called Air Ads. He'd been hired by both sides.

Perhaps the only person who still considered Wenger truly a super-manager – and remained committed to spending eight figures a year to make that point – was the man paying his wages, Stan Kroenke. On the rare occasions when Silent Stan could be drawn to utter anything in public at all, his response to any mention of Wenger was always the same. 'A great man,' he said from beneath a bushy silver mustache. At Arsenal's 2016 AGM, with the club's fans out for blood, Kroenke responded by handing Wenger a framed portrait of Wenger. (The portrait never did make it to the walls of his house.)

At Manchester City, the mood was decidedly more upbeat. With the club's executives still obsessing over the question of how to bring superelite players back to the Premier League, City pushed the button on a scheme they'd been preparing for at least five years. Perhaps the only club in England that could afford someone like Lionel Messi settled on another international superstar, a bald midfielder from Barcelona with a grey beard and a bad back: Pep Guardiola. He was precisely what City's Catalan contingent, led by CEO Ferran Soriano and sporting director Txiki Begiristain, had been laying the groundwork for since the day they touched down in the north-west. 'It was always foreseen from the very beginning that we would try to bring Pep,' Soriano said. And now that they had their man, they were going to give him all the space and resources he needed to leave an indelible mark on the club.

Guardiola set himself an even larger mission. Not only did he want to win the Premier League – that would be an incidental consequence – he hoped to teach England a whole new way of conceptualizing football.

'Of course I think the coach sooner or later has to prove what it means to play in England,' Guardiola said at his introduction in Manchester. 'At the end what we want is so simple; when the opponent has the ball, take it back as quick as possible. When we have the ball, try to move as quick possible, to create as much chances as possible. That's all.'

At the opposite end of the Premier League, there was another group of managers without the pedigree or the trophies who didn't want to hear about football philosophies or Catalan gurus.

They were all older, battle worn, and invariably British. Not a single one of them was known for playing attractive football. But that hardly dented their employment prospects. Granted, they might not ever get near a club like Manchester City or Chelsea. But they were hardly ever out of work. In fact, they played a critical role in the Premier League ecosystem.

They were survival specialists – men like Sam Allardyce, Roy Hodgson, Tony Pulis, David Moyes, Mark Hughes, and Alan Pardew. With the kind of money that used to be available exclusively to Champions League teams now on offer just for staying up, a manager who could guarantee safety was potentially worth more than one who made the leap from mid table to the top four. For owners, they kept investments safe. For fans, they were sometimes necessary evils.

In a league where the average lifespan of a manager was sliding down towards thirteen months, the constant presence of these survivors in effect formed the Premier League's permanent bureaucracy. In 2013–14, nearly half the league finished the season with a different manager than the one they started with. Nine clubs burned through ten different coaches mid campaign – Fulham were the ones to achieve the rare feat of sacking two in a single season.

And in those situations, owners always went back to the well: the old reliables who had been in those scraps before. Allardyce, Hodgson, Hughes, Moyes, Pulis, and Pardew. At least four of those six managers were employed by a Premier League club or the England national team in the course of every season between 2008 and 2018. That's a decade's worth of immovability.

The clubs that ended up hiring them made up a list of usual suspects, too. Since 2006, Blackburn, Crystal Palace, Everton, Fulham, Newcastle, Stoke City, Sunderland, West Brom, and West Ham have all hired at least two of those men off the Premier League's merry-go-round of retreads.

'You can stand there and be the saviour of so many football clubs because there's so many sackings,' said Allardyce, who has managed seven different clubs in the league. 'You can pick up a job if you've got the experience now and you've got your track record.'

Fans don't exactly get excited when their club's owner unveils a relegation doctor. It's usually an admission that things have taken a turn for the catastrophic – or that the owners are content simply to stay afloat in the Premier League. Supporters always prefer to spend their season-ticket money to watch a team play stylish football with attacking verve and at least a vague promise of entertainment. Of course. And every so often, a club will hire a manager promising to deliver that fantasy. But when it starts to go wrong, if the prospect of relegation starts to creep in, questions of style go out the window. It's all well and good for owners to please the fans so long as it doesn't cost them £100 million in missed Premier League payments the following season. At that point, the thing that matters is hiring a manager who can make sure the club are better than just three other teams. Then the rescue job begins.

'You look at the squad that's available, you look at the opposition you're playing against, and you try and simplify the game,' Allardyce said. 'Say, "These are the simple basics, lads, you try and achieve those in the ninety minutes."'

At Stoke City, Pulis thought the path to overperformance was making sure the ball was in play for as little of those ninety minutes as possible. More skilful teams can't hurt you if the ball is somewhere off in the stands. David Moyes, before his unhappy adventure at Manchester United, helped Everton exceed expectations by putting the emphasis on corners and free kicks, where physicality was more likely to make up for a gap in talent. And Allardyce, in his permanent quest for simplicity, asks all of his clubs for only two things: play hard and play direct.

The result is never pretty. Mourinho famously called it 'nineteenth-century football'. But he couldn't argue that the approach didn't work. Allardyce has never been relegated from the Premier League. 'I tell the lads, "It can't happen,"' he said, '"You're not going to spoil my record. So we're going to survive."'

27

THIS WAS THE football that Guardiola, the game's philosopher king, was about to encounter. He had dismantled English clubs in the Champions League as a coach but never experienced it as a player week after week. The closest he came was standing in Arsène Wenger's north London kitchen in the early 2000s asking to sign for Arsenal. Except he was already in his thirties and Wenger had one of the most dominant central midfields in Europe – he didn't need Guardiola the player.

Shortly thereafter, following stints at Brescia, Roma, and Al-Ahli of Qatar, Guardiola the manager was born. His brain was always more valuable than his right foot anyway.

Steeped in the football culture of Barcelona since joining its youth academy/finishing school at the age of thirteen, Guardiola grew into the custodian of the club's ethos. Johan Cruyff had first brought it to Catalonia in the 1970s, and he perfected it during his tenure as manager of the Barça Dream Team of the 1990s – with Guardiola anchoring defensive midfield. Cruyff's entire edifice rested on a revolutionary understanding of space on a football pitch and intricate passing patterns, mistakenly dubbed 'tiki-taka', something Guardiola never stopped mulling over. The Barcelona brass took note. And though Guardiola had no previous experience in management, the club deemed him fluent enough in the Barça doctrine to teach it to the reserve team, Barça B, in 2007. 'Cruyff built the cathedral,' Guardiola said, 'our job is to maintain and renovate it.'

A season after being handed the keys to Barça B, he was promoted to manage the senior squad. The next nine years turned into a blur of trophies and brilliance and all-consuming stress for Guardiola. Three Spanish league titles; two Champions Leagues with a Barça side built around Lionel Messi, Andrés Iniesta, and Xavi; then three more league titles in Germany with Bayern Munich. 'Maybe it's true,' he said in 2010 as journalists showered him with praise. 'Maybe when I piss, I do piss perfume.' Storming up and down the touchlines of two of the most storied clubs in Europe, constantly rubbing his bald head as if to stimulate his synapses, Guardiola alternated between the roles of tortured genius and petulant child. In 2011, while receiving an award from the Catalan government, he described his process of tactical invention before a game – locked in his office with a stack of DVDs, a notepad, and music playing softly in the background. 'That's when it comes,' he said. 'The instant I know, for sure, that I've got it. I know how to win the match. It only lasts for about a minute, maybe eighty seconds, but it's the moment my job becomes truly meaningful to me.'

That moment might be his final taste of calm before kick-off. From the second the game begins until his customary glass of post-match champagne, the genius turns into a madman wound tighter than one of his slim-cut jumpers. His outbursts on the touchline were often so wild that they couldn't be contained by his clothes – in one Champions League match, he sprang so violently into the air that he ripped open his tailored suit trousers. When he left Barcelona in 2012, he felt exhausted. Four years at the club seemed an eternity to him. Which might have been the case for a man who barely sleeps.

That was the first time Ferran Soriano tried to convince him to join Manchester City.

Guardiola said no. Most coaches spend the time between jobs looking for new jobs. They advertise their expertise by moonlighting as TV pundits. They stay on the prowl – or at least in the country – should one of their mates with a more desirable gig get fired. But Guardiola is forcefully not 'most coaches'. Instead, he retreated to New York for a year-long sabbatical, where he lived on tree-lined Central Park West up the road from the American Museum of Natural History. Like a Manhattan novelist between opuses, the football manager was content to simply exist and contemplate and let his well of inspiration refill. He walked his children to their Upper West Side private school. He dined with chess champion

Garry Kasparov. He watched the Knicks at Madison Square Garden. His only concession to his future in soccer was taking secret German lessons in preparation for Bayern Munich.

But if he arrived in Germany rested and brimming with ideas, he left it exhausted again and somewhat unsatisfied. Guardiola's team crushed the Bundesliga in all three of his seasons there; but without a Champions League triumph to show for himself, he had missed out on proving to the world that he could build a European power-house without the Messi advantage. Soriano came calling again. And this time, Guardiola was ready to take the leap into the Premier League. (He would also be cashing yet another petrodollar pay cheque a decade after playing for Al-Ahli and six years after serving as an ambassador for Qatar's bid to host the 2022 World Cup.)

To Sheikh Mansour, who spoke to Guardiola on the phone, and to Soriano, who finally had his white whale, Guardiola was the biggest get in Manchester City's history, more impactful than any player, more sought-after than practically any human in football. Plus, Guardiola shared their view that the world's superelite talent needed to be lured back to the Premier League – and that a super-elite manager was the perfect bait. As Guardiola put it at his intro-duction in Manchester: 'Hopefully the best players can come here to England.'

This is what the whole City plan had been building towards since the Catalan invasion of 2011 and 2012. Manuel Pellegrini, a grave Chilean in his sixties, had always felt like a placeholder despite winning a championship in 2014 – a title that Sheikh Mansour celebrated from a distance, surrounded by white-robed royalty slicing a novelty cake with a sword. Pep was, just as City had always wanted, the true best in class. 'The time was right for him and the time was right for us,' City's Brian Marwood said. 'We were ready for some-body as great as him. If you'd have said, were we ready for Pep three, four years before? I don't think we were. He came into a ready-made environment for him. He didn't really have to make seismic changes.'

Guardiola may not have had to. But he did anyway.

For one, there was going to be a lot more Catalan echoing around the halls of City's training ground. Guardiola imported the backroom staff that had followed him since the Barcelona days, including the assistant coach who had never played professional football because he was Spain's greatest water-polo player, Manel Estiarte. Then he would have to get to his new squad – Guardiola's philosophy requires nothing less than total buy-in from his players. 'I know them from TV', he said at his introductory press conference in Manchester, 'but I must speak with them, hug them – and kick their asses.'

He wanted each of his players doing exactly the same thing to one another. In his first months at City, he banned the use of mobile phones and disabled the wi-fi at the training ground. He even 'forces us to have breakfast and lunch together', former defender Pablo Zabaleta said at the time. Team meals were only for emotional connection or high-minded debates about football strategy, not for browsing Instagram.

The whole experience can be taxing for players who, it must be said, often enjoy a quite laid-back existence, with a daily two-hour training session, some time in the gym, and most of the day spent recovering from games. Guardiola's charges at Bayern left his first few sessions terrified that he would exhaust them. The City squad could be forgiven for thinking the same. Guardiola is so obsessive that he had the lines on one pitch at the club's training facility redrawn to better illustrate his thoughts on using space. He had done the same in Germany, breaking down a pitch into twenty smaller boxes so he could push his players around like little chess pieces. 'I can see why he has these sabbaticals,' Marwood said. 'Because the energy that he brings to the job is amazing. From early in the morning to late at night, this guy never switches off.'

The difference now for Guardiola – and what set the challenge in England apart from what he faced in Spain and Germany – was that he was suddenly up against four or five other likely title contenders as opposed to the one or two he was used to. And every one of them was doing some version of City's plan to build around a supermanager. The tone was going to be different. And for that, from day one of the season, he had his old foe José Mourinho to thank. The pair had clashed almost everywhere – in Spain, when Mourinho managed Real Madrid, and in the Champions League before then, when Mourinho was at Inter.

'There are some managers that the last time they won a title was ten years ago,' Mourinho said at his Manchester United introduction, taking a shot at Wenger. 'Some of them have never won a title,' he added, in a drive-by on Pochettino. 'If I have a lot to prove, imagine the others.'

And on the topic of Guardiola, Mourinho was an expert at dodging the question, appearing to be the bigger man while still turning the screws. 'To speak about one manager, one club, one enemy, I hate the word in football and life, I don't think it is right. It is one thing to be in a two-horse race like I was in Spain, or in Italy it was three teams fighting for the title, then that kind of approach makes sense. In the Premier League it doesn't make sense at all. If you focus on one opponent, the others will be laughing so I am not going to be part of it . . . I am the manager of the biggest club in the UK.'

Guardiola's first season in England was a strange one. As he navigated the Premier League calendar, his every move under scrutiny, Conte's Chelsea quietly ran away with the title. No real challenge ever materialized. Guardiola's match-day attire changed from suits to hoodies, bomber jackets, and oversize scarves.

But the Premier League establishment struck back so hard in the wake of the Leicester City upset that the Big Six whipped the rest of the clubs with renewed violence. In finishing sixth, Manchester United left an eight-point gap between themselves and Everton in seventh place, followed by a further fifteen-point gap from seventh to eighth. The good vibes in Leicester, meanwhile, evaporated as quickly as they'd arrived. A miracle of that size in any other sport might earn a manager a long contract extension or at least a voucher so he'd never have to buy a drink in the city again. In the Premier League, the miracle bought Ranieri nine months.

With the Foxes in danger of relegation, the club's owners sacked Ranieri in mid February. No sentiment, however fuzzy and improbable, was worth dropping out of the Premier League for.

Key players had turned on Ranieri and lobbied the owners to replace him with his English assistant, Craig Shakespeare. The narrative gathered enough steam that, at Shakespeare's first game in charge, the Leicester fans unfurled a gigantic display urging their team to CRY HAVOC AND LET SLIP THE DOGS OF WAR. Their choice of a line from William Shakespeare's *Julius Caesar* was no accident.

'Okay, I was sacked. Okay!' Ranieri said. 'This is my life. My life is football. I know one day you are at the top, one day you are down.'

Maybe for Ranieri. The men in soccer management's A-list can't afford to ride such a rollercoaster. As the season came to a close, the Premier League's supermanagers took stock of what they'd achieved. Conte made the biggest impact, out-thinking the opposition with decisive tactical changes that won him the title. Pochettino pulled off a second straight second-place finish. Klopp secured a top-four spot and returned Liverpool to the Champions League. And Mourinho won the Europa League and a League Cup, Manchester United's first trophies in four years. Even Wenger, despite missing out on Champions League qualification for the first time in twenty-one years, had something to show for himself as Arsenal won the FA Cup.

Only Guardiola was left staring at a chasm between his club's season and his club's expectations. This was a strange new feeling for him. Third place and no tournament finals. Neither Barcelona nor Bayern had ever finished lower than second on his watch. And for the first time in his decade as a manager, spring had come and gone without a trophy.

'The 2016–17 season – the first under new manager Pep Guardiola – was something of a contradiction. It was a season in which no silverware was won by our first team and in which we finished third in the Premier League, only securing our Champions League position relatively late,' al-Mubarak, the club chairman, wrote in his annual report, as if it were City's end-of-year earnings.

'In the last seven seasons, we have won more trophies than any other team in the Premier League . . . Having set such high standards for ourselves it is inevitable that finishing a campaign empty-handed brought with it a raw sense of disappointment.'

Wide swathes of the football media, returning to their old suspicion of anything that had the misfortune of being highly regarded and foreign, were less circumspect. Despite having the largest budget in the league, Guardiola had failed to mount a serious challenge of any sort. And the press seized on his continued failure to reach a Champions League final without Messi, his on-field nuclear weapon. All of it was proof that his tippy-tappy tiki-taka might have worked in Spain or Germany, but Guardiola couldn't expect to try that stuff in Manchester and succeed. The phrase 'Welcome to the Premier League, Pep' was uttered and printed sarcastically more times that season than anyone could count.

The tabloids even had a new name for this delicate Catalan genius. *Fraudiola*.

It was a Sunday night in early December, and flecks of snow hung in the air over Manchester. The temperature was stuck somewhere south of zero, and Old Trafford was now mostly empty. Even some of the hardened locals had to admit that it felt a bit brisk. But for Pep Guardiola, this was no time to head indoors. The warmth of a steamy dressing room could wait. For now, he wanted to bask in the moment.

Out in the centre of the Old Trafford pitch, a dark wool scarf draped over his black bomber jacket and skinny trousers, Guardiola could barely contain himself. He bear-hugged his players as they made their way off the field, exchanged violent high fives with his assistant coaches on the sidelines, and he planted a big slobbery kiss on the head of midfielder David Silva. Finally, he pumped his fists, turned his gaze towards the skies overhead, and closed his eyes. For Guardiola, a year and a half into his Premier League journey, it was a moment to savour. This was validation.

His team had just closed out a 2–1 victory in the first Manchester derby of the 2017–18 season and stretched a fourteen-match winning streak in the Premier League. City were a runaway train atop the table. But none of that explained why Guardiola was bouncing around like a ping-pong ball. It wasn't the fact he'd just schooled Manchester United and his long-time nemesis José Mourinho either, although, if Guardiola was being completely honest, that didn't hurt. The real reason Guardiola was luxuriating in the frosty December air was that he finally felt vindicated. Ever since he had pitched up at Manchester City in 2016 promising to launch a sky-blue revolution with his blue-sky thinking, all Guardiola had heard was that his philosophy couldn't and wouldn't work in England. The Premier League was too rough-and-tumble for Guardiola-ball, too fast and physical to pass the ball around for minutes at a time. The English schedule, with no winter break, was too exhausting for it, the Premier League's strength of competition too deep for a ninety-minute *rondo* to succeed. Even the frigid British weather was supposed to be inhospitable to the pass-and-move style of a man who dreamed of his team having 100 per cent of the ball in every match.

But Guardiola never wavered. Not when City were eliminated in the Champions League round of sixteen during his tough first season at the club. Not when it took until the final day for Manchester City to clinch a top-four finish. Instead, he committed more faithfully to the fundamentals of his philosophy, and then, in classic Guardiola fashion, he doubled down.

City would keep the ball even more than any of his Barcelona or Bayern Munich teams. They would be faster and more powerful, too. And here they were, on course to break the Premier League record for consecutive wins, with the title all but wrapped up in early December, an attacking juggernaut operating in perfect sync. No one who knew a thing about football dared call him 'Fraudiola' now. Guardiola hadn't merely shown the world that his way could work in England. He had transformed Manchester City into the most Guardiola team of his career.

'This kind of play, we can do it in England. That's why I'm so happy,' Guardiola beamed as if he'd won an Oscar. 'The people said, "No, the way we tried to play in Barcelona, in England, it's not possible." It's possible! Always it's possible to play football, to try to keep the ball.'

Not everyone was quite so enamoured by Manchester City's new-found superiority. Naturally, José Mourinho was among the first to express his displeasure. Not long after the full-time whistle, the United manager barged into the Manchester City dressing room and accused Guardiola's players of celebrating their derby victory a little too loudly. 'You have no respect,' Mourinho admonished the City players, demonstrating his famous good manners. City didn't like that. They shot back in Spanish, English, and Portuguese. A multilingual skirmish of men in various states of undress broke out in the dressing room and spilled into the tunnel. Reinforcements scrambled from the United dressing room, and the brawl degenerated into a swarm of thirty players pushing and shoving and tossing whatever they could get their hands on in the Old Trafford tunnel. Once it was broken up by police, the teams surveyed the damage. Each side had taken some licks. Man City assistant coach Mikel Arteta suffered a nasty cut where an airborne bottle caught him above the eye. Mourinho finished doused in milk.

It was the sort of farcical episode that could occur only in a showdown between Mourinho and Guardiola. Except for the fact that the same thing had happened eight years before. On that day, it was Manchester United and Arsenal going at it in the Old Trafford tunnel, and instead of José Mourinho being on the wrong end of projectile post-match snacks, it was United manager Alex Ferguson. A slice of pizza nailed him square on the jacket, hurled by the Arsenal midfielder Cesc Fàbregas. The incident went down as the 'Battle of the Buffet'.

But just as a pepperoni slice couldn't fluster Alex Ferguson for long, no flying bottles were going to slow down Guardiola or Man City or their owner's boundless ambition in 2017. This wasn't just a dominant team blowing away opponents for a season. City were rattling all of English football.

28

WITH A SEEMINGLY insurmountable lead at the top of the table, and more than half the matches still to go, the rest of the 2017–18 campaign may have seemed like a Manchester City victory lap. But if that suggested a Premier League season devoid of suspense, the reality was far different. There was still intrigue, tension, and drama out there. You just had to know where to look.

For example, the dining rooms of hip Manhattan restaurants.

Because roughly six weeks before Manchester City's derby victory, on a warm night in the middle of October, an incongruous group of diners sat down to eat among the dark wood tables and black leather banquettes at Locanda Verde, a high-end Italian eatery in Tribeca.

The group of old white guys with not much hair between them didn't turn many heads amid the usual gaggle of well-tanned, well-Botoxed VIPs. But if anyone with a keen knowledge of English football executives had passed their table on the way to the restroom, they'd have recognized that this party represented the most unlikely gathering of enemies since the heads of New York's organized crime families held their regular meetings in red-sauce joints to keep the peace. Because around the table that night were Joel and Avram Glazer, the owners of Manchester United, along with the club's chief executive, Ed Woodward; Liverpool's principal owner John W. Henry; and Ivan Gazidis, the chief executive of Arsenal.

They weren't there for the blue crab.

How these clubs ended up brushing off more than a century of mutual loathing and sitting down to dinner was due to an emerging crisis that concerned all of them. Or to be more accurate, two emerging crises. The NFL happened to be holding its autumn owners meeting in the nearby Conrad New York hotel, hoping to tackle a bizarre national flare-up involving President Donald Trump and a group of NFL players who were protesting for social justice by kneeling during the national anthem. That's why the Glazers, owners of the Tampa Bay Buccaneers, were in New York along with Arsenal's Stan Kroenke, who owned the Los Angeles Rams and had summoned Gazidis across the pond.

But as they wrestled with an NFL public-relations imbroglio, they were also preoccupied by a developing impasse in the Premier League, and this one alarmed them a lot more than the rantings of the leader of the free world. This was about money.

Over the previous twelve months, the Premier League's Big Six had jointly reached the conclusion that the exorbitant sums the league were now raking in from the sale of overseas TV rights – currently worth £3.5 billion – should no longer be distributed equally among the league's twenty teams as they had been since the Premier League was first founded twenty-five years earlier.

The way the Big Six saw it, some clubs deserved a larger share. Specifically, them.

After all, they were the ones responsible for the league's explosive global popularity, weren't they? They were the ones crisscrossing the planet every summer to raise the profile of English football, the ones who boasted of absurd global followings in the hundreds of millions, driving international viewership from Trondheim to Tierra del Fuego. It was only right that they should be compensated accordingly. Nobody in the United States or Asia was wrenching themselves out of bed early or staying out of bed late to watch bloody Bournemouth.

Unfortunately for the Big Six, Bournemouth disagreed. So did the likes of Huddersfield, Brighton, Watford, and the rest of the league's smaller clubs. Which is why the executives around the table were slurping their pasta a little more sombrely than the chef intended.

John Henry, seated to the right of Joel Glazer, had come down from Boston to talk things through. Woodward and Gazidis, sitting opposite them, had been called to New York to add their input. But the group around the table knew that any hope of finding the fourteen votes they would need to rip up the existing revenue-sharing agreement and draft a new one was all but doomed.

The Premier League clubs were due to meet in seven days to discuss the matter, with a proposal on the table to ring-fence 35 per cent of future international broadcast money and divide it between clubs according to their final position in the league. But the ugly conclusion to the last meeting on the subject a few weeks earlier was a stark indication of how entrenched the divisions were. Richard Scudamore had worked around the clock to secure the necessary fourteen votes on behalf of the Big Six. But outside of their little clique, only Leicester, Everton, and West Ham seemed inclined to endorse the new formula. Newcastle were on the fence but by no means a sure thing. And besides, no one knew for sure if Newcastle's owner Mike Ashley would still be in charge by the time of the vote. Just a day earlier, the billionaire sporting-goods retailer had announced he was actively trying to sell.

Beyond that, the smaller clubs were united in opposition – and their resistance appeared to be a little stiffer than what the Big Six were used to steamrolling every Saturday afternoon. Within minutes of the topic being broached at the meeting earlier that month, it became obvious to the Big Six that they didn't have a path to the fourteen-vote threshold. At least half the league's twenty clubs were not going to budge. The consensus was so strong that Scudamore didn't even bother asking the clubs to go through the motions of a vote. There was no point. Instead, they had agreed to revisit the issue and try again three weeks later.

But now, seven days out, the diners at Locanda Verde had to admit there'd been no meaningful change. After years of attending Premier League meetings, Woodward and Gazidis had everyone's voting tendencies memorized as if they were political pollsters. But when Woodward and Gazidis tallied up the two camps, even if every swing vote broke their way, they couldn't make it work. The league was still gridlocked.

Which left Henry, the Glazers, and the rest of the Big Six owners backed into a corner. The Premier League's revenue-sharing model, the two-thirds majority required for rules changes, these had been core tenets of the league ever since Rick Parry wrote them down on a sheet of Ernst & Young notepaper twenty-five years before. They were the same tenets that had allowed English football to reach its position as the world's pre-eminent league. But now, in downtown Manhattan, those pillars began to look as if they'd have to come down.

If the league's top clubs couldn't secure a more reasonable revenue split through peaceful means, what option did they have left? Nobody at the table uttered the words 'European Super League', but then they didn't need to. Only hours earlier, the Glazers and Arsenal's Stan Kroenke had rubbed shoulders at the NFL owners' meetings with Stephen Ross, the New York real estate developer, Miami Dolphins owner, and founder of the International Champions Cup.

Because of his financial clout and his existing relationships with the clubs, Ross had been earmarked as the man who could make a European Super League happen ever since an ICC executive sat down with representatives from five of the Premier League's Big Six at London's Dorchester hotel in 2016. (Tottenham weren't invited, a fact that infuriated Daniel Levy so much that he probably had to poach one of his rivals' transfer targets just to feel better.) Ross had the money, he had the sporting background, and he had Charlie Stillitano, the promoter who appeared biologically incapable of passing up a chance to hold forth about the possibility of creating a new competitive tournament exclusively for the biggest clubs in Europe.

To be sure, the prospects still seemed improbable. But as the owners and executives from Manchester United, Liverpool, and Arsenal left the table at the end of an improbable sit-down of their own, it was clear that the upcoming league meeting was shaping up to be one of the most consequential in the Premier League's history. At stake was the one thing that had been the bedrock of the league since its establishment a quarter of a century earlier: its unity.

All of which made it awkward when that meeting was abruptly cancelled.

Just twenty-four hours before the second league-wide discussion on overseas TV revenues was due to take place, the Premier League issued a terse statement announcing that the gathering had been summarily called off. 'It has become clear that there is currently no consensus for change,' the statement noted. It didn't require a PhD in reading between the lines to work out what was left unsaid.

After twenty-five years of peaceful coexistence, in which English football's top clubs had made money hand over fist, built towering new stadiums, attracted huge global fan bases, and transformed themselves into billion-dollar businesses, the Premier League gravy train had come to an unexpected standstill, just as Britain's trains are wont to do. For the first time in a quarter of a century, its twenty clubs found themselves locked in a dispute that money alone couldn't solve. The whole thing was about money. And as the impasse dragged on and the two sides dug in, a series of smaller disagreements bubbled to the surface.

It soon became apparent that England's top flight – once a model of collective harmony and mutual benefit – was racked by division of its own, that the Premier League had split into a morass of feuding factions that were each blaming somebody else for threatening to blow the whole thing up.

The simmering tensions were mostly kept behind closed doors, in club boardrooms, in executive boxes, and in the conference rooms of swanky hotels. Outwardly, it appeared the Premier League was a picture of strength. The league was resurgent on the European stage, qualifying a record five clubs for the Champions League's last sixteen while negotiations over the latest sale of domestic TV rights meant the clubs were in line for another windfall.

But amid this outbreak of unseen hostility, there was one surprise. It turned out that the biggest agitator was the one club that seemingly had the least to worry about. Not content with laying waste to English football on the pitch, Manchester City and its Catalan-Emirati leadership were pushing to overturn the league's way of doing business.

In official league meetings and private discussions with other clubs, City railed against the league's revenue-sharing model and repeatedly challenged the age-old Founder Members Agreement, the document scrawled in Rick Parry's handwriting that held the status of Premier League Scripture. The reality is that when it was written up no one paid much attention to the overseas income. In fact, the league was losing money on international broadcasts back then as it was paying foreign networks to carry its games. 'Nobody envisaged that it would be as big as it is, so sharing those rights equally was a concession they thought wouldn't matter,' Parry said.

The way Manchester City saw it, the Founder Members Agreement was more like a relic that belonged in a glass case with acid-wash jeans, the Sega Genesis, and other treasured artifacts of the 1990s. The league's antique formula and their quaint old-fashioned ideas about competitive balance had allowed the Premier League to become the richest purveyor of the world's favourite sport. But for a club like Manchester City, whose modern history dated back to only 2008, that was all in the distant past.

In truth, no one should've been shocked to learn that City gave little thought to the overall strength of the league. Ferran Soriano had telegraphed exactly those sentiments a decade earlier in his book about running Barcelona. Midway through a meditation on the differences between professional sport in the United States and football in Europe, Soriano laid out his thoughts about the concept of competitive balance. 'A well-known American sports manager once said to me, "I don't understand why you don't see that what you should be doing is boosting teams like Seville FC and Villarreal FC to make the Spanish league more exciting and maximize income,"' Soriano wrote. 'While I was listening to him, I found it very difficult to think about maximizing any income of any kind, because all I wanted and cared for was for FC Barcelona to win all the matches and always win, independently of the "tournament overall income", or suchlike concepts.'

Those 'suchlike concepts' now applied to the Premier League's money-sharing mechanism. And if anything, Soriano's conviction was even stronger now. The Premier League's top clubs needed a greater share of the wealth if they were ever to hope of luring the world's best players back to England.

That much had been made clear to Soriano during the previous summer's transfer window. It wasn't that City lacked the funds to compete at the top end of the transfer market, of course. No team in world football spent more than the £221.5 million of Sheikh Mansour's fortune that Soriano plunked down on five new recruits for Pep Guardiola's squad. They weren't the only big spenders in the Premier League either. In sum, English clubs splurged more than

£1.4 billion in transfer fees, the fifth successive summer that their combined spending passed the billion-pound mark. That was all well and good. The issue for Soriano was that the summer's headline moves for the best players and the biggest fees had not involved Manchester City. Nor had they involved Manchester United, Chelsea, Liverpool, or any other English club for that matter. The juiciest transfer of the summer belonged to a different superpower in a different league controlled by a different Gulf state. Paris Saint-Germain, backed by Qatar's sovereign wealth fund, blew a world-record €222 million in a single instalment to sign the fleet-footed, flamboyantly coiffed Brazilian Neymar from Barcelona. If that wasn't bad enough, just a few weeks later, the French teenager widely tipped to be the game's next global superstar, an eighteen-year-old forward named Kylian Mbappé, had moved from Monaco for the second-highest transfer fee on record. He had signed for PSG, too.

For Soriano, this was a galling development. It was one thing if English clubs had to defer to Real Madrid or Barcelona when it came to signing the game's most prized players. The two Spanish superclubs had their domestic championships on lockdown as did Bayern Munich. Players who signed there knew they could spend most of the season beating up on the weaklings that made up the rest of the league, allowing them to conserve energy for the occasional big game, the later rounds of the Champions League, and the serious business of lifting a big trophy above their heads. By contrast, English football was a grind. So Soriano couldn't blame the likes of Lionel Messi and Cristiano Ronaldo if they chose to spend their careers somewhere a little more comfortable. But there are only so many world-class players to go around. If Paris Saint-Germain were getting in on the act now, too, that was a problem. And in football, there's only one sure-fire way to solve a problem. Soriano knew that if he threw enough money at them the world's best players could be persuaded to move to Manchester. The Premier League clubs were making more than enough cash for him to do so; he just needed to ensure a greater share of it flowed into Manchester City's coffers at the expense of those other clubs at the wrong end of the table. It made perfect sense to him. If English football wants to attract the world's best players, who could argue?

Pretty much everyone, as it happens. 'These Spaniards at Manchester City, they think they're superior to everyone else,' said David Sullivan, the co-owner of West Ham. 'I think it's just greed.' Sullivan has never been a man to mince his words. He once branded himself a 'freedom fighter' after he was convicted for living off immoral earnings and forced to spend seventy-one days in jail – thanks to his adult publishing business. But on this occasion, he might have been speaking for any number of Premier League chairmen, many of whom had privately taken issue with City's contemptuous attitude to the clubs outside the Big Six.

That only stoked the us-against-them dynamic inside the league, a rift that some owners traced back to a Premier League summit in 2016. It was then, during a routine meeting to rubber-stamp a £564 million TV deal with Chinese broadcaster PPTV, that Manchester United chief executive Ed Woodward brought a temporary halt to the proceedings in order to hold an impromptu huddle with the other Big Six representatives in the room. Once the pow-wow was over, the PPTV deal duly received unanimous support, but Woodward's powerplay exasperated the other fourteen clubs. Nearly two years later, the schism had deepened, with no real attempt made to repair the damage. Tottenham's Daniel Levy took it upon himself to explain the Big Six's position at a subsequent league meeting but only succeeded in further riling the rest of the league. As one owner recalled, Levy's explanation amounted to just five words – 'We only want what's fair' – which he repeated ad nauseam to every objection raised.

'Everyone is always talking in code,' that owner complained.

The Big Six may have been the most powerful clique in the Premier League, and the only one with a cool nickname, but they were not the only group frustrated by this internal stand-off. In recent years, another small but increasingly vocal subset had emerged that was particularly dismayed by the deteriorating relations inside the league: the Americans.

With five teams now under their control – a quarter of the league – the US owners had formed a sort of unofficial lobby. They arranged to meet on an ad hoc basis in New York or London to discuss issues, share insights, and frequently marvel at the eccentricities of English life. They saw the latest log jam as emblematic of a broader problem. The antagonistic attitude that prevailed in Premier League meetings made it all but impossible to have a serious business discussion. That wasn't how professional sport worked on the other side of the pond. It pained them to think how much better off all twenty clubs would be if they just adopted the sort of collaborative approach that characterized the NFL or the NBA.

The other Premier League owners had embraced the arrival of businessmen from across the Atlantic over the years, praising their commercial savvy and marketing teeth. But by now, the US owners were resigned to the fact that reaching an agreement on centralized commercial projects or mutually agreed-upon cost controls was all but impossible. The antagonistic attitude inside the Premier League meeting room meant they were more likely to vote for playing with the lights off.

The transatlantic contingent wasn't alone. A growing number of clubs were also alarmed by the explosion in player salaries, which were taking up a greater proportion of overall team revenues each year. In recent seasons, player wages have represented an average of 63 per cent of club revenues across the league according to Deloitte, though that figure climbs above 80 per cent for a handful of smaller clubs at the wrong end of the table. For them, any increase in television-rights payments is a double-edged sword – yes, it improves their cash flow, but they end up pushing nearly all of that extra money into player salaries and transfer fees just to keep up.

While clubs like Manchester United and Tottenham showed it was possible to operate with a fixed internal wage cap and still put a winning team on the pitch, some of the teams scrambling for survival at the bottom of the league found that so much of their income was being paid out to players that every increase in commercial or TV revenue was swallowed up before it was wired into their accounts. The league had floated proposals for a salary cap before and adopted some short-term cost-control measures, but as usual, the clubs hadn't been able to agree on a sweeping league-wide measure on a par with the salary caps in US pro sports.

There was, however, one topic nearly all of the league seemed to agree on. The 2017–18 season had made it plainly obvious to them that Manchester City were turning into an existential threat to English football.

It wasn't simply that City were in the midst of a historically dominant season. The Premier League had seen its share of dominant teams before. It wasn't the astronomical sums of money that they were spending either. As far back as Jack Walker and Blackburn Rovers, there had been individuals prepared to buy success on the pitch. The Premier League had welcomed them in, emptied their wallets, and continued along their merry way.

But there was something about the way Manchester City combined these two things that made this time feel different and more dangerous. It was partly the extremes that City were taking them to: thirteen points clear at Christmas, the largest margin in English top-flight history; eighteen league wins in a row, not merely a record for the Premier League but better than anything Real Madrid or Barcelona had ever done in La Liga. And off the pitch, they weren't merely outspending the rest of the league, they were spending them into oblivion to the tune of more than £1 billion in transfer fees in the past five years. The club had the most expensive squad ever assembled. Just the previous summer, City had flexed its muscle with a £200-million outlay – on fullbacks alone. All this and the world's most brilliant coach on the bench. And a youth academy stacked with top-class teenage talent. When would it all end?

Those inside English football had a different question on their minds: when does it start to undermine the whole point of showing up? The appeal of the Premier League, its fundamental selling point, is that it is among the most open and competitive leagues in sports, a fluctuating free-for-all that proved that the expression 'any given Sunday' should really refer to Saturdays. Now it was beginning to look like a large bunch of nobodies and one elite team way out in front.

It didn't take a marketing whiz to identify the problem.

'We don't want somebody winning the league by twenty points – it's not good for our brand,' said Sam Allardyce, hired by Everton in the 2017–18 season for another rescue job. 'The league loses its power, loses its product, loses its ability to get the worldwide audiences excited.'

It was another Premier League manager – the one with the economics degree – who really put his finger on what made the challenge posed by Manchester City so unprecedented in England. It wasn't the team on the field or the money in the bank. It was the vision. Unlimited ambition, laser-like focus, and all the cash in the world to execute it. No team had ever offered such a complete threat.

'We had no petrol and ideas,' Arsène Wenger said, looking back on Arsenal's lean years after building the Emirates Stadium. 'They have petrol and ideas, so that makes it more efficient.'

Wenger had once been the man to bridge the gap to richer teams with a radical approach to recruitment and training. But against a foe as overwhelming as City, that was no longer enough. It was no coincidence that the season Guardiola's plans came together happened to be the year Arsenal decided to nudge Wenger towards the exit.

29

FOR TWO DECADES, Richard Scudamore's professional life had been more or less smooth sailing. He promised the twenty owners of the Premier League that he would sell their game around the world, and for twenty years, that's what he did.

The audience kept growing, so did the sales figures, and so did Scudamore's own salary, from £900,000 in 2003 to £6 million with bonuses in 2015. There were some missteps along the way, not least the embarrassing episode in 2014 when a series of sexist emails sent from his work account were leaked by a former PA. But, by and large, Scudamore managed to sidestep trouble.

As he entered his third decade as the Premier League's top executive, however, trouble found Scudamore: the might of Manchester City, the split between the Big Six and the rest, the squabble over international rights fees, and the struggle to maintain competitive balance. These all represented hurdles not only for the league's continued success but also for Scudamore's authority over it. Could he keep his members, the twenty clubs that were really his bosses, from tearing at one another's throats?

More to the point: could he keep them in business with one another?

On a personal level, Scudamore knew that his answer to those questions would shape his legacy as the Premier League's longest-serving chief executive. But when it came to the bigger picture, he knew that it wasn't all in his control. Scudamore needed to reckon with shifts in the political, cultural, and technological forces that threatened the empire he had painstakingly erected.

For starters, the Brexit vote of 2016 had raised questions about how one of Britain's most successful cultural exports to the world would be affected by the country's decision to leave the European Union. Scudamore had spent more than a decade trying to insulate the Premier League from these sorts of specific external political pressures. Ever since the European Commission threatened to sue the Premier League in 2005 over the way it auctioned off its UK broadcast rights, arguing that Sky's deal to show all live matches amounted to a monopoly, Scudamore had found a way to keep a permanent eye on the various legislative bodies that could force the league to change the way they did business. That's why the league's only permanent employee based outside the UK was an individual based in Brussels, whose job was to monitor the policy papers and political debates inside the EU for signs of any detail, however minor, that could impact English football.

But now Scudamore faced a series of unknowns, any number of which could impact the Premier League's standing, from freedom of movement and visas for foreign players to the broader perception of Britain as a country that welcomed overseas investment.

Long before those questions could be resolved, the fallout had already started to jolt the Premier League as the pound's plunging valuation against the euro adversely impacted English clubs relative to their peers on the Continent. In 2016–17, for instance, figures from Deloitte show Manchester United's revenues fell by €13 million, a drop directly attributable to changes in the exchange rate, which cost the club €89 million, offsetting underlying growth of €77 million. United weren't alone. The combined £1.4 billion spent by English clubs in the summer transfer window in 2017 cost them an estimated £105 million more than they would have paid before the Brexit vote and the ensuing calamities in the foreign-exchange market – a worse deal than using the cash machines at the airport.

For Scudamore, these tectonic shifts struck at the fundamental business model that underpinned the Premier League's success. If English clubs were no longer able to attract the best players and managers, the league's star power would be diminished and the standard of play would suffer, which could potentially cut the value of future TV rights, further hampering English clubs' ability to sign star players, and on and on, unspooling all of the Premier League's progress.

But navigating the chaos of Brexit and the most unpredictable period in modern British history seemed like a tap-in compared with the other major political obstacle confronting Scudamore. Somehow, he had to find a way to reconcile a push by club owners to play meaningful Premier League games overseas with the suspicious mood of the British public, which regarded the mere suggestion of moving games abroad as the most heinous act of treason since Guy Fawkes tried to blow up the Houses of Parliament.

This was a crisis years in the making. Ever since Scudamore opened the eyes of Premier League owners to the popularity of their product beyond England's shores and the riches on offer there, they had been fixated on the idea of taking league fixtures to key international markets. After all, they had already seen how much pre-season tours and exhibition games boosted their international revenues. What sort of windfall could they expect if the games they gave away actually counted for something? This was a question the league first sought to answer in 2008 when the owners approved a proposal to tack on an additional round of matches – a so-called thirty-ninth game – to the Premier League season, to be played in stadiums around the globe. The league's internal calculations suggested the plan would net each of its twenty teams an additional £5 million, all but ensuring the unanimous support of the club owners. It was, Scudamore declared when he unveiled the scheme, 'an idea whose time has come'.

Unfortunately, it turned out that the idea had come before anyone thought to inform the Football Association, FIFA, the government, or the country's football supporters. One by one, those groups expressed immediate and violent opposition to international matches. Their reservations ranged from the practical – the addition of a thirty-ninth game would destroy the symmetry of the league – to the political. The Football Supporters' Federation launched a petition in conjunction with the *Daily Mail* to oppose 'the outrageous desecration of our national game'. It wasn't long before FIFA president Sepp Blatter had his say. 'Football cannot be like the Harlem Globetrotters or a circus,' world football's ringmaster announced.

And with that, the thirty-ninth game was no more. By 2010, Scudamore confirmed that whole concept was dead on arrival.

Or so it seemed. Because sometime after 2016, the Premier League quietly revived the idea of playing an international round of matches.

Not necessarily a thirty-ninth game. Just one round of fixtures, likely early in the season, played at neutral venues in five cities around the world. In truth, the league's owners never really forgot the idea. They would still stand to make money, which was something they could usually get behind. And now, nearly a decade after the possibility was first raised, there was a sense that the time might finally be right to revisit it. Not to the extent that they would publicly announce anything. They learned that lesson the first time. But there was a concerted effort among the clubs, led by Manchester City, to finally make it happen. 'This is a great idea,' Soriano said after Spain's La Liga beat the Premier League to the punch by announcing it would stage a competitive league fixture in Miami. 'This is an idea that takes the business to another dimension.'

If the Premier League took the leap, they could be sure the ICC folks were waiting around the corner to help them execute the project. Their vision was for something similar to the annual set of games the NFL hosted in London, which go far beyond just an afternoon's entertainment. Each one is attached to a week of events, promotions, and gaudy marketing displays all the way down Regent Street.

'If the league decides to come here, we have our hand up,' Stillitano said. 'We're ready to do it. We're uniquely qualified to make it a big event.'

In public, Scudamore remained coy whenever the subject came up. 'Is there still a burning desire? The clubs would like to do it,' he said in Hong Kong at an event to promote the 2017 Premier League Asia Trophy, 'but we are also realistic, which says until the fan, political, and media reaction is any more warm towards it, it won't happen.'

Privately, however, Scudamore had spoken to overseas broadcasters, including NBC, about what it would take to stage a round of international games. 'We're working with the league, and we've got our fingers crossed,' said Jon Miller, NBC's president of programming. 'I think there's some challenges, but we've offered and I know they're looking at it.'

It would fall to Scudamore to sell all this to the same sceptical public that knocked it back the previous time – the administrators, the politicians, and even the league's managers.

But most of all, it was up to him to sell it to English football fans at a time when the connection between the clubs and the communities they were born into had never felt more uncertain. As the Premier League's owners increasingly focused on overseas territories to keep the cash registers humming, local supporters were beginning to feel that they were a diminishing concern.

Partly it was due to the rising cost of attending live games. In the Premier League era, the value of the league's teams and the zeros at the end of the players' pay cheques had soared, but so had the ticket prices. The most expensive season tickets in English football in 2018 went for more than £1,700, an increase of more than 1,000 per cent from the previous two decades. The result was that thousands of fans were priced out of attending while those who could afford it tended to be older and more affluent – two traits that no one anywhere had ever considered conducive to sparking the atmosphere in a stadium. Clubs could have capped their ticket prices, of course. They could have entirely subsidized tickets for the price of a decent centre-forward. But, with a few rare exceptions, they seemed uninterested in doing so. The perception was of a game increasingly divorced from its working-class roots.

Perhaps no episode highlighted this disconnect quite as clearly as the case of West Ham, which had embarked on their latest attempt to gatecrash the upper reaches of the Premier League in 2014. This time, the blueprint they followed wasn't Manchester United's scheme for building a dynasty around a bunch of youth-team graduates. It was Manchester City's model for self-improvement. The Hammers upped sticks and moved into a new home paid for by the British taxpayer: London's Olympic Stadium.

Since January 2010, the club had belonged to David Gold and David Sullivan, who had made their fortunes in one of the few businesses seedier than English football – sex toys and smutty magazines. They had shelled out £110 million to buy the team and soon identified the stadium move as their best chance of turbocharging West Ham's fortunes and cracking the Premier League elite. After an exhausting three-year bidding process tied up in red tape and legal challenges, West Ham finally secured the keys to the building in 2013. That would allow the Hammers to move three miles from their gritty Upton Park home into a modern £750-million arena. All West Ham would have to pay for a ninety-nine-year lease was an annual rent of £2.5 million. As far as real estate coups go, this was like inheriting a flat in Knightsbridge from an uncle you'd never met. Arsène Wenger, aged by his own move to the Emirates, summed up the Hammers' stroke of fortune: 'I say to West Ham: "Well done. You have won in the lottery." You do not need to sweat like I did for long years, and fight for every pound.'

Not everyone saw it that way. Specifically, the West Ham supporters, many of whom viewed the move from Upton Park like a forced eviction. They didn't care that West Ham's 60,000-seat capacity was now the fourth largest in the Premier League or that their new home benefited from first-class transport links and had all the comforts of a twenty-first-century arena, from huge video screens to lavish hospitality boxes. What they did care about was that the new stadium was miles from the East End pubs and greasy spoons where they used to congregate before kick-off, that getting there involved a long detour around an upmarket shopping centre, and that the London Stadium athletics track formed a thirty-foot barrier between the fans in their seats and the players they could barely tell apart on the pitch. 'We never said it was a perfect stadium,' Sullivan said. 'But it was such a good deal.'

The West Ham fans showed their disgust the only way they knew how: by fighting. The opening months in the new stadium were marred by repeated outbreaks of violence as the home fans fought with Chelsea supporters, Bournemouth supporters, Middlesbrough supporters, and even, during a loss to Watford, with one another. By the second season in the club's new home, the atmosphere inside the London Stadium was positively toxic, the team on the pitch was flailing in the lower reaches of the table, and the ire of the fans had settled on the executive boxes. In March 2018, during an ugly loss to Burnley, tensions finally boiled over. Protesters carried out four separate pitch invasions, and fans surrounded the directors' box to pelt the owners with vitriol – and two-pound coins. Police had to ask Gold and Sullivan to leave.

It was obvious that repairing broken relationships between increasingly alienated fans and the businessmen who ran their clubs now stood among the league's most urgent issues. In the twenty years it spent courting investment, it forgot to make supporters feel that they were along for the ride.

Scudamore knew all of this. He pointed out that the Premier League has invested more than £1 billion in grassroots and community projects aimed at strengthening ties between the clubs and their local communities. But the growing disconnect showed on the terraces. The average attendance during the 2016–17 season fell 1.8 per cent from the season before, and that was despite huge increases in capacity at Liverpool and West Ham. One year later, in the twilight of Arsenal's Wenger era, large pockets of empty seats gaped at the Emirates Stadium – a sight that so alarmed Stan Kroenke that it was one factor in his decision to begin the search for Wenger's replacement.

League-wide, things weren't so dramatic. More than 95 per cent of seats were filled in 2016–17, down from 96 per cent in the two years before. But no one better understood the importance of full stadiums than Scudamore. The intensity of the match-day experience was the Premier League's magnet for top players and global audiences. Packed, heaving stands were the essential set dressing for its golden television product.

'The whole economic model only works when the grounds are pretty full,' Scudamore told the *Daily Telegraph* in 2014. 'No actor likes to play in front of an empty hall.'

The lesson was as true in 2018 as it was in 1992 when Rupert Murdoch found that the surest way to grab a piece of the Premier League was to write the biggest cheque. Money was English football's true built-in advantage. For two decades, Scudamore had been all but bulletproof thanks to his singular ability to negotiate eye-popping deals on behalf of the twenty owners who paid his wages.

Yet how much further could the TV market grow before hitting saturation? The sale of UK broadcast rights in February of 2018 raised £4.4 billion but translated to a drop in the valuation of individual matches for the first time in fifteen years. Given that the Premier League had already upped the number of games available for live broadcast to 200 of its total inventory of 380 matches each season, it looked as though the days of huge inflationary jumps in TV rights fees had come to an end. And that was before they reckoned with the shortening attention spans and cord-cutting customers reshaping the rest of the entertainment industry.

Much like leagues across the Atlantic had begun to do, the Premier League hoped to turn to streaming services to plug the gap. Scudamore had held discussions with Amazon, Facebook, and Netflix about bidding for rights packages, and as an avowed technophile who once described himself as 'dwelling in the future', he had a plan to bring online video services on board – something he pulled off in 2018 by selling a small package of rights to Amazon. There was even talk of the Premier League's operating as a platform itself, charging a monthly fee for live matches to subscribers across the world.

But amid the brouhaha over international rights, it was possible that such a move would only increase the league's internal divisions instead of solving them. A move to on-demand broadcasting risked highlighting how much more popular the Big Six were among global viewers than the rest of the competition, which would increase their demands to do away with the league's collective revenue-sharing model altogether. When Amazon wanted to produce a behind-the-scenes documentary with a Premier League club, it was no surprise that they inked a £10 million deal with Manchester City.

The pressure was building on Scudamore to come up with a new way forward. His failure to quickly come up with an overseas rights formula that a majority of clubs found agreeable had angered the Big Six, especially since he'd had months to lobby the league's smaller clubs. Alternate proposals had been discussed, including one that was believed to have support from as many as twelve clubs – a sliding scale that would see the top ten clubs increase their share of international revenues based on their final league positions. Another model suggested awarding the Big Six 35 per cent of all overseas revenues above £3 billion, but that proved more popular with the smaller clubs than the giants it was supposed to placate.

And all the time, the stakes for failing to quell the league's internal divisions had never been starker. From the moment executives from Arsenal, Liverpool, Chelsea, and the Manchester clubs gathered in secret at the Dorchester hotel, the message was clear. 'They threaten it all the time: "We're going to break away,"' said one Premier League owner. 'Sometimes they vaguely hint at it, sometimes they outwardly threaten it. But every time they want more money, it's "Well, we'll just go and play the big European teams."' The spectre of a break-away by the Big Six had been invoked so often during the previous decade that the Premier League now operated in a constant state of high alert, leaving even the most sober observers on edge. Which is how *The Times* ended up publishing a juicy front-page exclusive in March 2013 outlining secret plans for a Qatar-based 'Dream Football League', a new tournament to be played every two years and featuring twenty-four of Europe's elite clubs, including Manchester United and a handful of other top Premier League teams. The DFL had the potential to 'change the face of world football', the *Times* story noted. Doubtless that would have been true but for one minor detail: the whole thing was a hoax dreamed up by a blogger on a satirical French website.

The episode was embarrassing for Britain's paper of record, but there was one thing the bogus report got right: the desire from forces inside the game to blow up the existing structures and re-organize around the most powerful clubs. In 2018, FIFA president Gianni Infantino was motivated to cook up a proposal for an expanded Club World Cup by an international consortium dangling more than $20 billion. At the same time, Juventus chairman Andrea Agnelli was trying to convince his fellow superclubs to back a larger Champions League that would play on the weekends and shunt domestic league play into midweek.

The Big Six were not shy about expressing their interest. So Scudamore responded the only way he could. Two weeks after the end of the season, he gathered the clubs again at the league's annual general meeting in Yorkshire. Scudamore had begun to think of the year-long international rights debate as a boil that needed lancing. This time, nothing was off the table.

The solution they agreed on distributed roughly one-third of all future international rights fees according to each club's finishing position, meaning that the Big Six were almost certainly guaranteed a raise. To assuage the other fourteen teams, they agreed that the ratio between the highest earner and the lowest earner's payments would never exceed 1.8 to 1, a minor increase on the previous ratio of 1.6 to 1. The smaller clubs could tell themselves that the Premier League was still far more equitable than La Liga or Serie A. But as far as the Big Six were concerned, they were finally on their way to righting a great injustice.

In the interest of peace, the twenty clubs voted for it 18–2 and left Harrogate feeling relieved. But few gave much thought to the precedent they had just set. For the first time in twenty-six years, they had ratified a change to the Founder Members Agreement, the document that had governed the Premier League since its creation and provided the framework for its remarkable growth.

In the world of English football, it was as if they'd taken a chisel to the Ten Commandments.

Scudamore didn't think the league would need to revisit the issue anytime soon, but he wasn't about to stick around to find out. Within hours of the Premier League's announcement about the new revenue-sharing model, it followed up with a notice that Scudamore would step down by the end of the year.

His battle to quell the Big Six was behind him. His UK television rights were sold – he'd even brought in Amazon. And his international television rights were heading for another jackpot haul. It was time to punch out before the whole edifice started to wobble.

'The stronger the Premier League is, the more successful the Premier League is, the more international rights go and generate, the more the TV deals go up, the less incentive there is for any of our clubs to go "Well, I'm going to leave the Premier League",' Scudamore said. 'The biggest antidote to chaos is a strong Premier League, for our clubs in England. And that's the bottom line of it.'

But he knew all too well that those outside forces would keep chipping away at the Premier League's *raison d'être*, that those twenty businesses had less and less in common with one another and that they might soon wonder why they were in business together at all. Whether those outside forces were Qatari or Saudi or Japanese investors, or even FIFA, hardly mattered. Because everyone could already see the broad strokes of what a break-away future might look like.

Picture a Champions League-type tournament featuring the

biggest clubs in Europe supercharged by a fresh influx of television rights money playing one another year-round and not bothering to deal with the smaller clubs that used to clog up their schedule – not unlike what goes on stateside every summer in the ICC.

But above all, it would look like the richest clubs in England deciding once and for all that they weren't getting their due; that they simply wouldn't carry the burden of the poorer, smaller, less popular teams any longer.

In other words, it would look an awful lot like 1992.

Epilogue

Two Nights in May, 2019

ANFIELD WAS TURNED up to maximum Anfield.

When it's full – and it always is – no stadium captures the essence of English football quite as powerfully as the home of Liverpool Football Club, from the narrow streets in its shadow to the telegenic sweep of the Kop end. There's a reason the waiting list for season tickets is 25,000 names and several decades long. Since the pitch markings were first laid down in 1884, Anfield has seen more trophies raised to the sky than perhaps any other ground in the country. And the locals don't let you forget it. But on this crisp night in early May, under floodlights that projected the stadium across Stanley Park, those packed inside witnessed something their fathers and grandfathers had never imagined. Anfield was as loud as anyone could remember.

Clouds of red smoke billowed through the stands, the diehards stood on their seats to sing till their throats were raw and, before them, victorious players in red shirts lined up to lead another rendition of 'You'll Never Walk Alone'. Even in an age when Anfield has become the shop window of a slick, global business, this was an outpouring of genuine local ecstasy, unprompted and unplanned, a timeless snapshot no different from all those other memorable nights through the years – only this one came with 10,000 smartphones held in the air.

No one in this iconic ground, not the thousands in the stands, nor the twenty-two players on the field, could quite believe what they had just seen. Even the greatest footballer on the planet no longer seemed to understand exactly how the game of football worked. Shaking his head, Lionel Messi marched straight to the tunnel without a word or a handshake.

On this wild night in north-west England, even he couldn't make sense of it: Liverpool 4, Barcelona 0. With a comeback for the ages, they had overturned a 3–0 deficit from the first leg and seemingly ripped up the fabric of football space-time.

There were systemic reasons why such a thing was *possible*. In eight years under Fenway Sports Group's ownership, Liverpool had become one of the smartest run clubs in the world, using its Premier League bounty to hire a project-minded manager and assemble a squad of high-priced stars and undervalued assets. The club had also shown the humility to ditch ideas that didn't work out. None of those, however, made the Barcelona turnaround any more *probable*. A few bookmakers had offered odds of more than 100–1 on a turnaround. In truth, the prospect of a Liverpool comeback seemed even more far-fetched than that.

Immediately the debates started over whether this was the most outrageous victory an English outfit had ever managed in Europe, right up there with Manchester United snatching the 1999 Champions League final and Admiral Lord Nelson beating France away at Trafalgar.

It didn't matter. The question was only relevant for twenty-four hours, because the next night in Amsterdam was even more bonkers.

Tottenham travelled to the Netherlands to play Ajax in the second Champions League semi-final, already trailing by one goal. When they shipped two more in the first forty-five minutes at the Johan Cruyff Arena, that looked to be that. There was no great shame in losing at this stage, of course. For one thing, Spurs entered the game without their star striker, Harry Kane, who was injured. And, besides, this season wasn't supposed to bring glory on the pitch. Tottenham's primary objective was to pay for the new 61,000-seat stadium they had opened a few weeks earlier. In the long run, the new ground would boost Tottenham's match-day revenue threefold and, just as importantly, appeal to the club's newest business partner, a little foreign concern known as the National Football League. But, in the short term, it turned the club into an experiment in Premier League football on a budget: Spurs were the only team in Europe's top five leagues not to spend as much as a penny on new players in 2018–19. Simply reaching the Champions League semi-finals was already a staggering overachievement. On paper, the season was already a hit.

Forty-five minutes later, the opening of a £1 billion stadium had been relegated to a mere footnote. In the second half, Tottenham stunned Ajax by scoring three goals – the last in the final minute of stoppage time – to complete another head-wrecking comeback. Just like Liverpool, they had returned from the dead, only Spurs did it in half the time.

The suddenness wasn't the only difference. Where Liverpool's triumph was met with an ear-splitting noise, this one played out to near silence inside the stadium. Only one corner of the stands, packed with a few thousand unreasonably optimistic Tottenham supporters, could match the elation of the players on the pitch.

Back in London, the mood at Premier League HQ was one of quiet satisfaction. They knew that no matter which way the final broke, one of their members would be crowned champions of Europe.

But further afield, the reaction to Liverpool's and Tottenham's successes was a little less muted. Each night, the teams were joined in their celebrations by thousands of far-flung fans who couldn't pinpoint Liverpool on a map. In a Midtown Manhattan bar run by a former Liverpool defender, in the middle of a Tuesday afternoon they partied as if it was Mardi Gras. The moment the game ended in Ghana, students poured out of a university campus waving red Liverpool flags over their heads. In pre-dawn Singapore, even government officials rubbed the sleep from their eyes to post messages of support on Facebook. And in Los Angeles, Tottenham fans poured out of dimly lit bars squinting into the California sunshine and snarled traffic on the freeway. No one had missed it, from Prince William to World Cup winners to NBA champions. LeBron James, somehow a minority stakeholder in the club, couldn't help but tweet about it in all caps.

English football was back on top of the world and the whole world was watching.

This was precisely what the Premier League's founders had dreamed of, but never dared imagine. Back when Irving Scholar, David Dein and Martin Edwards first cooked up their vision for a breakaway league in the late 1980s, English clubs weren't even *allowed* in Europe. Those men thought they could help English football make more money, and maybe that would lead to a better calibre of player landing on their shores, and maybe those players could help English sides rediscover their swagger abroad. But this? Premier League clubs weren't just the strongest on the playing fields of Europe. They were even stronger off the pitch, with annual turnovers in the hundreds of millions and valuations in the billions. The Premier League's genius for raking in TV money, which had once set it apart from the rest of English football, now set it apart from every other professional league on the planet. The founders' audacious play to drag the sport they loved out of the nineteenth century and rebuild it for the twenty-first had transformed English football, then English society and now the very landscape of global sports.

Almost as an afterthought, twenty-four hours after Spurs made their date with Liverpool, two more English clubs would set up their own European final. Arsenal and Chelsea won semi-finals of their own to advance to the Europa League final. For the first time in the history of European competitions, its two most important finals featured four finalists from a single country.

No wonder the rest of European football was losing its collective mind. Resentment over the Premier League's immense wealth had been building for years. Now the leaders of some of the most powerful clubs in Europe began agitating for sweeping changes to European competitions. Led by Juventus, they wanted more Champions League matches between the superclubs and guaranteed qualification year after year, all in the name of a bigger TV windfall. To the owners who seemed more like boxing promoters than the chairmen of local institutions, this was the logical next step. And, above all, it was the only solution they could envisage for a problem that vexed them more with each passing year: closing the gap to the Premier League.

Even those English sides that got nowhere near European finals lorded it over the rest of the continent. The Premier League had reached into its pot of television cash and doled out at least £100 million to nineteen of its twenty clubs this season. Liverpool, which had had twenty-six of its thirty-eight league games aired live on TV, led the way with a £152.4 million payday. The only one to take home any less than £100 million was last-placed Huddersfield Town, which had to settle for £96 million – still more than the French league paid out to its champion, Paris Saint-Germain.

'It is hard to think of a season that has been better,' the semi-retired Richard Scudamore said, admiring his handiwork.

But for some, it was also hard to think of a season that had been worse. What the rest of Europe couldn't see was that inside the league, twenty-six years of unchecked economic growth, vicious competition, unrestrained spending and next to no oversight had left English football with a serious problem.

Its name was Manchester City.

Liverpool and Spurs reached the Champions League final, Arsenal and Chelsea had their Europa League showdown, but none of them could claim to be the best team in England. That was reserved for City, on their way to a second straight Premier League title. This one couldn't match the mind-boggling numbers of their 2017–18 triumph, when they scored 106 goals and amassed a record one hundred points to leave a field of deeply flawed rivals in their wake. But in some ways, this one was more ominous. Because City's 2018–19 campaign managed to make one of the great seasons in English football history – Liverpool's ninety-seven-point, one-defeat campaign – completely meaningless.

The turning point came on the night before Liverpool's miracle against Barcelona, thirty-five miles east of Anfield. Vincent Kompany, the only City player to predate the Abu Dhabi takeover, had given the club a nervous victory in its toughest remaining game with a shot that his teammates had begged him not to take. They didn't know precisely that it had just a 3 per cent chance of going in, just that a Kompany shot was more likely to smack some fan in the head than the back of Leicester's net. Once it left his foot, though, there was no stopping it. And now, there was no stopping Man City either.

One week after posting ninety-eight points to pip Liverpool to the league title, City stuck six goals past Watford to lift the FA Cup, completing a clean sweep of the domestic trophies following the club's League Cup triumph over Chelsea in February, all of which prompted a new kind of collective freak-out in English football. There had been shades of it in 2006, after Chelsea's second consecutive title backed by Roman Abramovich, but City's project seemed altogether more sustainable, more structurally sound and more menacing to the game's future. If this club was really prepared to spend everyone into oblivion for ever, and if it really had the smarts to use those riches to build for the future, would City ever lose again? The club wasn't shy when it came to questions of competitive balance – the short answer was always that it wasn't City's problem. Leave it to the rest of the Premier League to raise their game.

The championship was now a race of billionaire tax exiles, hedge-fund tycoons and real-estate magnates, all outspent by a high-ranking member of the ruling family of Abu Dhabi. But, in many ways, it was also the ethos of the Premier League writ large. Because the same vision that had allowed a small group of club owners to imagine a future in which English football conquered the globe – the notion that the future of pro sports wasn't the US approach of cooperative socialism, but an aggressive and unrestrained style of capitalism – was exactly what had drawn Sheikh Mansour, John Henry and dozens of other millionaires and billionaires into English football. It just turned out that their pockets were deeper and their visions were broader, which allowed them to carry that idea to its logical extreme.

And behind them, the league was more stratified than ever. Even the Big Six seemed to be bursting apart, falling into a Big Two of City and Liverpool and the Other Four. As its members' interests diverged, it was harder and harder for the people running the show to convince the twenty disparate owners that they all shared the same business interests. It didn't help matters that the Premier League's ringmaster had quit the stage with no permanent candidate to replace him. Almost a year on from Scudamore announcing his intention to step down, the league was still casting around for his successor. At least two candidates were offered the job and turned it down, perhaps spooked by the power of the owners and signs that domestic broadcasters might tighten their budgets. Scudamore was always going to be a tough act to follow.

None of which was of any concern to Manchester City's owner,

Sheikh Mansour, whose record of attending a grand total of one game in England during his eleven years as owner had survived the season intact. As his project closed in yet another title, he watched from afar, while a pastry chef in a kitchen somewhere in Abu Dhabi probably worked overtime on designs for a fourth Premier League championship cake.

It was an utterly absurd situation: English football clubs, established over a century ago by local labourers and factory workers, now transformed into trophy investments. The Premier League's pioneers had dared to conceive of English football as a form of family entertainment. The next generation came to see it as a global media property. But as the stakes grew higher and the owners got richer, they came to realize that the Premier League's greatest asset was its very framework. It wasn't about England's football heritage or its style of play, and it had nothing to do with authenticity or narrow, cobbled streets around crumbling stadiums.

It was the idea that a football club could be the face of an empire.

A quarter-century after a handful of frustrated owners looked across the Atlantic and tried to mould their product on the NFL model, it turned out their rogue project had wider global appeal than its American cousin and none of those annoying socialist constraints. Salary caps? A draft for the best young players? An incomprehensible rulebook? Not for the Premier League. This club of owners and executives would let in pretty much anyone who could stump up the money to compete.

Only now the same instinct for empire-building that had turned English football into the world's most watched sports property was in danger of tearing the league apart. Just as the British Empire prospered on the back of free trade until its control became unsustainable, so the Premier League had conquered the world on the back of its very English, outsized global ambition. Now its supremacy was threatening to fall apart. Because when it comes to outsized global ambition, the best empire builders turned out to be from places like Abu Dhabi. And they weren't interested in trifling details like competitive balance, or the health of the league or the way things had always been done.

They were interested in building monuments.

Acknowledgements

A BOOK OF this scope, about the most popular sports league on the planet, wouldn't have been possible without the cooperation of the Premier League's biggest clubs, who opened their doors and sometimes their books to show us how they took over the world. So we have to first thank Manchester City, Manchester United, Liverpool, Arsenal, Chelsea, and Tottenham Hotspur – along with their press offices – for making so much time for us and sharing their insights.

Of course, there wouldn't even be a Premier League – and we wouldn't have had a story to tell – were it not for the original architects of this whole experiment. David Dein, Martin Edwards, Irving Scholar, and Rick Parry all generously searched through their memories for us, opened doors, passed along phone numbers, and vouched for us inside the club of owners and decision makers who pull the strings of English soccer's leading institutions. None of the founders could have ever foreseen what the Premier League would become, but no one had a clearer understanding of why it exploded the way it did.

In doing the reporting for this book, we conducted hundreds of interviews. But we would be remiss if we didn't single out a few of the most helpful people we spoke to for special thanks: Arsène Wenger, John W. Henry, David Gill, Daniel Levy, Randy Lerner, Peter Kenyon, Pini Zahavi, Sam Allardyce, David Sullivan, David Gold, Steve Parish, David Blitzer, Jason Levien, Chris Pearlman, Stan Kroenke, Charlie Stillitano, Carlos Queiroz, Claudio Ranieri, Gareth Southgate, Garry Cook, Greg Dyke, Trevor Birch, Richard Wiseman, the current front office at Manchester City, the talented 'Premier League on NBC' crew, and the football finance team at Deloitte.

Particular thanks also go to the dozens of anonymous team executives, owners, managers, agents, ex-players, and football operatives who asked to remain unnamed but were equally essential to the project.

We also received assistance from the Premier League itself. Inside the halls of 30 Gloucester Place, we owe credit to Richard Scudamore, Nick Noble, Paul Stringer, and Emma Wilkinson.

Writing the book was one thing. Putting it into the world was another. And for that, we have to thank the incredible team at Houghton Mifflin Harcourt in the US led by the fantastically supportive Susan Canavan. Her enthusiasm for the book was contagious – and apparent from the first moment we spoke to her. We also owe a debt of gratitude to Jenny Xu, who helped shepherd us through the production process. And we were floored by David Hough and his astonishing attention to detail as he pored over every word of the manuscript.

With us at every step, from the original kernel of an idea to the finished product, was our brilliant agent, Eric Lupfer of Fletcher & Company. Despite being a Manchester City fan, he showed exceptional judgment in helping us to identify the structure we needed to turn a gargantuan story that spanned nearly three decades into a clear, compelling narrative. Throughout the writing process, Eric was constantly there to keep us on the right track and to keep us from losing our minds. Also at Fletcher & Company, Christy Fletcher and Grainne Fox were instrumental in helping this book find an audience.

In the UK, huge thanks are due to Joe Zigmond at John Murray, who saw from the beginning that the tale of the Premier League could be told in a new way, even in the country that invented it.

We never would have been in a position to wrap our arms around this story had it not been for Sam Walker, our former captain on the *Wall Street Journal* sports desk, who provided thoughtful feedback on early drafts. Sam also put us in a position to cover the Premier League in the first place by hiring us, dispatching us all over the soccer world, and teaching us how to write about sports with the irreverence it deserved. His starting point was always to ask, 'What would get us fired?' So when it came to writing our own book, our first question was always 'What would Walker do?'

At the *Journal*, we received immeasurable support from our Anglophile bosses and erstwhile Londoners, Bruce Orwall and Lydia Serota, who gave us the time and latitude to pull off a project about the most famous English export this side of the monarchy. Across the *Journal*'s New York and London offices, we are also indebted to Gerry Baker, Gráinne McCarthy, Thorold Barker, Jenn Hicks, Phil Izzo, Brittany Hite, Christopher Chung, Elena Chiriboga, and to Jason Gay, Ben Cohen and the rest of our all-star colleagues at WSJ Sports.

Finally, and most important, we want to thank our home teams.

Joshua wouldn't have survived this process without the support of his parents, Jeffrey and Aline, or his sister, Céline – who provided edits and encouragement during all of his midnight calls from London – or his wife, Daniella, whose superhuman drive is a source of constant inspiration.

And Jon would never have dreamed of starting it but for the encouragement of his wife, Katie, who heroically endured months of missing weekends and movable deadlines, all while attending to the much more important business of looking after their newborn daughter, Evie. Special thanks also to his brother, Dan, for his thoughtful advice.

For all of those people, we finally have proof: twenty-five years of watching English soccer wasn't a complete waste.

Select Bibliography

Allardyce, Sam, *Big Sam: My Autobiography*, London: Headline, 2015

Balague, Guillem, *Cristiano Ronaldo: The Biography*, London: Orion, 2015

Bose, Mihir, *Game Changer: How the English Premier League Came to Dominate the World*, Singapore: Marshall Cavendish, 2012

Bower, Tom, *Broken Dreams: Vanity, Greed and the Souring of British Football*, London: Simon & Schuster, 2007

Chenoweth, Neil, *Rupert Murdoch: The Untold Story of the World's Greatest Media Wizard*, New York: Crown Business, 2002

Chippindale, Peter, and Suzanne Franks, *Dished! The Rise and Fall of British Satellite Broadcasting*, London: Simon & Schuster, 1991

Cole, Ashley, *My Defence: Winning, Losing, Scandals and the Drama of Germany 2006*, London: Headline, 2006

Conn, David, *The Beautiful Game? Searching for the Soul of English Football*, London: Yellow Jersey 2004

——, *Richer than God: Manchester City, Modern Football and Growing Up*, London: Quercus, 2012

Duff, Alex, and Tariq Panja, *Football's Secret Trade: How the Player Transfer Market Was Infiltrated*, Chichester Wiley, 2017

Edwards, Martin, *Red Glory: Manchester United and Me*, London: Michael O'Mara, 2017

Ferguson, Alex, *Managing My Life*, London: Hodder & Stoughton, 1999

——, *My Autobiography*, London: Hodder & Stoughton, 2013

Goldblatt, David, *The Game of Our Lives: The English Premier League and the Making of Modern Britain*, London: Viking, 2014

Horsman, Mathew, *Sky High: BSkyB and the Digital Revolution*, London: Orion Business, 1997

Hourani, Albert, *A History of the Arab Peoples*, London: Faber, 2013

Kelly, Graham, *Sweet F.A.*, London: Collins, 1999

Lisners, John, *The Rise and Fall of the Murdoch Empire*, London: John Blake, 2012

Lovejoy, Joe, *Glory, Goals & Greed: Twenty Years of the Premier League*, Edinburgh: Mainstream, 2011

Marcotti, Gabriele, and Alberto Polverosi, *Hail, Claudio! The Man, the Manager, the Miracle*, London: Yellow Jersey, 2016

Perarnau, Martí, *Pep Confidential: The Inside Story of Pep Guardiola's First Season at Bayern Munich*, Edinburgh: Arena Sport, 2014

——, *Pep Guardiola: The Evolution*, Edinburgh: Arena Sport, 2016

Soriano, Ferran, *Goal: The Ball Doesn't Go In by Chance*, Basingstoke: Palgrave Macmillan, 2012

Vialli, Gianluca, and Gabriele Marcotti, *The Italian Job: A Journey to the Heart of Two Great Footballing Cultures*, London: Bantam, 2006

Yergin, Daniel, *The Prize: The Epic Quest for Oil, Money, & Power*, New York: Simon & Schuster, 1991

Index

Index

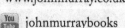
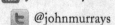
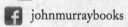